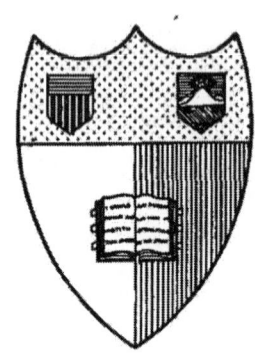

Cornell University Library
Ithaca, New York

CHARLES WILLIAM WASON
COLLECTION
CHINA AND THE CHINESE

THE GIFT OF
CHARLES WILLIAM WASON
CLASS OF 1876
1918

Cornell University Library
DS 517.C48
A study of the Russo-Japanese War /

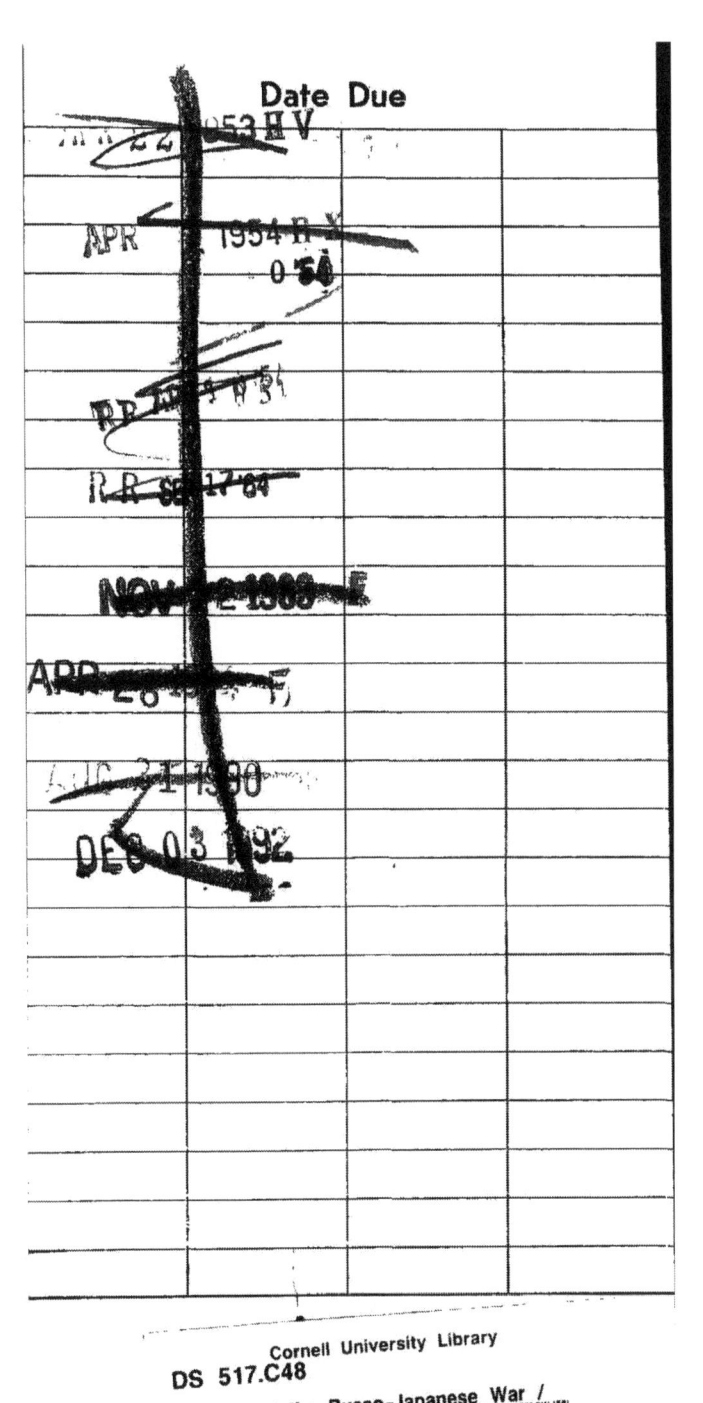

Wason
DS 517
C 48

A STUDY OF THE RUSSO-JAPANESE WAR

A Study

OF THE

Russo-Japanese War

BY

CHASSEUR

WITH MAPS AND PLANS

WILLIAM BLACKWOOD AND SONS
EDINBURGH AND LONDON
MCMV

All Rights reserved

26/II/20

Wason
DS 517

W 1410

FOREWORD.

In putting this short summary of the great struggle which has taken place in the Far East before the public, the author has only attempted to outline and arrange in some sort of convenient sequence the broad issues of the campaign. But he has tried to make full use of all available information, and having an intimate knowledge of the theatre of operations and of the armies of both belligerents, is ambitious enough to believe that a consecutive narrative will be acceptable even in its present defective form. He takes this opportunity of thanking the proprietors of 'Blackwood's Magazine' for having accorded him the hospitality of 'Maga's' pages in the compilation of his narrative.

CONTENTS.

		PAGE
I.	THE NAVAL CAMPAIGN	1
II.	THE LAND CAMPAIGN TO THE PASSAGE OF THE YALU	63
III.	THE LAND CAMPAIGN UP TO THE END OF JUNE 1904	95
IV.	THE ADVANCE TO LIAUYANG	117
V.	PORT ARTHUR	162
VI.	ROJDESTVENSKY'S ARMADA	201
VII.	THE OVERTHROW OF THE ARMADA	230
VIII.	THE BATTLE ON THE SHA-HO	251
IX.	THE BATTLE OF HEI-KOU-TAI	277
X.	THE BATTLE OF MUKDEN	299

A STUDY OF
THE RUSSO-JAPANESE WAR.

I. THE NAVAL CAMPAIGN.

As was the case during the South African War, before the first twelve months of hostilities had passed, publishers began to rush out volumes dealing in an ephemeral manner with the war, so also with regard to the present struggle in the Far East, we had amongst last winter's publications three bulky and expensive volumes which dealt with the Russo-Japanese War. At the present moment we have these three volumes before us. Two may be said to deal with the war from the Japanese standpoint and one from that of Russia. Of the three, the one that seems to be the least partisan, and consequently the most valuable, is Mr Palmer's, while in literary attainment it surpasses both its contemporaries.

It would be both wearisome and uninstructive to

examine these works[1] purely as narratives of the war; but as we have now been able with their help, and with the help of the fuller reports which have come tardily from the front, to form a more accurate perspective of the situation in the Far East than was possible in 1904, the moment is not ill-advised for the purpose of studying the operations as a whole. With this object in view, the volumes under consideration serve a purpose, for even though in many cases they express opinions with which we are not in agreement, and make statements the accuracy of which we are at liberty to doubt, yet they refresh our memory on many points which might otherwise have escaped us. For this purpose we will take Mr T. Cowen's book first. It is the most prodigious volume of the three, and covers not only the operations on sea and land as far as the battle of Liauyang, but also deals with the past diplomatic history of Japan and Russia in the Far East.

In fact, we do not scruple to say that these introductory chapters furnish the only really valuable reading matter in the work, since it is obvious to the most cursory reader who has taken the slightest interest in the operations that the latter chapters are simply a compilation from the more or less inaccurate

---

[1] The Russo-Japanese War, by T. Cowen (Arnold). With Kuroki in Manchuria, by Frederick Palmer (Methuen). The Campaign with Kuropatkin, by Douglas Story (T. Werner Laurie).

press accounts of the various operations, and such meagre official reports as the author had access to. Nevertheless, the volume is written in a manner which would beguile the unwary into believing that the author had been present at the various battles and engagements which he describes. We will later quote inaccuracies, which definitely show the sources from which these descriptions have been compiled.

Mr Cowen has approached the difficult question of the diplomatic relations which led up to this deplorable war with considerable skill, and it is evident that his long residence in the Far East makes him conversant with many phases of both Russian, Japanese, and Chinese intrigue, which on the surface are not apparent to us here in the West. But for all that, his attitude is so partisan that we cannot but think he injures the case for Japan by the exuberance of the language in which he paints her virtues. This attitude will of course appeal to the sentimental enthusiasm which is prevalent in this country.

And it is quite possible that the author had this in view when he over-painted his picture. But we hope, when the first enthusiasm has worn off, and increased interest in the Far East has encouraged increased study of that portion of the globe, the people of this country will take a less hysterical view of the operations, and will realise how great an influence the issues at stake must have upon our future foreign policy.

The pith of Mr Cowen's argument in favour of this sudden war is in the clap-trap diplomatic statement which shields Japan under the pretence that the whole of her policy is defensive. On the surface this is a truism, because preparedness for war is the strongest and most pacific defence that any nation could have, provided that nation is not stimulated with the piratical tendencies which have built up our own Empire.

Mr Cowen reverts so often to what he is pleased to call this "defensive instinct," that we shall be constrained to quote him against himself before entering into a study of Japan's past foreign policy. This instinct for defence is so nearly allied to the desire for national aggrandisement, that it is hard to say which inclination prompted her to make herself a first-class naval and military power. Mr Cowen takes it for granted that Japan's object in demanding a cession of Port Arthur from China after the Chinese war was simply a defensive measure against possible advances of Russia from the north. Of course, in a way, this is again a plausible truism; but the main object of Japan in desiring Port Arthur was to be able to place herself in a position to prevent a dismemberment of the Chinese Empire. Not so much on the defensive line—although this of course sounds well in diplomatic statements,—but in order that she might lay the first stone in her schemes for predominance in Pekin. The determination to be the great Power in the Far East has so permeated through every rank and walk of life in Japan, that it almost upset the well-balanced plans of the better-informed statesmen. Writing of these stormy days when Japan, flushed with her victory over China, was compelled by European intervention to relinquish much of her fruits of victory, Mr Cowen says:—

Many and bitter were the newspaper articles and pamphlets published in Japan against the three Powers and against giving up Port Arthur. Feeling ran so high that there must have been war in any other country less carefully controlled. The Press censors had to work like a fire brigade; newspapers were suspended right and left; the prisons were filled with indignant patriots; and wherever one publication was stopped others would come to light in its place. When a printing plant was placed under lock and key some neighbour would buy a few dollars' worth of materials, and publish one defiant protest before going proudly to prison.

This public outburst, though it was quelled by the more far-seeing statesmen of the time, became a valuable instrument for the furthering of Japanese policy. To show the key-note of this policy, we will quote the Japanese themselves. 'Japan by the Japanese' clearly shows that Japan fastened a quarrel upon China, not because she had any particular grievance with the Chinese, but simply because the time was ripe for her to commence expansion. The Marquis Ito, according to this work, formulated the Japanese claim to Korea as follows:—

The claims of China over Korea were historical only—*i.e.*, as the history of China reckons Korea among her tributaries; and as China had the greatest repugnance of changing the face of history as the worthy legacy of ancestral Emperors, so she was intent on claiming Korea as her vassal State. The claims of Japan over Korea were economical—*i.e.*, she did not claim any regal authority over Korea; but from her geographical position and the necessity of providing for her constantly increasing population, she was intent on utilising Korea as the best source from which the defect in the home produce of rice was to be supplied, as well as the nearest field in which the future sons of Japan might find employment.

Does not such a statement, coming from the Japanese themselves, remind us that there are two sides to every question? Does not the memory of the Seoul plot and its murderous issues sound a note of warning, which should qualify to some degree the warm appreciation with which we acknowledge the many virtues of our allies?

A book like Mr Cowen's is calculated to mislead the judgment of those who, if they had really studied the facts, would prefer to steer a more moderate course than one of blind adulation of our allies. Not that we as a nation have any right to throw stones at either of these Powers, who are really struggling for an expansion which is economically necessary to both.

The means by which we have built up this great Empire will not permit in us a policy of cant. But although we have no cause to throw stones, yet that is no reason why we, with our experience behind us, should not be able to judge more truly of passing events in cases where recent history in the East has striven to emulate the past history of the West. It were foolish not to profit for ourselves from the precedents in piracy which we ourselves established. For this reason sentiments expressed as Mr Cowen has expressed them, although doubtless at one time they helped to sell his book, will not tend to make this country more alive to the great issues which will be thrust upon it when the effects of the struggle begin to crystallise.

We have studied Mr Cowen at this length for the purpose of exposing certain fallacies of opinion which we know to exist, in order that we may approach the more important subject of this treatise—the study of the nineteen months' war—with an open and unbiassed mind. It is necessary to do this, because no one can say that this war has up to date been studied dispassionately; and as we proceed we will endeavour to illuminate the drier portions of the narrative with extracts from the contemporary works which have accumulated upon the table. But before commencing this study it must clearly be understood that the standpoint which we take is, that Japan has for the last twenty years realised that the partition of China would kill her own progress in the Far East. She had had proof of this in the case of Germany's action in Shantung, following immediately upon Russia's occupation of Port Arthur. She saw clearly that Russia's expansion in Manchuria unopposed would without doubt bring about the partition of China within a few years. She determined, therefore, to use her whole strength and the whole of her resources to check Russia, and thus delay the partition, which was imminent, until her influence, power, and prestige were sufficient in China to render a partition impossible.

For the purpose of a brief study, the affairs of the past year in the Far East divide themselves conveniently into three phases — namely, the preparations before hostilities, the naval, and the land campaigns.

We have abundant evidence that Japan, even though hers was a purely defensive instinct, was preparing for many years against the eventuality of this war with Russia. We have abundant evidence of the state of efficiency existing in her Navy and her Army. We have also now sufficient evidence to show us that although the little island Power was preparing in every detail to await a war against Russia in Manchuria and in the Far Eastern waters, yet the great military Power which Japan had made up her mind to face was in no wise as well prepared to undertake a struggle in which its opponent possessed most of the essential strategic advantages. On the face of it, it seemed absurd that a little country, whose total population did not yet reach fifty millions, and which sixty years ago was existing in a state of civilisation so opposed to the Western development that it could not even for a single moment have held up its head as one of the nations of the world, should dare to enter into a conflict with a great military Power which for twenty years had, in the terror born of its unfathomed strength, carried colossal weight in Western politics.

This want of proportion and disparity of strength between the belligerents has doubtless been responsible for much of the sympathy and enthusiasm vested in Japan. But really Japan's numerical weakness, and her comparatively recent insignificance, has been the main cause of her success. Russia, dwelling secure in the knowledge of her size and reputation, had never taken in serious part the opposition she was receiving from Japan. Even her most far-seeing statesmen could not bring themselves to believe that this little nation of dwarfs would ever dare to risk political and national effacement by breaking a lance against the solidity of the Russian Empire. Thus it was that Russia hoped, by an adequate show of naval and military strength in Manchuria and the Pacific, to convince Japan of the impossibility of ever really interfering with Russia's plans and projects.

Consequently, while Japan was steeling herself for years for this very struggle, Russia was content to smile at the warnings which came to her, and never until the last moment did she make any real effort to render herself invulnerable against an offensive Japan. Japan, however, took a different view of Russia's strength to that held by the rest of the world. And her military and naval advisers, at the time when she induced the British Government to enter into an alliance, argued that when once they had secured a powerful ring-keeper they would be able to handle any naval and military force that the Russians could bring against them in the Far East.

Events have proved that these naval and military advisers were right. Their only fear lay in the question of command of the seas: they felt confident that if once they gained a supremacy over the Russian naval forces in the Far East, their armies would be able to undertake the discomfiture within a specified time of such troops as Russia could place in the field against them. Their counsellors argued that if, on paper, they could place a fleet in opposition to the Russian fleets in the Chinese waters equal in fighting strength, they would be able to beat the Russians on the score of efficiency.

Once they had the command of the sea, for the time being every advantage lay with them for a land campaign. They could calculate upon being able to place between four and five hundred thousand men in the field, long before the Siberian railway could reinforce the existing strength of the Russian garrisons in the Far East. This would give them a numerical advantage at once, and they felt confident that man for man the Japanese soldier was as good as the Russian, and that the Japanese officers were superior. Moreover, they had an intimate knowledge of the theatre of operations, and, with the command of the sea, they would be able to make the Russians fight on ground of their own selection. They would be able, owing to their close connection with the people of Manchuria, to furnish intelligence of their enemies' movement which no European army in the Far East could hope to equal, and they had always at the back of their heads the belief that their initial success on sea and land would plunge Russia internally into such a disorder, that long before the great strength of the Empire could be drawn upon she would be forced to relinquish the conflict. Thus it was that, on 6th February 1904, almost with a light heart, the Japanese people entered upon this colossal struggle. And to a considerable extent their estimate of their enemy has proved correct. Russia's naval power has proved to be despicable,—so much so, that the Japanese were able to throw their armies into Manchuria even more rapidly than they had anticipated in the best appreciation of their chances.

We will now deal with the circumstances in which Russia found herself when, towards the end of January, it was evident that there would be no means of avoiding hostilities. We have not the slightest hesitation in saying that Russia was in no measure prepared for such a war as Japan was making ready to bring against her, either in Manchuria or in Chinese waters. It is impossible even now to say whether this want of preparedness was due to a general disbelief in St Petersburg that Japan would ever be bold enough to risk this stupendous issue of the war with a great European power, or whether Admiral Alexieff, the Czar's viceroy in the Far East, had underrated the powers of the island nation.

Judging from Mr Cowen's very correct appreciation of the Czar's feelings towards Japan, we would be inclined to think that the real blame rested with Alexieff, although we have recently had this official's disclaimer to such a suggestion.

Mr Cowen believes that the attack made upon the Czarevitch in 1891 has, to a large extent, been responsible for the Czar's present policy towards Japan. He refers to it in the following manner:—

As usual in such cases, the outrage had not the effect it was intended to have, but rather the contrary: it reduced to silence, for very shame, all who would have spoken reasonably of the Russian Peril, and it gave the present ruler of Russia a lifelong conviction that the Japanese are a dangerous race. In fact, the act of Tsuda Sanzo helped to popularise throughout the Western world the outcry against the Yellow Peril. This effect was intensified when a very similar attack was made on Li Hung Chang in 1895, at Shimonoseki, during the negotiations for the cession of Port Arthur to Japan. Again the intending assassin thought to do his country a service by removing in a merely mediæval way a dangerous man. The Czarevitch Nicholas had just become Czar, and this affair in Shimonoseki must have appealed to him as it could not to any other. As if to remind him again, a year or two later the Kaiser sent his famous cartoon to the Czar, and the nations of Europe were confirmed in their combined action against the Yellow Peril, and against Japan. It is undeniable that the Japanese in certain moods are as terrible as any one can paint them. . . . Under provocation or under apprehension of danger they are liable to develop a volcanic temper, comparable with Mont Pêlée in fury and utter destructiveness.

Therefore it will not be unreasonable if we trace the Russian unpreparedness to the old sin of which we ourselves have so often been guilty—of underestimating the prowess of our enemy. The Japanese, on the other hand, made a very fair and correct estimate of the strength of the Russian forces in Manchuria. It has been agreed on all hands, both by the Russians and by disinterested spectators of this struggle, that the system of the Japanese espionage has been unequalled. It must be borne in mind that the opportunities for this very espionage, which their close affiliation with China afforded them, have been unequalled. But we may also safely say that Japanese expert officers have gone to much further lengths in their desire to compile faithful information for the use of their country than has ever been contemplated in European countries. We have countless records of Japanese officers, often of considerable rank, undertaking menial posts in all quarters of the globe in the service of those from whom they have something to learn.

But the Russians' occupation of Manchuria furnished them with unequalled opportunities in this respect. With a little property artist's work there is not much to choose between a Chinese and a Japanese servant. We have reliable information that even while the Russians were building their fortifications at Liauyang, Port Arthur, and Yongampo before the war, though for diplomatic reasons they were denying the existence of such works, at the very moment when these denials were handed to Baron Komura in Tokio, reports were lying on the table of the War Minister from Japanese officers, who, in the character of labourers, were helping to build these works. Therefore, when a nation is prepared to go to this length in order to pursue its national schemes, it is not surprising that they should have been the first to understand where Russia's weakness lay. That they have finally, to use a vulgar expression, pricked the Russian bubble, we are not prepared to allow. But that they have shown that there was much to warrant the use of the expression we readily admit, though we venture the opinion that there is a vast difference between pricking a bubble and emptying the whole of the washing-tub.

The main cause for Russia's unpreparedness for war in her newly acquired province was not only the paucity in numbers of troops, the want of munitions of war, or the inefficiency of the railway communications. What the Russian army in the Far East lacked was system. There is undeniable proof that much of the moneys which should have been expended against possible hostilities found its way into the pockets of superior officers. Where venality exists, it is impossible to have discipline. Dishonest direction means a rotten company. Therefore, as far more time had been spent by the superior officers in Manchuria in lining their own pockets than in preparing against a possible Japanese invasion, when that moment came there was practically no machinery to make profitable use of such military and naval material as existed.

It has been seriously stated on the authority of a Russian naval officer that none of the battleships in the Far East had ever attempted gun-practice with their primary armaments. By collusion with accomplices in St Petersburg, the money which should have supplied ammunition for the heavy guns disappeared as cash into somebody's banking account. As a proof that such scandals were possible, we have the disgraceful affair of the Royal Hospital train. But it would be useless to follow up the long list of official venality: it will suffice to say that, although it may have been hid from the knowledge of such superior officers as did not participate in it, yet it had never escaped the vigilance of the Japanese, and it doubtless to a large extent accounted for the sanguine manner in which they entered upon the campaign.

Yet in spite of their knowledge of these deficiencies, the administrators in Manchuria pinned extraordinary confidence in their naval supremacy. And it must be borne in mind that the prevailing influence at the moment in Manchuria was naval rather than military. On paper the Russian fleet showed a slight superiority in power over the naval strength of Japan. But as this total tonnage in the case of Japan was distributed over many ships of inferior class, and the prevailing impression in Western naval schools was that the battleship would be the decisive factor in modern naval warfare, and as on paper the Japanese were considerably inferior to the Russians in this class of vessel, the Russian officers were satisfied that their Pacific fleet would be able to carry the war to the coasts of Japan until the time was ripe to engage upon a land campaign. And until they were disillusioned on the fateful evening of 8th February, they rested secure in this belief. This has been proved to a great extent by Admiral Alexieff's statements made for publication after his recent return to St Petersburg. For he then readily allowed that if the Japanese had pressed their initial advantage with more vigour, they would have found the defences of Port Arthur in poor condition.

But from all this, it must not be imagined that Russia was overtaken in a hopeless state of unpreparedness. Although the character of her system allowed of enormous pilfering of public money, yet that state of venality had not been reached that the whole of the public funds were embezzled. We know that towards the end of 1903 Russia was making large purchases of warlike stores, — she was even purchasing canned meats in Japan,—and large orders were lodged in America and elsewhere: even it was possible to see in Tokio in January a considerable museum of samples of various preserved fruit-stuffs which Russia was then importing into Manchuria from over-sea; and it was doubtless the fact that Alexieff had awakened to the serious nature of the Japanese preparations which determined Japan to open hostilities as soon as the season should be favourable, in spite of the very strenuous endeavours of her more peacefully inclined ally.

Of the Manchurian railway we shall have more to

say when we deal with the land operations, though we are inclined to believe that the Japanese, in common with the several military theorists in this country and the Continent, were misguided in their estimates of the capabilities of that communication.

We will not enter here into the diplomatic relations which actually preceded the outbreak of hostilities. It is definitely apparent that although the quaint code of false morality which rules diplomatic relations throughout the whole world required a certain amount of formal representation, yet Japan had determined upon war while the season was propitious, before Russia had awakened to the full significance of the peril of her position in Manchuria.

That there was a considerable apprehension in Japanese naval circles that Russia would forestall them in striking the first blow is proved by the nature of the telegraphic correspondence received by the commanders of the *Nisshin* and *Kasuga* at the later ports called at on their journey outwards. Also by the state of consternation into which Sasebo was thrown when it was announced on 4th February that the Russian fleet had sailed from Port Arthur for an unknown destination. Until the return of the fleet to Port Arthur was reported, it looked as if Admiral Starck was bringing his fleet to force matters in Japanese waters, and at that moment such a stroke might have altered the entire complexion of the first year's hostilities.

JAPANESE MOBILISATION.

But this bubble burst almost as soon as it appeared, and on 6th February Admiral Togo sailed from Sasebo. Mr Cowen has graphically described this great occasion :—

Like a great, complex, perfect machine, every section set in motion simultaneously by the simple act of pressing a button, the entire fighting force began to move at the moment the signal was given. Soldiers who had been for days and weeks waiting for the "cue," quietly and methodically filed out of barracks and into boats to board the waiting troop-ships at Sasebo. Provisions and ammunition, field equipment, and all other necessaries had been stowed on board in advance, and the flotilla of troop-ships for the invasion of Korea moved out of Sasebo before daylight on February 6th, the main body of the fleet accompanying.

One can well imagine the feelings of anxiety which must have exercised the Cabinet Ministers in Tokio on this momentous occasion. In the existence of that fleet was vested the whole of the scheme of expansion which had inspired all their labours and ambitions of the last twenty years. Would their deductions and planning prove to be correct, or had they committed the Western sin of over-appreciation of their own powers. That they were confident there is no doubt. But war is a series of surprises, and it could not, at that moment, have been a confidence untempered with apprehension. In Admiral Togo's hands were vested the very destinies of the new-born nation.

The first objective of the Japanese offensive was Korea. A glance at the map will show the soundness of this first venture. At the moment the Russians were reinforcing their outposts on the river Yalu, and had even pushed south a mounted force into Korea proper. It was therefore essential that Russia should be forced from the "hermit kingdom" before she might gain a hold sufficient to upset the Japanese plan of campaign. It must be understood that Korea was just as essential to Japan for the purpose of naval strategy as for the military campaign. Togo required the west coast of the peninsula for his offensive strategy; while it was absolutely essential that Admiral Starck should not secure one of the many harbours to aid him in an attack against Japan. That this was contemplated by the Russian schemes is suggested by the large stores of coal accumulated by the Russians at Chemulpo. Therefore Japan's object was to land an expeditionary force on the coast of Korea, to establish itself first at Seoul, the capital, and then as quickly as possible at Ping-yang, the main strategic point in the north of the peninsula. This force having established itself, would then prove the advance point of the first invading army. If successful, this move would prevent the Russians from establishing a land supremacy which would control the harbours in the north.

With this object the fleet of transports carrying a portion of the 2nd Division, under the escort of Admiral Uriu's cruiser squadron, entered Chemulpo, and effected a landing under the bows of two Russian warships at anchor in the harbour: another transport deflected to the north, landed a company of infantry at Haiju, whose mission was to make a forced march upon Ping-yang. Both these forces successfully carried out their missions.

The situation in Chemulpo was of extraordinary interest. Owing to the incapacity of the Port Arthur command, the *Variag*, the fastest cruiser on the Pacific station, the gunboat *Korietz*, and the Volunteer steamship *Sungari* were lying at anchor amid the international squadron of warships, unapprised of the fact that hostilities existed. The commander of the *Variag* was unprepared to act in the circumstance of an obviously hostile landing in a treaty port. Moreover, he was trapped at his anchorage by the appearance of Uriu's superior squadron in the outer harbour. In these circumstances one is inclined to think that if he had been a man of grit he would have opposed the landing. But it is evident that he was as slow in arriving at a conclusion as he was in directing the fighting qualities of the ship. The *Korietz*, on the first appearance of the transports, had steamed out to the open harbour, and here, being confronted by Uriu's fleet, had fired at a torpedo-boat. This is claimed by Japan to have been the first act of war. An obviously absurd assertion, since the music of the windlasses of Togo's fleet in Sasebo harbour as they up-anchored to escort the transports was the opening act of war. But we are not concerned with such trivial details. The Russian ships were trapped, though if the commander had been a man of any moment, the very fact that the evening before Uriu's squadron arrived the Japanese cruiser *Chiyoda* slipped out of the Chemulpo anchorage without lights should have been sufficient indication to him to have rejoined his admiral in Port Arthur without a moment's delay.

As it was, when the landing had been completed, Uriu sent a request to the commander of the *Variag* that he should come out and fight, together with a notice to the commanders of the foreign war-vessels that they should move from the anchorage, as it was his intention to attack the Russians in the harbour. We do not for a moment think that Admiral Uriu intended to put in practice this bold threat, since there was no precedent which would warrant his carrying war into a treaty port. But it had the desired effect, for the weak little Russian squadron steamed out of the harbour to accept battle amid the enthusiastic acclamations of the other naval forces collected there.

This action of the commander of the *Variag* has been claimed by Russia and her sympathisers as a very gallant proceeding. Doubtless it was gallant in its conception. There is, however, a tradition in our own navy—a tradition which we trust will never pass into oblivion—that if a ship has to fight, no matter the odds, she will fight and sink with her battle-flags aloft. It was doubtless the intention of the commander of the *Variag* to do likewise. Although Uriu's squadron was so superior, be it said to his credit and the credit of the Japanese navy that it did not bring the whole of its gun-power to bear upon the solitary Russian cruiser. We say solitary, because she rapidly out-distanced the little *Korietz*. Uriu engaged the *Variag* with his flag-ship, the *Asama*, alone. After a brief exchange of shots, the courage of the commander of the *Variag* forsook him, and he turned and made for his late anchorage, the gunboat turning with him, and it was during this homeward journey that he suffered so severely from the *Asama's* fire. Back he went to his anchorage, and immediately opened the sea-cocks in his vessel and ordered the destruction by explosion of the *Korietz* and the *Sungari*. A dismal ending!

It may be pointed out here, as an aside, that in the enthusiasm of this first success the nature of the engagement was much exaggerated, for we read in the Japanese reports that the little *Korietz* was riddled with holes. She was never in action at all. Also we heard of the devastating effect of the Japanese shrapnel. It may be pointed out that shrapnel forms no part of Japanese marine artillery, except in the case of 9-pounder field-guns for landing-parties. It is evident from Mr Cowen's description of the affair, as in all his other battle descriptions, that he has drawn on the local official and newspaper reports for his information. Speaking of the *Korietz*, he says:—

> Then came the Japanese answer. Only half a dozen more shells from the *Asama*, and the *Korietz* was pierced through and through, leaking so rapidly that it seemed she must sink before she could get back into shelter. She certainly could not go on, she would not haul down her flag, and she did not want to sink out there. So back she came less than a half-hour after she had started. She just managed to reach shallow water in time, and sank on the mud on an even keel, her deck still standing out of the water.

Again, speaking of the same occasion, "Shrapnel shells were bursting all the time with deadly accuracy, filling the air like rain." Later on he forgets that he has already sunk the *Korietz*, for he says, "Though the *Korietz* was by no means so badly shattered as the bigger ships, it was decided to blow her up, so that she should not fall into the enemy's hands."

We will now deal with the first naval attack on Port Arthur. This really took place before the destruction of the Russian ships in Chemulpo—in fact, the first hostile act against the main Russian fleet occurred while the Japanese troops were disembarking in Korea. It may be taken for granted that Admiral Togo was kept informed up to the last moment of the movements of the Russian ships at Port Arthur. He knew that the battleship squadron preferred to anchor in the outer roadstead owing to the difficulties of negotiating the narrow channel of the harbour proper. The fighting power of its ships was then an unknown quantity, and their paper superiority to his own squadron of battleships warranted his attempting to reduce this superiority by any means that would still keep the striking power of his own battleships intact. Unless it were forced upon him, he would not have been justified in engaging in a fleet action. Being well aware of the naval custom prevailing in Port Arthur, and trusting in the fact that his rapidity of action would find Port Arthur still doubtful as to whether a state of war existed or not, he despatched two divisions of destroyers, with the object, if the circumstances proved favourable, of delivering his first blow against the Russian battle squadron as it lay at anchor in its own roadstead. It is not our object to enter upon any discussion as to the morality of the Japanese stroke: we will confine ourselves to the bare statement that, judging by the precedent contained in the history of past declarations of war, and remembering that the whole of the Japanese success depended upon rapidity of action, they were justified in using any means calculated to place them upon an equality with their enemy in a struggle which has well been called a life-or-death struggle.

Togo's information proved to be as correct as his conjecture, and the result rang through the length and breadth of the world with galvanic effect. The

Russians were caught napping; but that they had apprehensions was shown in the movements of their own destroyer flotilla. Two divisions were patrolling in the vicinity of Shantung promontory. These were sighted by the Japanese destroyers as they steered for Port Arthur, and, according to the most reliable information, the result was a race for the roadstead, and, as has proved so fatal in many land engagements, the Russians suffered from the attack because their retreating outposts and the attacking forces arrived simultaneously. This would account for the Russian statement that the Japanese torpedo craft made the Russian signals.

The attack, which was made about midnight, was over in a few minutes. Accurate accounts are conflicting; but there is sufficient reason to believe that the great Russian battleships were lying in line ahead with their anchor lights lit, that the crews were not even at quarters, and that several of the senior deck officers were on shore. Never before, and never possibly again, had torpedo craft such an opportunity.

But the dramatic side of the scene is painful in the extreme. The silence of the night broken first with the chime of the fleet bells sounding the hour; then, as the anchor-watch is changed, the sudden suspicion of the panting breath of torpedo craft; the indistinct lights of their own returning flotilla, and the dark moving bodies sweeping in from the seaboard; the dull reverberation as two torpedoes take effect on the largest of the Russian leviathans. One can almost feel the convulsive shudder that must have quickened that sleeping fleet. The frenzied rush to quarters, the anxious glances cast by the more responsible officers towards the flag-ship, for some signal to apprise them of the meaning of this sudden uproar. The ignorance of the said flag-ship, ringing with the cry for collision-mats, and then the sudden tumult of guns fired blindly into the appalling darkness out of which the attack had come.

But before the Russian crews had recovered from their panic the perpetrators of the trouble had disappeared into the great unknown. All that remained were two huge battleships in helpless distress, the unparalleled situation of a powerful fleet reduced to impotent consternation.

Although one cannot help being moved to admiration of the spirit which prompted the Japanese in this splendid effort, yet one cannot help thinking that they made a very small use of their unique opportunity. The destroyers, having passed down the line of battleships, sped away into the darkness, nor did they renew their attack until much later in the night. If they had returned again and again, they would have maintained the panic which their first appearance had caused, and it is impossible to estimate what other damage they might have achieved. As it was, at the time that they saw fit to renew the attack some semblance of order had been restored; so much so, that their second appearance produced no further results but an expenditure of ammunition from both ships and land forts. But although in this first instance the fullest advantage was not taken of the opportunity, yet the moral effect of this attack, aside from the fact that the two most powerful ships in the Russian fleet had been temporarily damaged, was a great achievement, and it may safely be said that the Japanese navy that night established its moral supremacy.

The scope of this work will not allow of our following in similar detail all the naval actions. We can only hope to quote enough to establish the broad lines of the general strategy employed. On the day following the torpedo attack Togo steamed in towards Port Arthur and demonstrated in front of the Russian stronghold. The Russian fleet was still at anchor, though the two injured battleships had been temporarily beached at the entrance of the harbour. It is probable that, as soon as Togo was informed of the success of the night-raid, he considered he would be strong enough to risk a fleet action with the remainder of the Russian ships. Anyway, he gave Admiral Starck this opportunity. But the paralysis which has marked the attitude of the Russian Pacific squadron throughout the war had already set in, and the demonstration developed into an exchange of shots at long range, and to a certain amount of bombardment between the Japanese fleet and the shore defences.

It had been arranged that as soon as the Japanese fleet left Sasebo it would first base itself at Mokpo, a suitable bay at the south-west corner of the Korean peninsula. To this place already the cable-boats and the naval transports had been sent. As long as there had been a possibility, however remote, of the Russian fleet attempting to take the offensive against Japan, Mokpo furnished an admirable base for the Japanese battle squadron, while the cruisers patrolled the one hundred and twenty miles of sea between the Shantung promontory and Sir James Hall group. Mokpo may therefore be considered as the defensive naval base chosen by Japan.

But Togo was now satisfied that he would be able to undertake the offensive without let or hindrance. It behoved him therefore to have an offensive base nearer to his objective than either Mokpo or Sasebo. This, of course, was laid down in the scheme of Japanese naval strategy, and instead of returning to Mokpo, Togo took his fleet into an indifferently charted bay behind the Sir

James Hall group, which brought him within ten hours' steam of Port Arthur. To this place all his necessary plant, supply, coal, and transports were brought, and the advance-base was established. Everything had been ready in Sasebo for this undertaking, and almost before the admiral's battle squadron first cast anchor, the wireless stations, which were to keep communication along the coast of Korea, were in working order, while his coal-supply was already awaiting him.

It would be well here to dilate upon the extraordinary secrecy with which these arrangements were carried out; and it is probable that, until this base was discarded as a primary base, not half a dozen Europeans knew the spot which had been chosen. Of course it was obvious that a base existed somewhere in the Yellow Sea, and the wildest speculations were current: even now the well-informed are at fault, for we find that Mr Cowen asserts, with a positiveness which might well convince the uninformed, that Togo's fleet returned to Sasebo, and that his primary base was at the Elliot Islands. He says: " Returning to Sasebo, two days' steam from Port Arthur, Admiral Togo sent ashore the dead and wounded, and quickly effected the repairs needed." And a few pages later he repeatedly refers to the Elliot Islands as Togo's base.

We will point out here that, although the moral effect of his initial success had been so great, it would have been foolhardy for the Admiral in the existing circumstances to have based himself nearer to Port Arthur—at least, as near to Port Arthur as the Elliot group. The Russian torpedo flotilla had yet to be reckoned with as an effective force. Togo had certainly reduced the Russian battle squadron by two ships, and by report by one or two others; but there was no evidence that he had done any harm to the torpedo flotilla, and it was therefore essential that his base should be at a sufficient distance from Port Arthur, in a sufficiently concealed position to place it beyond the possibility of an attack being made upon it similar to the one he had made himself. Also other considerations required caution. The outbreak of war had found the Russians with a cruiser squadron of four fast and powerful ships in Vladivostok. In order to cope with any movement undertaken by this squadron, either against the coast ports of Japan or in an attempt to concentrate at Port Arthur, it was necessary that Togo should weaken his own cruiser squadron. And he had had therefore to despatch a cruiser squadron more powerful than that of the Russians to watch Vladivostok. This so reduced his strength in cruisers with the main squadron, that in effect the Russian cruiser squadron at Port Arthur held the superiority over his own.

The result of Togo's first movement was a withdrawal of the Russian Port Arthur fleet into the haven of the narrower roadstead,—a certain number of the cruisers alone remaining outside. The weather, too, changed at this period, and from the 11th to the 20th of February fierce and continuous storms swept across the Yellow Sea. For a few days Admiral Togo contented himself with allowing Admiral Kamimura to make a demonstration against Vladivostok. On the night of the 13th, however, Togo despatched a division of destroyers to attempt a night-raid against the Russian cruisers guarding Port Arthur's entrance. These destroyers made the attack in a gale of wind through a blinding snow-blizzard. Two only of the four reached their destination, and they at wide intervals apart. They claimed to have torpedoed the many-funnelled and ofttimes-sunk *Askold;* but we think that the attack had no serious result except to the Japanese, who are debited with having lost a destroyer in the storm.

There was one hope that was high in the minds of the Japanese naval strategists—they were well aware of the value of the Russians' ships, and we are constrained to believe that after the 8th of February they rated the commercial value higher than the fighting value. And who shall deny that they had cause?

Now Japan coveted these ships, and already the Japanese naval experts were formulating a plan by which they might hope to possess the major portion of this powerful squadron. When once they felt that their moral supremacy over the Russian fleet was absolute they did not desire to bring about a fleet action, which, if unsuccessful, would ruin their own fighting strength, or very terribly impair it; and which, if successful, would not mean anything but an ultimate destruction of these magnificent ships which they so coveted. In the moment of success they would either be sunk in deep water or beached in despair on some rocky coast where their destruction would be inevitable.

In fact, the desire to possess these vessels has also to some extent dominated the military strategy of the war. The argument is as follows: Once Russia's fleet had slunk into Port Arthur for security, it had suggested to the Japanese a plan which they considered worth pursuing to the last effort. If they could effectually blockade the entrance to Port Arthur and keep this fleet immured, they might then be able, by combined naval and military operations, to possess themselves of it. Even if the Russians had to destroy their ships as a last resource, they would be sunk in shallow water, upon mud, in which case there was every probability that some, at least, of them might be salvaged at leisure. But there was also another governing factor, that whether they could be salvaged or not they could be destroyed without running the risk of impairing the striking power of Togo's battle squadron.

It was this policy which induced Togo to undertake the repeated hazardous endeavours to block the entrance to the port with ballast-laden vessels. It would be wearisome to follow in detail each of these gallant and brilliant attempts. They were three in number, and although they failed to absolutely close the entrance, yet they so impaired the fairway that indirectly Togo may be said to have attained his object. If for the moment we may anticipate, we may point out that the cardinal reason why the Russian fleet failed to escape on both occasions when it attempted to break away from Port Arthur, was that the navigation of the channel had become so difficult that it was impossible for the Russian squadron to clear all its ships in sufficient time to move off as a whole without the Japanese observation craft being able to transmit the information of the project to Togo. Consequently Togo, having moved up to his nearer base, was always in position to frustrate each effort.

In the meantime, although we are not yet dealing with the land campaign, in order to keep sequence of events we must refer to the movements which were taking place in Korea. Since Togo had established himself behind the Sir James Hall group, the ice which bound the northern coast-line of Korea began to break up. As soon as the Ping-yang inlet was navigable Togo sent up his fourth squadron, consisting of coast-defence vessels and second-class torpedo craft, to the Ping-yang inlet. This was then secured, and with it the treaty port of Chinampo. Togo had already informed the military department that it would be safe to transport troops to Chinampo, and thereupon the main portion of the 1st Army Corps (Kuroki's) was despatched from Japan, and proceeded to disembark at Chinampo. Thence it moved at once to reinforce the Division, which, after having occupied Seoul, had moved up to hold the strategic point which the company they had disembarked at Haiju had already seized. By March 15 Kuroki's army corps had all been landed in Korea.

To return to the naval operations. Russia had been convulsed by the news of her initial disasters. It was realised, now too late, that there had been nothing of unjustified bravado in the Japanese attitude. A movement was made at once to place the direction of affairs in the Far East in more capable hands. Admiral Makaroff, who possessed a world-wide reputation, was despatched post-haste to take supreme command of the Pacific Squadron, whose disasters were traced, and not unfairly, to the incompetency of Admiral Starck, the existing naval commander. General Kuropatkin, who was considered even by German authorities to be one of the ablest soldiers in Europe, was appointed to the chief command of the military forces in Manchuria; whilst orders were given that the home fleet should at once be mobilised, and as soon as the necessary naval arrangements could be perfected, despatched to the Far East.

The Japanese on their part, while waiting on the weather to enable them to proceed with their plans, entered into a political arrangement with the court at Seoul, tantamount to a protectorate over the peninsula, which, in order to forestall the Russian movements, they had found it necessary to invade. They were busy also mobilising their reserves, as the success of the naval operations now warranted their making their further movements without fear of interference, as soon as the ice should have broken up on the northern shores of the Yellow Sea.

Their successes had been extraordinary, and it is not a matter for surprise, in a country such as this, where we are bound to Japan not only by a solemn compact of alliance but also by that sentiment which is inseparable from this nation when it views a weaker in conflict with a greater, that the enthusiasm to some degree warped our comprehension of the due proportions of the struggle. Thus we failed to consider the limitations of Japan, nor stopped to analyse the remaining energy of Russia.

March was more or less marked by a lull in the sea operations. The Russians were engaged in an attempt to repair the disasters of the first month's war, while the Japanese were pressing on their invasion of Korea, which in itself was a co-operation with the naval strategy of Admiral Togo. Togo's fleet, however, was not absolutely idle: at stated intervals it appeared off Port Arthur and attempted to maintain the state of demoralisation within the fortress by long-range shelling; also further torpedo and blockading attacks were put into force.

Admiral Makaroff, the hope of the Russian navy, had arrived. His presence had an electrical effect upon the naval forces: the injured ships were placed under repair, the entrance was surveyed for a passage, and such obstacles as had become effective by the Japanese action were removed by blasting. By the 20th of March a passage was declared practicable, and Makaroff at once took such ships of his squadron as were seaworthy out to sea. What his ultimate intentions may have been it is impossible to say, but we know that after his first cruise in the open sea he returned to port, and Togo, who was apprised of every movement of the Russian ships, again swooped down on Port Arthur before the new Russian activity could effect anything.

On the night of 26th March a further fleet of merchantmen was convoyed to Port Arthur, and a third attempt made to block the channel. It was claimed at the time that the enterprise had been entirely successful; but in light of subsequent events it would appear that the Russian destroyers succeeded in torpedoing the two leading vessels, and thus diverted the course of those which followed. It is evident that from this time forward Admiral Togo was of the opinion that although he had not succeeded in absolutely choking the entrance channel to Port Arthur, yet he had sufficiently obstructed it to make the passage of ships of large displacement a tardy and difficult proceeding. Other plans were maturing in his mind: a Japanese naval officer belonging to the Scientific Research Department had invented a marine mine, for which he claimed most devastating powers. Togo determined to employ these mines in conjunction with a scheme of simple strategy, by which he hoped either to entice the Russian squadron out to sea, or, if he failed to destroy it in a fleet action, at least be able to drive it back to Port Arthur through an area sown with these blockade mines.

On April 12 a specially constructed mine-laying vessel, accompanied by two destroyer divisions and escorted by a cruiser squadron consisting of two first-class and four second-class cruisers, left the base at Haiju. They were calculated to arrive off Port Arthur about midnight. In the meantime Togo took his battle squadron and his squadron of first-class cruisers to a rendezvous twenty miles south-east of Port Arthur, timing himself to arrive at this rendezvous at daybreak on the 13th. The set scheme was as follows: The mine-laying craft was to sow an area in front of Port Arthur with a quantity of contact mines; at daybreak the escorting squadron was to sail in towards the fortress as near as possible without running undue risks from the shore batteries.

It was conjectured that as Makaroff now had a considerable fleet of seaworthy ships, and was, moreover, anxious to bring about some event that would more or less balance Russia's lost naval prestige, he would bring his squadron out, and attempt to get on terms with this weak decoy-squadron. The latter would then steer a south-westerly course, so calculated as to bring the Russians over the mine-field. If, however, they failed to come to grief upon the mines, and continued to pursue, Togo with his battle squadron would be in a position, provided the pursuit was sufficiently maintained, to cut them off.

Simple as this trap was in its conception, yet Makaroff fell into it. The mine-laying ship successfully distributed her engines of destruction in spite of the fact that the *Bayan*, the Russian guard-ship, discovered her and her attendant torpedo craft at daybreak. The weak Japanese squadron was descried dangerously close in under the forts. Makaroff personally took out a powerful squadron to pursue. The Japanese squadron at once steered its false course, and for fifteen miles the Russians pursued it, and even engaged it with long-range fire.

At this juncture an innovation in naval strategy and warfare was brought into play. It had been agreed that, when the admiral commanding the Japanese decoy-squadron should consider that he had enticed the Russian fleet far enough away from the support of Port Arthur, he should communicate by wireless telegraphy with the *Mikasa*,[1] and thus acquaint the commander-in-chief when the moment was propitious for him to appear upon the scene. It is not certain whether this message reached Admiral Togo or not. An impression prevailed at the time that it did so; also that Admiral Makaroff, on the *Petropavlovsk*, intercepted the message, and had his suspicions aroused. But from the statement of a Russian officer who was present, it would seem that the look-out on Golden Hill descried the smoke of the Japanese fleet at Togo's rendezvous, and reported the danger to the Russian admiral by wireless telegraphy.

Whatever the cause, this part of the plan missed

[1] Admiral Togo's flag-ship.

fire; for though Admiral Togo, about eight o'clock, took his battle squadron forward at full steam, he arrived on the scene too late to intercept the retreating Russians. The other alternative to the plan had, however, fatal effect. As the Russians in line ahead, with the *Petropavlovsk* in the van, were nearing their haven, the great flag-ship struck one of the blockade mines amidships. As these mines are so weighted that they lie about fifteen feet below the surface, it is probable that the *Petropavlovsk* was hit below the armoured belt. She reeled and listed from the stroke, and then her heavy superstructure took her over so that she sank, practically with all hands, within five minutes, taking the gallant admiral and his staff with her.

By good fortune rather than by good management, the rest of the Russian squadron was able to reach port safely. Although it was impossible to do other than acclaim the astuteness of the Japanese strategy, yet a thrill of horror passed through the whole world when for the first time the enormity of the calamities possible in modern naval warfare were realised. Although the Japanese were naturally jubilant over this success, which so materially reduced the fighting vigour of their opponents, still they received the news of the death of the Russian commander-in-chief in a most honourable and sympathetic manner.

During the foregoing narrative we have purposely

omitted making reference to many of the small naval encounters which took place before Port Arthur. But we must make reference to the first appearance of the Russian Vladivostok squadron on the scene of operations. Within a few days of the declaration of war it had effected nothing beyond the sinking of a wretched little packet-boat, but on the 25th of April it appeared off Gensen: its torpedo-boats entered the roadstead and did some damage. On the following day the fleet intercepted a Japanese troop-transport, which they sank under circumstances which, at the time, when judged from Japan's point of consideration, appeared distressing. In reality, the loss of troop-ships will always be distressing when the transportation of troops is undertaken before a nation has complete command of the seas.

The true story of the sinking of the *Kinshu Maru* shows that the Russian commander had no choice in the matter. He parleyed with the officers of the transport, and allowed them a time limit to remove into the boats. But, intoxicated by the obligations ingrained by a past fanaticism, the troops on the *Kinshu Maru*, of their own accord, opened a rifle fusilade upon their captor. In such case the Russians had no alternative but to sink the vessel as she was.

With the demoralisation which set in upon the Russian navy after the disaster to Makaroff and the *Petropavlovsk*, and with the proof of the superiority of his own destroyer flotilla both in speed and material which he had gained through the success of the three or four destroyer encounters, Togo felt justified in removing his base from the coast of Korea to the Elliot Islands, and making a last desperate effort to effectually seal Port Arthur.

The sealing expedition failed through the activity of the Russian destroyers, and Togo made no further attempt of this kind. The naval and military calculations had synchronised admirably—in fact, the whole programme for the initial invasion had dovetailed far better than the Japanese, even in their most optimistic mood, could ever have imagined. And here a point should be remembered which is of importance later— the military department was not fully prepared for this very rapid breakdown of the Russian naval defence: they were ready at the moment for the 1st Army Corps to cross the Yalu; their second army was waiting to be conveyed to the Liautung peninsula, but the third and fourth armies, including the material for siege operations against Port Arthur, were not so far progressed. It was while these were being pushed forward with fever haste that that procrastination occurred which we fancy in the long-run militated against the complete success of the Japanese land forces. It was the old story of a military organisation being prepared against every contingency except unchecked success.

About the middle of April the coast-defence squadron, which has been already mentioned as occupying Chinampo, moved up north and established itself at the mouth of the Yalu. Its northward movement was calculated to fit in with the advance of Kuroki's army from Ping-yang. This force, steadily driving the few Russian observation posts before it, had established itself firmly on the south bank of the Yalu during the last week in April.

In the meantime a great fleet of transports, with the second invading army on board, had assembled, half at Chinampo and half under the escort of Togo in his new base, and was waiting for the moment when Kuroki should successfully effect the passage of the Yalu. This was accomplished, as will be shown in a subsequent chapter, at the beginning of May.

As soon as the General Staff realised that Kuroki had for the time being effectively crushed all opposition on his immediate front, the fiat went forward for the second army to land. The movement of this second army was the movement upon which Japan's main hope of success hung. It was a movement destined to effect a complete isolation of Port Arthur, and consequently was intimately connected with Togo's naval strategy.

It had always been realised by the Japanese naval experts that, although they might be able to cope with the Russian Pacific Squadron as they found it when the war broke out, yet they had ever to face the possibility of Russia's receiving naval reinforcements from Europe. They had also to calculate that although they had been eminently successful so far, and had been able to inflict great damage to the enemy's naval strength without serious loss to themselves, yet it was always possible, as the result of a fleet action or accident, that their own numbers might be reduced, while it was impossible for them, situated as they were, not to suffer from deterioration after a prolonged sea struggle.

Port Arthur was the only Russian ice-free base in the Far East. If they could succeed in gaining possession of this stronghold, they at once quadrupled the difficulties of any attempt on Russia's part to regain her lost sea supremacy. Added to this was the sentiment with regard to Port Arthur which is very deeply ingrained in the Japanese nation, to say nothing of the hope of being able to acquire on the mud bottom of the Port Arthur reaches magnificent vessels which would add to Japanese strength and power in the future.

The duty of the second army, once Kuroki had established himself in south-east Manchuria, was the isolation of Port Arthur. Having effected this, it could then march northwards to frustrate any endeavour made by the Russians to raise the investment, while behind it the necessary forces would be able to land to carry out combined operations against the fortress. It was in the landing and equipping of the Port Arthur forces that the Japanese organisation was not yet fully prepared.

The second army landed in May, and during that month carried out the splendid campaign in which it not only isolated the fortress but beat the garrison back from its first line of defence at the fortified position of Nanshan. This gave the Japanese possession of Dalny, the landing base which, being an ice-free port, was essential both for the maintenance of the armies advancing to the north and for the organisation of siege operations against Port Arthur.

We have thus followed in outline the main features of the operations in May, in order to keep a continuity of the whole strategy of the campaign as it affects both services. We will now return to the naval operations proper. From the occupation of Pulientien by the land forces it may be said that for a while fickle fortune turned against the Imperial Japanese navy: hitherto its successes had been unprecedented, but from this point onwards to a very considerable degree the pendulum began its backward swing.

To begin with, Togo was obliged to again augment Admiral Kamimura's squadron, watching the Russian Vladivostok cruisers. This Russian force, which consisted of the four cruisers *Gromovoi, Rossia, Rurik,* and *Bogatyr,* was causing considerable anxiety in Japan.

The vessels were the fastest on the Pacific coast; they were handled far more expeditiously than the ill-fated Port Arthur fleet had been; and they had successfully outwitted the Japanese squadron which had been told off to prevent them from harrying the Japanese sea-communications.

Togo himself, based in the Elliot group, had always to keep a sufficient portion of his main squadron under steam to enable him to meet any sortie from Port Arthur; he had also from May 26 to maintain the blockade of the Kwantung peninsula, which he declared on this date. All this entailed enormous strain both on the *personnel* and *matériel* of his forces. Much as his ships required docking and attendance, he could only spare them when the necessity became extreme. As it was, although his gunboats and torpedo craft did their best, the blockade was very ineffective. But this was not his worst case. On May 12 mine-dragging operations in Talien Bay cost him a torpedo-boat; two days later the same work overwhelmed in destruction the gunboat *Miyako*. But his tonnage casualties did not cease here. In one fatal period of forty-eight hours he sustained losses which at the time were not appreciated in this country.

On May 15 he lost a second-class cruiser while dragging for mines in Dalny harbour, and on the same day a terrific disaster befell his battle squadron. The lesson which he had taught the Russians on 13th

April was to rebound upon him with double significance. Four battleships were cruising off Port Arthur when they were overtaken by one of those dense fogs which are common in the Yellow Sea during this season of the year. The Russian mine-laying vessel, the *Amur*, was out taking advantage of the fog, and was laying blockade mines in a similar fashion to that in which the Japanese themselves had laid them. Unsuspecting of the danger, the line of Japanese battleships, with the *Hatsuse* leading, steamed into the mine-field: the *Hatsuse* sank almost as rapidly as the *Petropavlovsk* had done; and almost immediately the *Yashima*,[1] who came to the flag-ship's assistance, exploded another mine. The *Hatsuse* sank in thirty fathoms of water, but the *Yashima* was towed in a sinking condition to the rendezvous. It was impossible to bring her into a secure position, and she sank somewhere near the Elliot Group.

To return to the brighter side: on May 17 a coast-defence squadron reconnoitred into Kinchau Bay (Port Adams inlet), and shelled the advanced position which the Port Arthur garrison was holding at Nanshan. They demonstrated that their fire could take the Russian works on the Kwantung isthmus

[1] Owing to the splendid secrecy which the Japanese have been able to maintain with regard to both their naval and military operations, there was some doubt with regard to the loss of the *Yashima*. At the conclusion of peace the loss was officially confirmed in Tokio.

in reverse, and then, satisfied with this discovery, steamed away to report their success to the military authorities. As a result of this reconnaissance, the attack on Kinchau town and the Nanshan position was proceeded with at once, the same flotilla of gunboats co-operating with complete success on May 26.

June opened with opportunities for the Russian fleet, which, we believe, if Admiral Makaroff had been spared, would have been turned to serious effect against Togo's force. Owing to the resource of a Scottish naval engineer, the damage to the *Tsarevitch* and *Retvisan* had been repaired. Admiral Witgeft had therefore six seaworthy battleships, five cruisers, and four divisions of destroyers. As Admiral Togo had detached three first-class and three second-class cruisers to watch Vladivostok, he would only have been able to oppose four battleships and six first-class cruisers against a Russian sortie in full force.

The situation, therefore, was one of anxiety, for although the Japanese possessed the moral advantages, yet the strain of four months' activity had not failed to deteriorate the steaming-power of the ships. The recent disasters, too, counselled caution, for their secret service from Europe had warned them that the powerful squadron in the Baltic was a real menace; that the delay at which many in this country jeered was not due so much to want of seaworthiness as to the necessity of completing a coaling scheme which would not break down during the passage to Far Eastern waters. A disastrous fleet action would have placed Japan at the mercy of the Baltic fleet, however inferior its *personnel*. It was considerations such as these that dominated Admiral Togo's strategy throughout the campaign, and more especially so after the *Hatsuse* incident.

By the middle of June there were evidences of activity in the Port Arthur roadstead. Mine-clearing operations had been diligently pursued, and a passage cleared. On June the 14th several of the larger ships, including the *Retvisan*, negotiated the passage and anchored in the outer roadstead. The value of the Japanese blockading operations was here demonstrated. It took so long for large-draught vessels to clear the sunken obstacles that it was impossible for the Russian admiral to get his squadron to sea without detection. Moreover, and this was even more important, it was impossible to navigate the now intricate fairway during thick weather.

While the Port Arthur squadron was again showing activity, the Vladivostok cruisers made a daring raid right down to the straits of Tsushima. Here they intercepted three of the Japanese troop-transports, and the incident of the *Kinshu Maru* was repeated. The Russian squadron had caught Admiral Kamimura unawares, and although he succeeded in getting into touch with the retreating Russians, yet he had not been able to move against them with his whole strength, and his chase was purposely abortive. This incident, which was the most daring exploit the Russians had yet engaged in, raised a storm of feeling in Japan. It was the first direct evidence that the country had, that sea-supremacy is not effected until the open sea is absolutely closed to your enemy. Chagrin for the loss of their soldiers on the transports, and consternation for the safety of their shores, blinded them against making allowances for the strain and wear which had been the price by which their navy had won success. There was a general outcry against Admiral Kamimura,—one rabid newspaper displaying in its window the knife which it proposed sending to the admiral to aid him in self-destruction.

It is evident that the Vladivostok squadron had come so far south to carry out some preconcerted co-operation with the Port Arthur fleet. That Admiral Witgeft essayed some movement is proved by the appearance of his fleet in the outer anchorage. What deterred him we shall never know; but it is safe to conjecture that the object of the movement was a concentration of the two squadrons in the Korean Straits, concerted action against the coastline of Japan, and a final withdrawal to Vladivostok. It is likewise admissible to conjecture that this was frustrated by the vigilance of Togo's blockading squadron.

It may be remarked here that no recent reference has been made to our books of reference. We may point out that as both Mr Palmer's and Mr Story's works refer almost exclusively to the land operations, they will be dealt with in a subsequent chapter. We have quoted sufficient from Mr Cowen's book to show that he has culled his naval information from sensational newspaper reports and meagre official statements. As he is inaccurate in his descriptive detail, and as neither official reports nor Japanese newspaper articles dilate upon the strategical conditions which we have discussed, we have failed to find anything illuminating on the subject in his volume.

Although Admiral Witgeft failed to put to sea when he first cleared the entrance, it was evident that if the effort to escape was to be made, it must be soon. The investing army was rapidly being converted into a besieging force, and it could only be a matter of weeks before the Port Arthur harbour ceased to be a haven from the fire of the shore batteries.

On June 23 the Russian admiral made his first effort. It was clumsy,—but it was an effort. The blockading squadron noticed that the Russian battleships were making the passage of the entrance in the evening of June 22. It was a ponderous undertaking, for the majority were towed out. It was not until the forenoon of the 23rd that the squadron was anchored in entirety in the outer roadstead. Togo had been apprised of the movement on the previous evening. His desire was to shepherd the Russians, when they took to the open sea, until the time was propitious to engage them. Japanese strategists say that until he had proved the fighting energy remaining with the Russians, he intended to avoid a decisive fleet action. His subsequent tactics go far to confirm this assumption.

Knowing that he was discovered, and consequently the risks he ran, the Russian admiral acted as if he were prepared to engage Togo. His squadron upanchored and steered for the Shantung promontory before midday. The story is short and dispiriting. Togo, who was stationed again at his old *point d'appui*, Encounter Rock, as soon as his scouts informed him of the Russian movements, steered a course which would have brought him across the *Tsarevitch's* bows. The Russians had six battleships, the Japanese four with six armoured cruisers. Bold as Admiral Witgeft's intentions may have been, yet he made the "fatal half-turn" which discloses moral inferiority. He modified his course to avoid closing with the Japanese,—that is, he allowed Togo to effect his object of shepherding him. By three in the afternoon, unless Witgeft contemplated a bold tactical move, and an engagement, his original course was lost to him. His object does not matter. Togo was between him and the Shantung coast when the Russian squadron suddenly disintegrated, and made its best speed back to Port Arthur.

Whether the admiral ordered this manœuvre, whether the crews mutinied, we do not know. Togo launched his destroyers after them, as his battleships had not now the pace of the Russians. However, only a moral success had been gained. The incapacity of the Pacific Squadron was, however, definitely ascertained. To regain sea supremacy Russia would have to look to her European reinforcements.

July was not marked with great naval activity. The Vladivostok destroyers paid a visit to Gensen, and the cruisers carried out a buccaneering raid into the Pacific, their successes being gained mainly over unarmed neutral shipping.

It was in August that the day of reckoning was to come. No fleet had yet sailed from the Baltic to turn the balance in Witgeft's favour. General Nogi's army was steadily drawing its siege tentacles round Port Arthur. The last moment for enterprise on the part of the Pacific Squadron had arrived. They must make their bid for freedom now—or be prepared to share the fate of the garrison that was grimly keeping the covetous yellow hands off them.

On August the 10th Admiral Witgeft made his expiring effort. The premises are very similar to those in the last previous sortie. The Russian squadron left the outer anchorage at Port Arthur about the same time, and Togo was waiting with his four battleships, two armoured cruisers, four protected cruisers, and several divisions of destroyers at Encounter Rock. The Russian squadron, consisting of six battleships, four cruisers, and two destroyer divisions, was steering for the promontory. On paper the Russian was the stronger force. Togo, however, had taken into account the deterioration both in *moral* and *matériel* which his successful operations had caused, and this time he was determined upon a fleet action. But he was determined, if possible, to prevent an escape similar to the last. He therefore manœuvred in front of the Russian vessels, which were in line-ahead, with the *Tsarevitch* as flag-ship in the van. By changing his formation from line-ahead to line-abreast, and back again three times, and then making a sweep to the south, at 2.30 P.M. he had the Russians steering a westerly course, while his own squadron, in line-ahead, was steering a like course 9000 yards south of them.

An hour and a half previous to this there had been some ineffective firing, but it was not until 2.30 P.M. that the real fleet action opened. We have only Japanese accounts, and the sketch published in the December number of 'Blackwood's Magazine,'[1] upon

---

[1] "The War in the Far East: V., The Fall of the Mighty," in 'Maga' for December 1904.

which to base our study of the detail of this action; for the Russian official accounts were of the sketchiest, and the information hitherto supplied by the officers of the ill-fated Russian flag-ship have not been of high professional value. But it is certain that for a considerable period the Russian squadron held its own, and we know now that one Japanese battleship was seriously damaged.

It must have been a grand spectacle, this the first fleet-action of modern warships in the world's history. Is it not a trenchant lesson that the victory should have gone to a nation that sixty years ago knew nothing, and cared less, about our Western civilisation? There seems something uncanny in the thought that the blood-red battle-flag, the emblem of a rising Eastern sun, should have triumphed over the blue St Andrew's Cross. But one can see the picture of those ponderous leviathans closing on each other as they rose and fell to the leaden sea. How their dull sombre-painted hulls suddenly belched out the flashes of lurid yellow that have taken the place of Nelson's smoke. The splash and ricochet of giant projectiles. The din and tumult of thundering chase and bursting shell. The shivering of metal plates and pungent pall of picric fumes. Then the shambles on the decks, the carnage in the tops and casements.

The fight engrossed the squadrons all through the afternoon. The Japanese Admiral, feeling his superi-

THE RUSSIAN LINE BROKEN. 57

ority in accuracy of shooting, decreased the distance until the final issues were in the balance at 4000 yards. The sea was getting up, and Togo, who in the afternoon was joined by two more of his armoured cruisers, feared that a gale of wind might enable the Russians to break through him.

About half-past six the climax was reached. A 12-inch shell hit the *Tsarevitch* just at the base of the foremast. Its burst killed the Russian Admiral and made a clean sweep of his flag-officers. At the same moment the Russian flag-ship ceased to steer. She made a sweep to port; the ships following her conformed to her erratic manœuvre. There was no one in authority to correct the formation, and in five minutes the cohesion of the Russian squadron, which up to this moment had been admirable, was lost. Once lost it was never regained. The Japanese were not slow to seize their opportunity, and they poured a devastating fire into the medley of ironclads, which in their anxiety not to collide were furnishing a perfect target at a murderous range.

At this juncture the Japanese were joined by the coast-defence battleship *Fuso* and two more cruisers. The Russians broke up, and individually sought safety in flight, pursued into the darkness of night by the Japanese destroyers. Five of the Russian battleships and one cruiser returned to Port Arthur: the *Tsarevitch*, the *Novik*, and three destroyers escaped to

German waters; the *Askold* and a destroyer fled to Shanghai, and the *Diana* to Saigon.

Thus ended the luckless Witgeft's bid for freedom. Although we readily admit that Togo out-manœuvred his adversary, yet we cannot but think that the chances of war favoured the Japanese. There had been no diminution in the Russian fire, no sign of waning strength, until the lucky shot destroyed both the admiral and the steering-gear of the flag-ship. The combination destroyed the cohesion of the fighting line and caused a climax which, with ordinary fortune, even if the Japanese were in every way superior, might have been staved off until darkness or increasing weather saved them from a decisive issue. The damage sustained by the *Tsarevitch* was not great. Although she had been hit by fifteen large calibre projectiles, her thick armour was not pierced. Two large shells had entered her superstructure forward and another had exploded on her after-turret. That was all she showed after a five-hours' engagement, with the fire of the Japanese fleet concentrated on her at effective ranges.

The damage to the other Russian battleships is not definitely known, neither does it matter, as they returned to Port Arthur, if all reports are true, to be ignominiously destroyed as disarmed hulks by the fire from shore batteries. The damage sustained by the Japanese fleet has been jealously concealed. The casualties, however, on the *Mikasa* were 111: that is more than on any Russian ship.

It was a dismal ending to the glory of a battle squadron. Two-thirds of its strength lying down to die in Port Arthur, the other third ignominiously fleeing to the shelter of a neutral flag, and accepting emasculation as the price of protection.

A curious incident occurred with regard to the Russian destroyers which escaped from this action. Two, pursued by Japanese boats of similar type, were deliberately beached on the Shantung coast a few miles from Wei-hai-wei. The stranded officers marched into the British port and craved protection from the naval commander-in-chief. Admiral Noel refused to have anything to do with them unless they complied with the international usage with regard to neutral zones. Having no choice, the Russians surrendered their arms, and claimed the surrender privileges of distressed belligerents.

In Chefoo, however, another precedent was established. A Russian destroyer, the *Reshitelni*, sought a haven in this port. It was followed to its anchorage by two Japanese destroyers, and after twenty-four hours a Japanese officer boarded the *Reshitelni* and claimed her as a prize, since he insisted that the vessel had coaled, and had failed to comply with the demands of the Chinese authorities that she should disarm. An altercation followed between the Russian commander and the Japanese boarding officer, with the result that, in Mr Cowen's picturesque language, " The Russians, thereupon, heaved the Japanese off the deck into the sea, and exploded the ship's powder-magazine, the crew all swimming ashore. The Japanese then took the *Reshitelni* in tow, and put to sea, claiming her as a lawful prize."

Before concluding the obsequies of the Russian Pacific fleet, we must place on record the expiring effort of the Vladivostok squadron. Doubtless, hoping that on this occasion they would not be disappointed in making a junction with the Port Arthur fleet, the three Vladivostok cruisers left port on August the 12th. Early in the morning of the 14th they were in the Korean Straits. On this occasion Admiral Kamimura was ready for them with a squadron consisting of four armoured and two second-class cruisers.

The Russians, naturally enough, tried to avoid an action against such a superior force. But the best pace of the troop is that of the slowest horse, and the slow *Rurik* brought the Russian squadron to battle. The Russian commodore stood gallantly by his consort, whose steering-gear was carried away by one of the first of the Japanese shells. Later, when the *Rurik's* case was seen to be hopeless, the *Gromovoi* and *Rossia*, badly damaged, steamed away. Kamimura left the lame Russian duck to his two second-class cruisers, and pursued the major portion of the Russian squadron. The Russians were in bad case. Three of the boilers in the *Rossia* had been rendered useless, and she had eleven hits below the water-line, while the *Gromovoi* had six. The collective casualties amounted to 25 per cent of the united ships' companies. But for some reason, hitherto unexplained, about ten o'clock the pursuing squadron sheered off. One can only conjecture that the Russian shooting had been too effective to warrant Kamimura continuing the action, or that in the five hours' engagement he had expended either his ammunition or his coal. He returned to the scene of the first encounter to find that the buccaneering *Rurik* had ceased to exist, having been sunk by the *Naniwa*.

Six days later the gallant little *Novik*, which before all the Russian ships in the Far East has covered herself with glory, was engaged and destroyed by two Japanese cruisers while endeavouring to make Vladivostok. The long sweep which she had made after leaving Shanghai had almost exhausted her coal: this, and the many hurts she had received in action, had impaired her speed, otherwise she would never have been caught. Her history in this war should serve as a lesson to our naval architects.

The ignominious destruction of the five battleships and two cruisers in Port Arthur roadstead by the Japanese shore batteries closes the naval operations for 1904. The result is the most signal demonstration of the triumph of skill, discreet enterprise, and seamanship that the naval history of the world records, if perhaps we except the Armada. In ten months the united efforts of Japan's naval and military forces have succeeded, while maintaining their own fleet as a serviceable striking force, in totally destroying six first-class battleships, eight cruisers, and a dozen lesser craft. They have also driven out of the field into neutral ports one first-class battleship, two cruisers, and four destroyers. The only remnants of the magnificent Russian Pacific fleet are the *Gromovoi* and *Rossia*, the fighting value of which is materially reduced. The cost to Japan has been infinitesimal in comparison with the results attained. We believe Admiral Togo's fleet at the present moment to comprise four battleships and eight armoured cruisers, irrespective of his smaller vessels, which have suffered about ten per cent in casualties. How far the power of this fleet has been impaired by the stress of war it is impossible to estimate. It may have deteriorated something if the Russian gun-practice was as good on the 10th and 14th of August as we have reason to believe it was.

II. THE LAND CAMPAIGN TO THE PASSAGE OF THE YALU.

WE have shown in the previous chapter the considerations which prompted the Naval Department of Japan to throw down the gauntlet to the Russian Pacific Squadron. It was prepared to carry out to the letter all it promised to the Cabinet. The subsequent campaign has proved that it did not under-estimate the task which stood in front of it. It is now our intention to make a brief and cursory study of the land operations as conducted by the Japanese War Department.

Considering the high estimate which the Western world placed upon Russia's military organisation, it was not so much the fact that the Japanese were prepared to face the Russians on the water that impressed Europe, as that they should also contemplate land operations on a large scale. As far as we can judge, it was the Japanese navy that was the less confident of the two services. The War Department in Tokio entertained little apprehension with regard to the success of their land operations, provided the navy could carry out its share in the general scheme. We will presently show the reason for this confidence. Meanwhile we will study the Russian military attitude towards Japan.

Not unnaturally the Russian military attitude was based upon political assurances, and, as was pointed out in the previous chapter, the political interests prevailing in the Far East were naval, and the Russian navy was optimistic to an extent wholly unjustified except by its paper value. As a consequence of this optimism, Russia suddenly found herself confronted with a situation for which her preparation was practically nil. We in the West do not understand this; but there was not a single Russian weakness in the Far East hidden from the knowledge of the Japanese Intelligence Department.

Politically, Russia did not believe that Japan would ever dare make the venture; navally, Russia classed a conflict with Japan as a picnic; and, militarily, Russia never gave the matter serious consideration. It is difficult to understand how Russia could have been so misinformed as to the genuine character of the Japanese attitude throughout the negotiations. It is almost impossible for the essayist to wrestle with all the conflicting reasons which underlay Russia's foreign policy. But we feel sure that to some degree Russia's disaster may be traced to their representative in Tokio. Baron Rosen, the Russian Minister, had been in Japan during the early days of his service. Since his return, after a lapse of years, as Minister to the reformed capital, he had never been able to disassociate from the Japanese character impressions which he had formed when the people were swaying in the throes of a national reformation. In those days it was almost impossible to take the nation seriously, and Baron Rosen as Minister never emancipated himself from the views which he formed when a junior secretary. Consequently we may surmise that the Foreign Office in St Petersburg read their naval and military attachés' estimate of preparation and progress through the Minister's spectacles.

On the 1st of February 1904 the Japanese Government were determined to take the fateful step. The Japanese War Office was prepared, as soon as the navy should have succeeded in obtaining reasonable command of the seas, to throw into Manchuria an army of 220,000. Although on this date this force was not already mobilised, yet the mobilisation warnings were in circulation, and every preparation was ready to allow of an instant embarkation.

In Russian Manchuria there existed a very different state of affairs. We have seen no published estimate of the Russian garrison in their trans-Amur province that has not been 50 per cent above the estimate existing in the Japanese Intelligence Department. We were told by some authorities that, on the outbreak of war, Russia had 200,000 men east of the Amur; by others that she had 150,000; and by all that 200,000 was the full limit which the carrying capacity of the trans-Siberian Railway could maintain. It may therefore come as a shock to the majority of military experts in this country to learn that the Japanese estimate of the Russian forces east of the Amur, on the 1st of February 1904, was under 100,000 men. These numbers included railway-guard troops—11,000 infantry, 8400 cavalry, and 1200 gunners. Of the whole force 26,000, inclusive of railway-guards, were south of Mukden, 15,000 between Tie-ling, Kirin, and Harbin inclusive, 11,000 scattered between Nikolsk and Bukhatu, 16,000 between Possiet Bay and Khabarovsk; of the rest of the total, 1000 were at Blagoveschensk, perhaps 10,000 in outlying posts, and just over 10,000 on the line of the Amur.[1]

These figures, in conjunction with the poor estimate which European experts had made of the carrying capabilities of the trans-Siberian railway, are sufficient to explain the optimism of the Japanese War Department. They will further, to a very considerable degree, explain the phenomena of the Japanese initial successes.

[1] Mr Greener, in his book, 'A Secret Agent in Port Arthur' (Constable), states that there were 202,150 men east of Baikal. We prefer to believe the Japanese War Department, of whose estimate we have documentary evidence, as to the force south of the line of the Amur.

We will now study the Japanese plan of campaign. Although it is impossible for any one at this period to make an authoritative statement, yet in view of the sequence in which events have followed each other in Manchuria during the past year, it is possible to arrive at a very accurate surmise. Three main objectives stand out in the Japanese campaign. The first and essential is the command of the sea; the second the occupation of Mukden; and the third the isolation, and incidentally the reduction, of Port Arthur. It was without doubt the intention of the Japanese, when they so rapidly gained a working command of the sea, to isolate Port Arthur, drive the Russians out of the rest of the Liautung peninsula, and to occupy Mukden before the severity of a Manchurian winter should paralyse military movements on a large scale. The impression also remains that, once this end had been accomplished, the Japanese would have been willing that diplomacy should end the struggle.

We now turn to the Russian plan of campaign. At the period the present chapter covers we can almost dismiss it in a line, for until General Kuropatkin arrived to infuse some cohesion into the nerveless military organisation no plan existed beyond a feeble endeavour to reinforce the threatened area of invasion, and a fevered haste to pour a garrison into Port Arthur. The Japanese opened their campaign with every component part of their armies in working order, while the similar organisation of Russia was in a state of chaos.

Before entering into the web of the land campaign, it may be as well, with the aid of the published statements of professional observers, to make some small study of the material which both belligerents employed to hew out their destinies in this fight for national expansion. We readily turn to Mr Palmer for his pen-sketches both of the Japanese officer and private.[1] Mr Palmer is an enthusiast, and though his descriptions, perhaps, point to exuberance, yet we can forgive that in the pen of a man who has written his essays in the camp of a victorious army. But with this slight discount his pictures seem to us lifelike. Take, for instance, his estimate of a Japanese general:—

> The general whom we see in paintings—the general of the old days of shock tactics—used to swing his sword and charge. The brigade commander, Okasawa, was at this time watching the fight from the Conical Hill. Across the space of the valley was the white tower, where no doubt the Russian general in command looked on. And by the work of the armies that lay between them, you may know the two. Our Japanese generals

---

[1] The Russo-Japanese War, by T. Cowen (Arnold). With Kuroki in Manchuria, by Frederick Palmer (Methuen). The Campaign with Kuropatkin, by Douglas Story (T. Werner Laurie). A Secret Agent in Port Arthur, by William Greener (Constable). A Modern Campaign, by David Fraser (Methuen).

know their ground and their men; and instead of becoming intent on any one piece, they follow the game as a whole. They make generalship as simple as a good approach from the green. Not until you see the sweaty effort of wasted energy on the part of a bad player do you realise the skill of the good one. Let dashing heroes who place themselves with their point take note; let general staffs whose machine is not ready sue for peace before war begins.

We will now take another view. It has been fashionable in this country to jeer at the Russian senior officers. We have also had the reports of several special correspondents, who, chafing under the restrictions which the Russian Staff placed upon their movements, and anxious to pander to the most profitable market, returned to this country to paint their late hosts in desperate colours. It would be well for the unprejudiced student of this campaign to discount to a considerable degree these ill-natured reports concerning the Russian officer, as well as much of the eulogistic vapouring in which lickspittlers have qualified the excellence of all things Japanese. From Mr Palmer's writings we judge him to be a man of the world as well as an artist. He sees the best in everything about him. It is because his eulogies of the Japanese are tempered with some restraint that we accept him as the best witness among those who have hitherto testified from personal knowledge of the character of the Japanese soldier.

We will now turn to Mr Douglas Story, and

present his view of the Russian officer. Not because we altogether agree with the thesis of his work, not because we admire the selfish motives which threw him into the Russian camp, but because we think that he feels that many of his *confrères* with the Russian Army have been untruthful, not to say vicious, in the seed of abuse which they have sown in the ready soil awaiting them in this country. Between these two authorities, and with our own observation, we may help the reader to arrive at a fairer estimate than at the present moment would appear to exist. Mr Story says:—

As a student the Russian staff officer is a gentleman and a soldier of rare intellectual attainment. He has been allowed to follow his bent, has been stimulated in the study of tongues, has been encouraged to investigate the psychology of the people dwelling upon the borders of the Czar's dominions.

A born linguist, among the French he is a Frenchman, among the Germans he is a German, even among the Chinese a Chinaman. . . .

The adaptability of the Russian is amazing,—the result of a wide humanity and ready sympathy. The Russian is as devout as was ever any commandant of Boers, as scrupulous in the observances of his religion. His nearness to nature is at all times apparent; his faults and his virtues are those of a strong race, of a man whose blood runs warm in his veins. . . . As a soldier, the Russian officer is a strangely nervous fighter, a thoroughbred pawing at the starting-point. His nerves are all a-tingle, his face flushed, his speech quick and voluble. There is none of the steady calm of the British company officer; but there is courage—plenty of it—dogged, as well as hot-blooded. He loves a fight at close quarters, and it is significant that in war-time the private goes about all his business with his bayonet fixed.

With all his excitability the Russian officer is commendably reticent with respect to the affairs of the War, and his own part in them. There is no boasting, no despondency, no unprofitable regret. He is content to do his duty as he sees it, leaving the extrication of the forces from their difficulties to those placed in authority over him. . . . One's general impression is, that the officers are a set of great-bodied, big-hearted, good-natured schoolboys, sadly pestered by the stone-throwing of the small boys from a neighbouring inferior, but rival, academy. I have not heard, in all these weeks of trial, one ungenerous word of their enemy from a Russian.

Judging from eighteen months' study of the reports from both sides during the progress of the war, we would be inclined to think that both these extracts are very near the truth. We know that the Japanese regimental officer enters upon his career as a business-in-life which knows no pastime unassociated with his profession. His ancestry and boyhood have given him a self-possession which is denied to the peoples of the Western Hemisphere. His training has made him a master of detail, and his blood is the pure heritage of a warlike race. We have in him consequently, perhaps, the finest type of regimental officer that modern history has ever known.

We will now make a short comparison, with the aid of our eyewitnesses' reports, of the fighting material in the ranks. Mr Palmer has the knack of turning happy sentences, and in the following few lines he has adequately summed up the Japanese soldier:—

Equally as well as he knows that his ammunition is good, a Japanese general knows that any force, however small, will stay where it is placed—stay alive or dead. One company is as much like another as peas in a pod. No special units; no Rough Riders; no King's Own; no stiffening of weak regiments with regiments of volunteers or regulars. There is an approximate level of courage and skill. A commander may choose the unit at hand as a mechanic takes down any one of a number of equally tempered tools from a rack. If you want a Horatius at the bridge take the nearest sergeant.

Again—

Nowhere do you better show that you are a true Samurai than on the march and in camp. You are obedience itself. Your officer provides for everything in the text-book, and you do as he says. The fault with most armies is that human nature does not permit of everything in the text-book. If you are tired, you do not throw off your blanket and knapsack, you keep on with it. The road behind a regiment is as clean of Japanese equipment as that before it. You have a marvellous way of making yourself comfortable when you break ranks. That is because you squat instead of sit, and some corn-stalks tied together make a shady place for you. A true Samurai private bathes frequently, washes his clothes, and observes sanitary regulations. You do. That is one of the pleasures of being attached to your army. Very rarely do you take too much *saké*. Property may be left about carelessly. It is safe from your hands. Not even horses are "taken" if not watched in this army. . . .

You are impersonal to the last degree; in your impersonality lies one of the causes of Japanese efficiency. The Japanese seems to think of himself always as one of many;

his squad, his company, his regiment—not himself! That makes team play easy. On the march when ranks are broken, the officers of European armies stand apart. It is bad for discipline not to keep the gulf between rank and line always in evidence. I have often seen the Japanese officer sitting among his men by the roadside and chatting with them; but always he is the officer, and so clear is the definition of feudalism that they do not think of presuming. You like to fight as squads, companies, and regiments, just as well as some white men that I know like to fight individually. One common weakness you have with every soldier of the world is home-sickness.

Mr Palmer might have added, "And you win victories."

We will now see what Mr Story has to relate of Ivan Ivanovitch, the prototype of the Russian private :—

"Ivan Ivanovitch is a big, burly, bovine type of fighting man. He is docile and respectful, long-suffering and slow to anger, simple of faith, and altogether lacking in the arrogance of the professional soldier. He will cook a meal or whitewash his officer's dwelling, nurse the child of his captain's lady, or stand long hours outside a restaurant waiting, as willingly as he will shoulder a rifle against an enemy or present arms at a review. The Russian private is never absolutely the soldier. He is the peasant in arms—dogged, loyal, and formidable. . . . He marches with the swing of a man accustomed to tramping, chanting his folk-songs. He laughs at fatigue, he cares little for extremes of temperature. Peasant-like, he drinks when vodka is obtainable; but at the front there is no vodka, and Ivan Ivanovitch lives a cleaner and healthier life as soldier in camp than ever he does as farmer on the steppes of Siberia. . . . Much vile libel has been spread about the Russian soldier's treatment of the Chinese in the war area. So far as

I have seen—and I have seen most of the country he has traversed—the Russian soldier has behaved to the Chinese with remarkable restraint and a simple-hearted good fellowship. There has been no commandeering in this war and marvellously little looting. John Chinaman and Ivan Ivanovitch are friends, with all the advantage of the friendship on the Chinaman's side. In their hours of ease Muscovite and Manchurian stroll arm in arm through the streets of the villages. There is no brutality on the part of the one and no distrust on the part of the other. The Chinaman is intellectually the Russian peasant's superior, and he uses his intelligence to curb the muscularity of Ivan the good-tempered. . . . The Russians possessed magnificent fighting material—great strong sons of the soil, who wasted no time in asking questions, who troubled not about comment or criticism, but who lacked the fierce fanaticism or the scientific direction which made their enemy irresistible.

There is little fault to be found with either of these summaries; but although on the surface they seem to differ widely, yet those of our readers who are soldiers will realise that, as food for powder, their opposite qualities bring them both to a very similar level. The Japanese is a fine fighting-man on account of his inherent discipline and patriotism; the Russian on account of his want of intelligence. Therefore, as both these critics agree that both armies possess the same military quality of dependence upon their immediate superiors, and as we have already allowed that the Japanese regimental officer possesses many points which are superior to the similar rank in the army of his enemies, we may safely venture the opinion that in the raw material necessary for warmaking the Japanese had other advantages besides numbers.

On February 9 the Japanese opened the land campaign by throwing a division into Korea. Twelve days later, General Kuropatkin was appointed to supreme military command in Russian Manchuria. As it was at least three weeks before he could arrive in the Far East to take up his appointment, we cannot consider that any military arrangements existing on the Russian side participated in any definite plan to counter this invasion of Korea. The only very sincere military undertaking was the frenzied endeavour to make Port Arthur, in the matter of works and garrison, impregnable, and a reinforcement of the weak garrison existing at Feng-hwang-cheng.

As the first two months of the land campaign only concern the 1st Army Corps of the Japanese army, we will, for the time being, confine our examination to the operations of this force. The first rôle of this army corps, which, in the beginning, consisted of 40,000 men commanded by General Kuroki, was to secure Korea against Russian invasion. It was composed of three divisions—the 2nd, the 12th, and the Guards. The 12th Division landed at Chemulpo on February 8, under the protection of Admiral Uriu's squadron. At the same time one company landed in the vicinity of Haiju, with the special object of making a forced march to Ping-yang, which was the first main strategical point that the Japanese wished to hold in Northern Korea. It was judged that if they could reach this point before the Russians, its possession would enable Kuroki to consolidate his strength in the northern area of the "Hermit Kingdom." This would answer the dual purpose of strengthening Japan's political hold over the Korean Court, and of guarding the land approaches of the advanced base which had been selected by the Navy.

At this period the winter had barely broken in Northern Korea, and the march to Ping-yang by the advance company was made in the teeth of almost arctic weather. The case of the rest of the division was not so strenuous. They immediately seized the railway and telegraphic communications of the whole peninsula. They established themselves in the capital, and, cantoning there for a few days, ensured sufficient political ascendancy to enable Mr Hayashi, the Japanese Minister, to render a final and crushing blow to Russian prestige and influence by the expulsion of Mr Pavloff, the Tzar's Plenipotentiary. This end effected, the division pushed up by brigades to Ping-yang, and established itself upon the northern strategic line.

Climatic considerations necessitated a temporary halt at Ping-yang. Chemulpo was not destined to be the sea-base of Kuroki's army. Chinampo, a treaty port, 120 miles north-west of Chemulpo, and 40 miles from Ping-yang, had been selected for this purpose; but, unlike Chemulpo, Chinampo is an icebound port, and the Japanese therefore had to await the breaking up of the ice in the Ping-yang inlet. But for the time being the object desired had been attained, and Japan had ample time to complete the more intricate arrangements for the general invasion of Manchuria.

Although we have found Mr Cowen so inaccurate that he is often ludicrous, yet we think that in matters which deal with Japan itself and of the China coast treaty ports he is worthy of attention. We may, therefore, safely quote him for the detail of the military movements which were taking place in Japan during the brief interval in the land operations, after the first dash for Ping-yang. He says :—

The soldiers of Japan were all on the move, some already crossing the water to Korea, others coming down by train to the point of embarkation. The ships had been in readiness for days, some for weeks, to take troops on board. The railway companies throughout the land had been notified, and in the flash of a single simultaneous telegram the ordinary running of trains was changed wherever necessary, and steady streams of armed men began to gravitate towards Sasebo, Nagasaki, Moji, Ujina, as if they had been so many streams of lava pouring simultaneously down the furrowed hillside of some mighty volcano which had slumbered for centuries and then suddenly began to pour out fire and molten metal.

From the above it will be seen that the Japanese machine was working perfectly from the central lever in Tokio. What a terrible parallel we find at this period in the ranks of the Russians. A fevered effort to pour every available man and all available stores into Port Arthur, that fatal siren of the Pacific Fleet. A crude and almost purposeless attempt to counterbalance the loss of prestige in Korea by a hasty reinforcement of the miserable force at Feng-hwang-cheng, the latter reinforcement to be followed by a tepid excursion by timorous Cossack patrols south of the Yalu river.

On February 28 a force of these Cossacks, more enterprising than their fellows, arrived within range of Ping-yang, to be hustled back by the Japanese force which had already been in occupation of that town over a fortnight. On the same day that the Cossacks reached the most southern point in their Korean expedition the ice in the Ping-yang inlet showed signs of disintegration, and three days later the entrance channel to the treaty port became navigable. Already the Japanese transports were at hand, and on March 4 the advance-guards of the two remaining divisions commenced to disembark.

There are few appliances in the dangerous roadsteads of the inlet calculated to faciliate disembarkation either of troops or stores. The Japanese brought everything with them: they erected landing-piers of bamboo, the better to negotiate the mud-flats; they brought a flotilla of tugs and lighters from Japan; and in one week they had converted the wretched little Korean town which fringes the mud-flats into a veritable military emporium, complete in every department, with go-downs, repository works, and even a light railway.

Mr Palmer gives a further illustration of the Japanese genius in mastering detail. Writing of Chinampo as a military sea-base, he says:—

> From the steamer we could see the new unpainted barracks and storehouses, which rose with the magic that forethought and preparedness command, soon after the first transports dropped anchor. Beyond the piled stores, beyond the artillerymen scattered in the streets or taking their horses for exercise, there is nothing of the commotion to be expected of a great military debarkation.

Each unit, as it landed, pushed forward to Ping-yang or in the direction of Anju, as the case might be. This army had its particular function to carry out. The hand on the lever in Tokio was still waiting on the climate. Although the ice had drifted down from the Ping-yang river, yet for a matter of three weeks or more the sea-entrance to the river Yalu would still be frozen. Kuroki's army, therefore, was detailed to push forward, and so establish itself within striking distance of the river Yalu, there to remain passive until its mouth should become practicable. For the time being everything that Kuroki's army required was landed at Chinampo, even to the pontoons, which were forwarded from Japan in sufficient numbers to enable the Yalu, if necessary, to be spanned in at least twelve places.

The student cannot fail to notice the similitude which existed between the Japanese first move and the strategy they employed in their campaign against China in 1894.

The Russians pushed down a force which they, in their present undermanned condition, doubtless considered adequate to delay the blow which was threatening from Korea. A certain number of elementary works, in spite of assurances to the opposite, had been commenced on the right bank of the Yalu before the outbreak of war. These were hastily improved, and for reasons which the officer commanding on the spot alone could give: these works were constructed to dispute a passage of the Yalu between the town of Chiu-lien-cheng and the sea.

Observation posts of Cossacks still remained south of the Yalu; but they fell back immediately the advancing Japanese gained touch with them. The first recorded skirmish of any importance between these Russian observation groups and the Japanese advance screen took place at Teishu on March 27.

On April 3, as the Japanese approached, the Russians evacuated Wiju, a more important village on the south bank of the Yalu; and by April 10, when the entrance of the river became practicable for navigation, General Kuroki was in possession of every approach which separated him from the Russians' selected position, and was prepared, as soon as the lever in Tokio should be turned, to attempt a passage at any of the selected points.

Before entering upon a study of the first actual decisive shock which took place between the rival armies, it will be as well to record a second step in the Japanese scheme. As soon as the Yalu became practicable, the whole of the northern coast-line of the Yellow Sea was free of ice. On April 13, true to his guarantee, Admiral Togo delivered the paralysing blow to the Russian Pacific Squadron which lost them Makaroff and a first-class line-of-battle ship, and so destroyed their *morale* that the Japanese admiral was able to inform Tokio that his supremacy was sufficient to warrant the military department in proceeding with its operations.

On this assurance, between April 15 and 20, a second great fleet of transports sailed from the Inland Sea and conveyed to the roadstead of Chinampo the *personnel* and *matériel* of the 2nd Army Corps. This force was to remain at anchor within the friendly shelter of Kuroki's base until the passage of the Yalu had been attempted. In this wise it served a double purpose: in the event of the first army being checked, a portion of the second army could be landed to reinforce it; if, however, the operations of Kuroki's force proved successful, the second army would then be free to carry out the second step in the Japanese offensive campaign.

Shortly after the Yalu became ice-free a portion of the fourth squadron—*i.e.*, the gunboat squadron of the Japanese fleet—steamed up towards Antung and took possession of Yongampo on the left bank of the river, and established it as an auxiliary base for the first army. The rival land forces were now in such juxtaposition that there was daily skirmishing. The Japanese general manœuvred so as to confirm the Russians in their false impression that the passage would be attempted between Chiu-lien-cheng and the sea.

The threatened battle on the Yalu had a wider significance than attaches to a mere preliminary clash of arms in the beginning of a great campaign. For the first time in the history of the world the Occidental had been defeated by the pure Oriental on the element which had secured the Occidental supremacy in the East. An Oriental Power, throwing aside the trammels of Asiatic traditions, had usurped the secrets responsible for Western superiority in arms: had moulded them to its own uses, and now entered the arena as the fully-diplomaed disciple. On sea the results had been disastrous to the Occidental. Would the working of Oriental evolution be crowned with similar results on land?

The West watched the issues with breathless expectation. They realised the far-reaching possibilities that were becoming unmasked in this remote corner of the globe. The Russian had never held a character as a sailor; but the West could remember a hundred incidents in evidence of his peculiar attributes as a soldier. His energies were not those of a vigorous foe; but the past had shown him to possess a quality of stubborn resistance, by which, in effect, he had attained results similar to those others gained by an exercise of military *élan*. A sympathetic Europe pinned its hopes upon Russian infantry. They had miscalculated the excellence of the similar arm in the Oriental metamorphosis. Sentimentally the battle of the Yalu was perhaps the most important incident in the first campaign. As a military incident it was far less noteworthy.

We cannot hope to do more than give an outline of the battle, and in passing correct many of the existing misconceptions concerning it. We will dispel the first, which is the estimate of the Russian numbers. On the outbreak of war the Russians had at Feng-hwang-cheng 1000 Siberian Rifles and some Cossacks. General Sassulitch was given the command of this threatened area, and during the next two months his command reached the total of 15,000 men with four batteries of field artillery.[1]

As has been suggested, he had surmised that the Japanese would attempt to cross between Wiju and Yongampo, and he distributed his force between Antung and Chiu-lien-cheng, protecting in all a front of about twelve miles. Now the main strategical feature in the Russian position was the juncture of the river Ai, with the many streams which furnish the delta of the Yalu. Roughly speaking, the Ai comes into the Yalu almost at right angles, its final westerly loop enclosing the cluster of rock which furnished the Russian main position. The angles thus formed contain, on the left, Conical Hill, the position just above Chiu-lien-cheng, and on the right, Tiger Hill, a great bluff which commands the whole theatre. Sassulitch, firm in his conviction that Kuroki intended to cross the Yalu lower down, rather than face a double passage of rivers, heavily prepared Conical Hill both as an artillery and infantry position, and only held the commanding bluff in the angle between the Ai and main stream as an outpost. The only rational interpretation that one can put upon Sassulitch's dispositions is that

[1] Thirty-two guns.

he had orders to make as brave a show as possible, in positions from which he could easily withdraw at the eleventh hour, with a force that was recognised to be numerically inferior both in men and artillery. Otherwise his dispositions are unintelligible. If he had intended seriously to dispute the passage of the Yalu, he could not have failed to have intrenched Tiger Hill. But we can understand that as the commander of a delaying force he would not care to jeopardise a large portion of his command across the Ai. This view is strengthened by the knowledge that on April 25 General Kuropatkin personally inspected the Russian positions. Thus when Kuroki was prepared to strike, the Russians simply reinforced their outposts on Tiger Hill with a weak battalion of infantry and half a battery of artillery.

Mr Fraser, an eyewitness, writes: "On 29th of April, however, it appeared as if the Russians began to suspect something. . . . Their outposts on Tiger Hill were reinforced by a battalion of infantry, two squadrons of Cossacks, and several guns." The bulk of their force remaining in the prepared position of Chiu-lien-cheng consisted of about 8000 rifles and two and a half batteries of artillery. Against this Kuroki was able to operate with a complete army corps.

A study of the handling of Kuroki's force shows very clearly that the great General Staff intended that he should carry out his operations much after the manner in which the passage of the Yalu was accomplished in the Chinese War; also that they calculated for Chiu-lien-cheng and its given outpost Tiger Hill being held in greater strength than ultimately proved to be the case. Before arriving at the Yalu the army divided into three columns: the 2nd Division deflected to the left, the Guards Division advanced upon Wiju, and the 12th Division upon Sucochin, six miles up-stream from Wiju; the latter division also detached a battalion which went to Chonson on the Yalu, forty miles above Wiju. This brought the centre of the Japanese force practically opposite Chiu-lien-cheng, a trifle below the point of the right angle Sassulitch had chosen as his main defence.

For nearly three weeks Kuroki coquetted with the Russians while he developed the Tokio plan. He made play with the 2nd Division, which had sent a detachment to Yongampo in order to confirm Sassulitch in his conviction that the passage would be attempted from this flank. The whole movements of this wing were disclosed to the Russians across the river, while the Guards Division was kept secreted as far as possible behind the town of Wiju.

In front of the Russian main position—in fact, all along the Yalu at this point—are the delta islands. By dint of clever skirmishing between the 20th and

29th, Kuroki possessed himself of the majority of these essentials to his plan. The Russians showed very little tenacity in holding the islands as advanced posts, and fell back as soon as the Japanese moved in any force. There is one island[1] which lies almost due north of Wiju, and consequently faces Conical Hill, the backbone of the Russian resistance. This island is covered with a certain amount of brush and foliage. As soon as the Japanese occupied it, they constructed, under cover of darkness, a series of gun-pits. The approaches to these earth-works were carefully hidden amongst the trees, and in such cases where a clear line of vision was possible, false-cover was fashioned from boughs and bamboos, in order to mask the movement from the Russians. The bulk of Kuroki's artillery, to which were added several batteries of howitzers, brought by sea to Yongampo, were massed behind Wiju, a certain proportion being masked in battery, the others held in readiness to cross over to the works prepared on Kintei.

Here you have the whole of the cut-and-dry Tokio plan. The defences on Conical and Tiger Hills were to be overwhelmed by a terrific concentration of the artillery fire from the direction of Wiju. Under cover of this, two divisions were to cross in the vicinity, while the 12th Division made the crossing

[1] Kintei.

higher up the Yalu, at the same spot as the Japanese had crossed in the Chinese campaign. As a plan there is no fault to find with its military arrangement. But competent European observers have expressed their opinion that when the Japanese found the Russians in such small force and only holding Tiger Hill as an outpost, the cumbrous and elaborate march from the flank might well have been modified.

On the night of the 29th the 12th Division, withdrawing its detachment from Chonson, concentrated at Sucochin, and threw itself across the Yalu by means of a pontoon-bridge. The same evening there crossed over to the island of Kintei the necessary armament for filling the prepared gun-pits, namely, twenty howitzers and twenty-six field-guns; while the Guards and the 2nd Division concentrated behind Wiju, with the intention of forcing a passage of the Yalu beneath Tiger Hill.

Hitherto the guns on Conical Hill had erratically shelled such movement as they had been able to discern in the vicinity of Wiju. This artillery practice had called forth no reply. But on the 30th all was to be changed; and suddenly, without warning, the Japanese gunners opened fire on the wretched Russian outpost on Tiger Hill, and having quickly silenced the few guns posted there, turned their attentions to the batteries in position on Conical Hill. This terrible onslaught absolutely pulverised any illusions that the Russians may have entertained as to their *rôle* of a detaining force. The gunners were swept from their pieces: the guns themselves were wrecked, and, what was even more effective, indirect fire found their horse-lines and destroyed or stampeded the teams. Practically without resistance both divisions were able to effect the passage.

Seeing that his little game of bluff had been overpowered by the first serious initiative that the Japanese undertook, Sassulitch commenced to withdraw his forces upon his reserves, which were concentrated at Hamatan, six miles in rear on the road to Feng-hwang-cheng, leaving about 4000 rifles on Conical Hill, and such of his guns as the day's misadventures had made it impossible to horse. Under the first fire the Russian outpost had evacuated Tiger Hill, and it was duly occupied when the three Japanese divisions concentrated in order to attack on the 1st of May. They had now only the river Ai, which is generally fordable, separating them from the Russian position. The howitzers were left in their pits in front of Wiju, while the field artillery was brought over into the plain east of the Ai to support the coming infantry attack.

During the early hours of May 1 the two Japanese divisions crossed from Oseki Island to Tiger Hill, and then forded the eastern branch of the Ai. This brought them on to the elongated island of Ransuto. In this ground they deployed, so that the 2nd Division faced Chiu-lien-cheng on the left, the Guards Conical Hill in the centre, while simultaneously the 12th Division appeared on the right, and debouched into the flats of the river Ai. The whole force was then committed to the attack, supported by the full blast of the corps' concentrated artillery fire. It was just a direct frontal attack all along the line. There was no cover. The blue winter uniforms of the infantrymen stood out in the sunlight against the yellow stretch of sands. The Ai was forded in full view, within eight hundred yards of the 4000 rifles which Sassulitch had left behind to detain an army corps. There could only be one result. The Japanese suffered severely until it was time for the Russians to retire. The latter then fell back rapidly on their reserves stationed at Hamatan, while the Japanese walked into possession of the Conical Hill position. At nine o'clock in the morning the Japanese standard was waving over Chiu-lien-cheng.

A portion of the 12th Japanese Division had been detached to strike the Russian communication with Feng-hwang-cheng. One gallant company of this force had pushed forward more rapidly than the others, and alone it tried to stem the tide of the retreating Russians. It lost two-thirds of its numbers, and just at the moment when the retreating Russians were about to overwhelm and destroy it, its own reinforcement arrived and in turn isolated the last of the Russian rearguard on the small hill above Hamatan. This rearguard is the force which surrendered to the Japanese. The rest of Sassulitch's army fell back on Feng-hwang-cheng. Half of his force—namely, those posted in the vicinity of Antung and the defences joining up that point with Chiu-lien-cheng—fell back without having fired a single shot.

Thus, in outline, you have the facts about the first Japanese victory on shore. As a feat of arms there was nothing extraordinary about it. The Japanese possibly caused the Russians to carry out their plan of retreat a little more precipitately than the latter had intended. That is about all that can be said. For the most casual observer must perceive that Kuroki put into force a far more elaborate design than the strength and condition of his enemy warranted, and, as a consequence, he was unable to pursue.

But, as we endeavoured to point out earlier in the paper, the significance of the Yalu does not rest with the military issue. It proved to the world that the Oriental was as prepared and organised to meet the Occidental on land as he had been on sea. For this reason, and for the sentimental reasons which we have already deplored, the importance of the initial success of the Yalu was contorted and exaggerated by Western admirers out of all proportion.

We have had occasion to take Mr Cowen to task on this subject already: we will quote him once again as an instance of the fanciful fiction which has been served up as authoritative material with regard to the battle of the Yalu, and then we will shelve him as a writer calculated to waste the military historian's time, except as an example of the extraordinary lengths to which sentiment may stimulate imagination in the discussion of international struggles.

Mr Cowen poses as an experienced war correspondent, and as a witness of this very battle — at least, this is what we would have gathered from a perusal of his narrative, if we had not chanced upon superior authorities. We have shown the reader that the Russians only held Tiger Hill as an outpost. At the most, up to mid-day on the 29th, they had three battalions and a half battery on that hill. There were no prepared entrenchments, or earth-works; also, we have shown that Tiger Hill is separated from Conical Hill and the works in front of Chiu-lien-cheng by the river Ai in double stream. Mr Cowen refers to this position as follows: "The principal Russian position was close to the river above Chiu-lien-cheng. At the junction of the Ai with the Yalu there is a bold promontory called Tiger Heads Hill. . . . This place the Russians had fortified with two earth redoubts, each having four batteries of eight guns, making sixty-four altogether. One of these forts was on a spur immediately overlooking the river, and the other on a higher hill farther back towards Chiu-lien-cheng."

The reader will see at once that Mr Cowen has made an unfortified hill, whose position in the map he does not even know, to be a prepared position of extraordinary strength, with an armament just twice as heavy as the Russians had with their whole army on the Yalu at that period. But that is nothing. A few pages farther on Mr Cowen, with much of that verbosity which, we believe, is called word-painting, describes how against this very hill, which the Japanese occupied practically without opposition on the 30th, the same troops on the 1st launched a magnificent attack. He describes in detail how the sweating and panting soldiers of the Mikado arrived at the summit, to show mercy to the hundreds of Russians who surrendered to them.

It may be fine prose, but it is not history, and it does not convince us of the sincerity animating the views and sentiments of the writer, when we find that he has rolled the fortifications of Conical Hill, the gallant assault of that position, and the bloody fight at Hamatan all on to one canvas, and placed them upon a fictitious fortress on the wrong bank of the river, a mile from the one fight and seven miles from the other. Moreover, the hill which he thus immortalises had been in the hands of the Japanese for over twenty-four hours before the various events he has saddled upon it took place. Further comment is hardly necessary: all we can say is that if Mr Cowen were, as the publisher's note leads us to believe, "in the thick of the struggle since the outbreak of hostilities," he has but small title to be taken seriously as a war correspondent. If he were not present, it would have been far better if he had confined himself to fiction than to have ruined his graphic diction by a ludicrous distortion of facts.

Having effected the passage of the Yalu, Kuroki pushed on to Feng-hwang-cheng, which the Russians had evacuated before him. Here he remained for weeks, changing his sea-base from Yongampo to Antung. The transports that were waiting at Chinampo were convoyed by the fourth naval squadron to the points selected for invasion, and the plan of the major land operations began to unroll.

III. THE LAND CAMPAIGN UP TO THE END OF JUNE 1904.

STUDENTS of modern war who have been compelled, for want of better material, into a study of the various volumes which the much-maligned war-correspondents have given us, will be unanimous in allowing that Mr Story's best effort is found in his portrait of Kuropatkin. Two sentences which he attributes to the Russian general seem to furnish a keynote to the lamentable history of Kuropatkin's campaign. He is credited with having said: "At the end of the first month they will call me inactive; at the end of the second month they will call me incapable; at the end of the third month they will call me a traitor; at the end of six months—*nous verrons!*" Again: "Ce n'est pas le moment d'acheter des maisons à Liauyang, à Mukden non plus, à Harbin—oui!"

Mr Story credits the Russian Commander-in-Chief with having uttered these sentiments on his first arrival in Manchuria. It is obvious from their tenor that Kuropatkin appreciated the magnitude of the task before him; that his mind was free from that blatant and aggressive optimism which characterised the Russian attitude early in 1904; that he was cognisant of the existing state of criminal inefficiency; that he was prepared, if necessary, to abandon Liauyang and even Mukden to his enemy until he had constructed a field army. "At the end of six months —*nous verrons!*" We have seen. And in spite of his many traducers we believe that Kuropatkin has proved himself a soldier of first rank. His task was not to engineer a railway across a desert, taking his own time and opportunity, and then to mow down a mob of unarmed fanatics with automatic weapons. He was required to construct his army in the face of a superior, aggressive, and victorious foe.

In these circumstances the military historian of the future, with the true facts and figures before him, will marvel that he escaped annihilation. The critics in this country are unanimous in the opinion that Kuropatkin should have withdrawn the garrison from Port Arthur, abandoned the whole of the Liautung peninsula, and, for the time being, ignoring the invasion, quietly organised his field army in Manchuria proper. It is easy to sit down and dogmatise after the event, and military critics are prone to forget that it is given to comparatively few commanders in the field to hold both the military and the political reins of a campaign. Even his most unfavourable critics confess that the veteran Kuropatkin realised the military disadvantages entailed in holding Port Arthur, but was controlled by a superior authority into its retention.

If this should be the case, it is hardly just to debit this action against his military ability. Surely, in judging a man, the nature of the task allotted him should be considered. The field of criticism is translated as soon as you judge upon the character of the allotted task.

But in order to be impartial, we will examine other considerations. When Kuropatkin reached Manchuria the Russians had practically lost the command of the sea. Naval considerations, therefore, however vexatious, irrespective of political prestige, sentiment, and Alexieff, could not fail to influence the Commander-in-Chief of the land forces. Another pregnant lesson of the influence of naval strategy over military co-operation. It is possible that, although during the journey between the War Bureau and Irkutsk, Kuropatkin may have counselled in his mind the evacuation of Port Arthur, yet once he reached Mukden such a course never came within the scope of his calculations. He had to cut his cloth to suit his pattern. His pattern included the Kwantung Promontory.

This pattern even had military advantages of its own. To some extent Port Arthur, if held, might prove a magnet to the Japanese in attack, as it had proved to the Russian sailors in defence. If the Russian fleet under its fighting flags could not save the army, yet its presence at Port Arthur might warp the Japanese into weakening their real striking force. Whether this was Kuropatkin's calculation it is impossible to say, but from the sentences already quoted it is evident that he realised that he would have to fall back, and that all his first dispositions were calculated to gain time,—to keep the Japanese striking at his extremities until his energy had made a staff, and the railway had given him an army.

We have shown, in a previous paper, that Sassulitch's was only a delaying force on the Yalu. The garrison of Port Arthur became the same, once the Japanese decided to invest it. The series of intrenched positions which Kuropatkin prepared along the Port Arthur-Mukden railway and on the Mandarin road were all to the same end, to prevent the Japanese striking at his heart before he had found his army.

We will endeavour to keep ourselves free from journalistic dogmatism, for the simple reason that the naval and military strategy of this campaign have been so intimately wedded, that without the full official records an absolutely fair judgment is impossible. However, we will strive to show that there has been more far-seeing method in Kuropatkin's much-jeered-at strategy than has found credit in the vulgar estimate, and leave the reader to form his own opinion of the opposing strategy which dallied with extremities while the heart was anæmic, and ultimately struck at the vitals when those organs were more robust.

The Japanese determined to land their second army on the east coast of the Liautung peninsula. Again we have an echo of the Chinese war. As has already been shown, when the Yalu engagement was won the transports conveying General Oku's army were at anchor in the Yellow Sea. The chances of a diversion by the Port Arthur fleet were remote; but to remove all chance of jeopardy to the enterprise, Togo, on May 3, made another effort to finally seal the entrance to Port Arthur, by sinking a further number of ballast-laden merchant-steamers in the entrance to the harbour.

On the following day the 4th squadron of the fleet, in the face of some puerile opposition from a few Cossacks, effected a landing at Pitsewo, and on May 5 General Oku's corps of three divisions began to disembark. We have very little information with regard to these most interesting operations. The official references are bald and unilluminating, while at this period the Japanese did not suffer foreign military attachés and correspondents to be present. We had hoped that Mr Greener's book would help us, since the author claims to have been engaged in secret service in Port Arthur or Yinkow about this period.

But his book, in spite of its pretentious title, is even less valuable to the historian than that of Mr Cowen. It is a light and, in patches, interesting record of indifferent war-correspondence. The author's value as a secret agent may be judged by the following sole reference to the highly interesting military developments we are now studying:—

"Then I received accounts of the landing of Japanese troops at Takushan; and at Pitsewo, and acting in conjunction with the force landed at Kinchow, on the other side of the peninsula, succeeded in cutting the line, and isolating Port Arthur, &c. . . ."

We do not, of course, insist upon correct grammatical construction as an essential in the work of a secret agent, but we have a right to expect more accuracy than is contained in the above garbled and senseless reference to this operation, containing as it does one gross misstatement, and a general misconception of the real movement. This is only one of the many evidences which the book contains, that the author missed his vocation when in the Far East.

The preliminaries of the Japanese strategy declared themselves during the first twenty days of May. Oku had landed at Pitsewo and Kerr Bay, and a third army corps under Nodzu was thrown into Manchuria at Takushan, on May 19.

Takushan lies practically midway between Pitsewo

THE INVASION ON MAY 20.

and the Yalu. There are three main roads in southern Manchuria, which converge upon Liauyang, the ancient capital of the Manchu conquerors. The first is the Mandarin road, from Seoul to Pekin, passing through Feng-hwang-cheng and Motienling, the distance between the former place and Liauyang being about 80 miles. The next road is from Takushan, 50 miles south-west of Feng-hwang-cheng, which passes through Siuyen to Liauyang, Takushan being about 100 miles south of Liauyang. The third main road is identical with the Port Arthur-Mukden railway, and Port Adams, which was Oku's first objective, is 140 miles from the Manchu capital. Pitsewo is 70 miles from Takushan.

Thus on May 20 the Japanese position was broadly as follows: Kuroki with 50,000 [1] men at Feng-hwang-cheng, Nodzu with an equal force at Takushan, and Oku with 60,000 men at Port Adams. That is, an army 160,000 strong on the three main roads converging on Liauyang, and covering a front of 120 miles. To meet this invasion, which obviously would develop sooner or later into a concentrated attack upon Liauyang, Kuropatkin had, by the end of May been reinforced from Russia to a total of 170,000 men. But these numbers did not yet represent his effective striking force: 40,000—viz., the garrison of Port

[1] Kuroki had been reinforced immediately after the Yalu by a Reserve Brigade.

Arthur—were south of the Japanese front, and had already, by the occupation of Port Adams, been reduced to the defensive *rôle* of an isolated force.

Of the remaining 130,000 nearly 20,000 were garrisoning the Pacific coast towns; at least 25,000 were either worthless or recently mobilised troops; and the whole system was disorganised. The balance of serviceable troops, such as it was, had to be employed in furnishing stops at Motienling, Siuyen, and Kaiping, the defensive positions which had been chosen upon the probable line of advance of the three invading armies. This left the Russian Commander-in-Chief with barely 30,000 reliable troops in hand, as a nucleus for the field-army he must construct if he hoped ever to be able to take the initiative. A truly parlous position for any general when the state of the Russian army at this period is considered.

We believe that at this moment the whole course of the subsequent campaign turned upon the operations which Oku was instructed to carry out. Would he, as soon as he had occupied Port Adams, turn north, leaving the 4th army under Nogi to deal with Stössel and Port Arthur, or would he be required to prepare the way for the 4th army: to secure Dalny before he was set free?

Unfortunately the strain of landing the 4th army was too great at the moment, or the magnet of Port Arthur, coupled with the attendant advantages of

Talien Bay, were too powerful, for instead of turning north and striking at the heart, Oku was directed to the south. Here we have the first evidence of the limitations which mark the higher strategy of the Japanese campaign. The battle of Nanshan, magnificent example as it proved of the fighting quality of the Japanese soldiers, saved the Russian arms from that total annihilation in the field which would, in our opinion, have terminated hostilities, with the subsequent destruction of the Pacific squadron and fall of Port Arthur.

Nanshan might have been just as well fought and won by Nogi's, or even at a pinch by Nodzu's army. If it was not the magnet, but transport difficulties which ruled this decision, then the Port Arthur army could have landed before the Takushan army. The interval of time between the landing of these two forces was not great, and of the three field-armies the Takushan army had the shortest distance to cover from the point of debarkation to the main objective.

This strategical suggestion is confirmed when it is remembered that when on June 27 the Takushan army occupied Fen-sui-ling, fifty or so miles from Liauyang, with two divisions, Oku was still 120 miles from the same objective. Oku was never able to recover the valuable time which his brilliant victory at Nanshan and its attendant military exhaustion cost him. It brought both Tehlitz and Tashichaou and their delaying influences into his calendar, and enabled Kuropatkin, though beaten, to ultimately show sufficient front to carry the war into its second year without having sustained a paralysing defeat.

We will now follow the fortunes of Oku's army. Its leading division landed at Pitsewo, and, as soon as the small Russian opposition was brushed aside, pushed forward a raiding party to cut the railway communication with Port Arthur. There is a direct road from Pitsewo to Port Adams. This crosses the railway at Pulientien. On May 9 the Japanese, after a short skirmish, possessed themselves of Pulientien, destroyed the railway, and on the following day occupied Port Adams, where Oku established his headquarters. This was the crucial juncture. The remainder of Oku's army was landed at Kerr Bay, which seems to point to a predesigned plan that it should deal with Stössel's command before commencing its march north. If only the Takushan army had landed at Kerr Bay, Oku, based for the time being either at Pitsewo or Port Adams, could have been at Tashichaou before Kuropatkin had half completed the concentration of his first field-army there.

The southern extremity of the Liautung peninsula is of peculiar formation. Dalny and Port Arthur lie in a lozenge-shaped sub-peninsula, which is joined to the mainland by a thin isthmus, which at its narrowest point is barely a mile and a half across. This neck of land is almost level with the sea; but just south of the narrowest point a cluster of small conical hills command the whole of the approaches from the north. There are five or six of these hills, which, correctly speaking, are mere knolls. This position had been selected by the Russian sappers as suitable to defend against a land attack from the north.

In all the reports published at the time, it was credited with being a position of incredible strength. In reality, according to a professional eyewitness, it was only strong in its natural approaches from the north, as considered with a view of an infantry assault. Otherwise it was a solitary citadel, with a circular trace containing three lines of trenches. These latter were field-works, and though the position was mounted with a large number of guns of various calibre, yet from the very nature of its isolation, shallow trenches, and circular trace, it was a veritable shrapnel-trap.

Added to these disadvantages, the Japanese gunboat flotilla, on May 14, discovered its reverse to be exposed to shell-fire from the seaboard. Into this ditch-enclosed charnel-house Stössel—or rather Kondrachenko, who commanded in the field—had crammed half his garrison, and trusting to wire entanglements and a natural slope to save them from shrapnel and naval guns, awaited the Japanese initiative to develop. Nor had he long to wait. As soon as the last troops had landed at Kerr Bay, Oku, who had steadily driven in the railway-guard cavalry, which were keeping touch with him north of the Kinchau isthmus, was ready to force the Russians from the few positions which they held, covering the walled Chinese town of Kinchau. This town stands on Kinchau Bay, in the plain which forms the northern approach to the isthmus, and is one mile from the left conical hill of the group making the Russian position.

On May 25 the Japanese gunboat flotilla again appeared in Kinchau Bay, and commenced to shell the left of the Russian position and the town of Kinchau, upon which the retreating Cossacks and railway-guards had rallied. In the meantime Oku had occupied the hills, which rise in a considerable mass, not unlike the rocky conformations of South Africa, two miles to the north-east of the isthmus on the far side of the arm of water from Talien Bay, which is responsible for the narrowness of the Kinchau neck.

Once a Japanese general undertakes a tactical movement he wastes no time. His fetich is to strike his enemy as soon as he finds him. It is in the genius of finding him in the least favourable condition that his limitations become evident.

Oku closed down upon Kinchau on the 25th. He determined to carry the town by assault that night, and the position on the isthmus[1] the following day.

[1] Nanshan.

Owing to the prevalence of fog the night attack miscarried, but early on the morning of the 26th a detachment of Japanese sappers gallantly blew in the north gate of the walled town; and after two hours' street-fighting of a particularly sanguinary character, the last live Russians were cleared out of Kinchau, and, under a final scourge from the Japanese artillery, were streaming up the Port Arthur road, which passes over the left of the Nanshan position. The story which follows is one of unparalleled bravery on the part of the Japanese infantry. After an artillery preparation of two hours' duration, in which the gunboats took a decisive part, a Japanese division was committed to the assault.

Contemporary writers on the subject of this war have shown a tendency to discount much of the theory which was put forward by Mr Bloch. We believe that insufficiency of information and misinterpretation of Japanese despatches have influenced these writers. An intimate study of Japanese tactics during the struggle leads us to believe that although Mr Bloch, in common with many other enthusiasts, may have been guilty of the sin of over-estimation, yet in the main the principle upon which he based his deductions has been substantiated. Oku launched attack after attack against the centre and left of Nanshan. Each of these failed, and in failure the carnage was desperate. The anonymous author "O," in 'The Yellow War,' gives the only realistic account of this great assault that we can find :—

An officer seizes the emblem of the Rising Sun, and, bending low to meet the leaden blizzard, dashes for the slope. Where ten minutes ago he had had a company to follow him, he now finds ten or fifteen men. To right and left little knots of desperate infantrymen dash out into the fury of the blast—only to wither before it. . . . Then as if by magic the firing stops, and for one second the Russians jump up upon their works, and wave their caps and shout the shout of victory. The two Japanese battalions which furnished the forlorn-hope have ceased to exist.

And so it has been throughout the war. Persistency in attack, indifference to losses, night attacks and concentrated artillery fire, have given the Japanese their victories; and though we cannot find evidence that in the actual advance to the assault they exhibit an endurance in face of modern fire that sets Mr Bloch's theories at naught, yet we find that they possess a peculiar nerve-recuperative power under failure. This is perhaps the most extraordinary military trait which they exhibit. Eyewitnesses from Nanshan, Tashichaou, and Liauyang submit evidence that Japanese infantry, checked and punished even more severely than was the Highland Brigade at Magersfontein, accept such punishment as the logical sequence of preliminary attack in war; and the survivors will cheerfully advance to similar failure, by day or night, time after time, steadfastly believing that the sacrifices they make are providing some benefit in another portion of the field. This is the true martial spirit. The same spirit was once the characteristic of British infantry, though recent experiences would suggest that it has been lost.

But although the fierce assaults on the Nanshan citadel cost Oku close on 7000 casualties, it was not his infantry that won him the position. The Russian garrison, cooped up and overcrowded in shallow trenches, devoid of adequate head-cover, and wanting in splinter-proofs, reached the limits of their endurance when the Japanese gunboats steamed in to short range and swept the reverse slopes of the hills, to which the men, scourged from the trenches by Oku's merciless shrapnel, were clinging in thousands. Artillery fire had beaten the Russians by two o'clock in the afternoon. The retreat was general two hours later.

But in spite of this, the Russian riflemen in the advanced trenches, who were so situated that they dare not retire before dark, checked each of the successive infantry assaults that were made throughout the afternoon. At sundown the Japanese possessed themselves of the position. It was occupied but not carried. At least, that is the evidence from the shipping in the bay. To what degree it proved or disproved Mr Bloch's theory with regard to infantry assault is immaterial. It was a decisive victory for the Japanese. From that day, unless it received outside assistance, the fate of Stössel's garrison was sealed. Of itself it was powerless except to defend the standard on a hill.

What was the effect of the victory upon the Japanese? For the time being it brought Oku almost to a standstill. He had expended a prodigious amount of ammunition, he had weakened himself by 7000 men, and he was called upon for the moment *to move south*, until a sufficient force from the Port Arthur army could be landed to set him free for his march northwards.

While Japan was thus warring with his extremities, Kuropatkin was moving heaven and earth to expedite the formation of his field-army. He was organising at Tashichaou a mobile force under Stackelberg.

The object of this force proved to be an attempt at counter-offensive against the invaders operating in the Liautung peninsula. All current reports at the time stated that the army with which at the beginning of June Stackelberg took the counter-offensive consisted of 40,000 men: 25,000, however, were the numbers when it marched through Kaiping on its way south. The Japanese had adequate information both of its strength and movement, and though every effort was made, the Russians were not able to move until after the landing of the two divisions of the Port Arthur army.

In order to be in time to meet this threatened counter-stroke, it was necessary to make some slight changes in the organisation of Oku's and Nodzu's armies. Oku left one of his divisions at Port Arthur, while to bring his force up to a strength sufficient to annihilate the Russian counter-stroke, the right division of Nodzu's army was deflected from the Takushan line of advance, with orders to join Oku at Pulientien.

Stackelberg reached Tehlitz, twenty miles south of Kaiping, on the 13th of June. The same day Oku's army, brought up to its original strength by the arrival of Nodzu's division, bivouacked at Pulientien, the scene of its initial success. The cavalry screens of the rival forces had made contact on the 12th. Stackelberg, as soon as he found himself in touch, immediately abandoned his offensive rôle, and threw himself into the nearest position that seemed to present defensive advantages.

He chose the hills which dominate as a portal the southern entrance to the valley through which the railway passes. It would be hard to imagine a worse position. At the best it furnished a front of six miles: the flanks were both vulnerable, as the walls of the valley were low and everywhere easy of access, while the northern exit to the valley, ten miles in rear of the main position, could be converted into a cul-de-sac by a very small hostile force.

Oku's dispositions were simple. In racing parlance

he was a "bold fencer" on the battlefield, and had as much disinclination to act on the defensive as his inferior enemy had inclination for the offensive. His scouts had informed him on the 13th of the nature and extent of Stackelberg's front. He therefore detached one division to work round Stackelberg's right from the direction of Fuchau, while his cavalry was sent round the Russian left, with orders to place itself across the line of communications, and command the northern exit of the Tehlitz valley.

Satisfied that these orders would be fulfilled, Oku, on the following day, opened the operations by engaging the enemy in the centre of his position, before, in the picturesque language of our American cousins, "butting in" with his frontal infantry assault. The next day the climax came. During the night the Japanese gunners, having previously marked down the opposing batteries, had moved their own guns into a closer range. They opened the ball with a terrific artillery preparation against the Russian centre. The Russian batteries were massed on a low tableland, and eyewitnesses describe the iron onslaught which the Japanese gunners made upon them as "terrific." Inside of an hour they were out of action—more, destroyed—and Oku, true to his precepts, committed his infantry to the assault. One division advanced west of the railway, the other east.

The flank attack from the direction of Fuchau was

in position as arranged, and by two in the afternoon the Japanese infantry were in possession of the position held by Stackelberg's right and centre. The Russian left, however, had stood firm, and not only repulsed the Japanese assault, but delivered a powerful counter-stroke, before which the Japanese broke, and retired with considerable confusion and casualty.

The impetus of this counter-stroke was arrested by the arrival, at a most opportune moment, of the Japanese cavalry on the Russian flank. Then it was that the Russian left learnt that their right had been driven in. Their late success became their immediate ruin, for they had to retreat past the two divisions now in occupation of the positions from which their own troops had been driven. There was but one road. This lay down the valley. Practically it was annihilation. It accounts for the gruesome disparity between the number of Russian dead, reported by the Japanese as buried, and the wounded,—a disparity into which it would be profitless to inquire.

The keenest disappointment was felt at headquarters in Tokio at the result of this battle. It had been confidently anticipated that the whole of Stackelberg's force would have been annihilated when it became known that he had elected to accept battle at the southern exit of the Tehlitz valley. But, as will have been realised from the account given above, the Japanese cavalry, though they gave timely assistance to

Oku's right when it was in difficulties, were not where they should have been. In fact, they were some fifteen miles away from the northern exit to the valley. The excuse was "difficult country," an excuse with which the British reader himself has become somewhat familiar during recent years.

Kuropatkin's attempt at the counter-offensive had terminated disastrously. But Oku's success was purchased at the price of a military exhaustion which permitted him to cover only fifty miles during the ensuing month. This fact alone discounts something from the Russian disaster. Whether Kuropatkin had counted on this effect we cannot say; but that he counted on the Japanese curious post-victory inertia at a later period in the campaign will be shown in a subsequent chapter. We must now turn to the other theatres of the land campaign.

On June 8 Nodzu's army, now consisting of two divisions, came into conflict with Mistchenko's 1500 Cossacks at Siuyen, and, driving them out, occupied the town. From here it made connection with Kuroki's left, and then working cautiously forward, after some desultory fighting, was able to possess itself of the important passes on the road to Liauyang at Fen-shuiling on 27th June.

It has been impossible for the closest observer to follow with any pretence of detail the operations which Kuroki undertook during the long weeks that his headquarters remained at Feng-hwang-cheng. There is, however, judging from the official reports of foreign experts that we have seen, every reason to believe that his long halt was not altogether due to the necessity of waiting on the operations taking place in the Liautung peninsula. It is certain that some comprehensive operation was attempted which had subsequently to be modified, if not altogether abandoned. We may, however, judge of the reticence which the Japanese maintained with regard to these operations in the interior by the following extract from Mr Fraser's work:—

> Early in June, however, the Russians appeared in force on the road running at right angles to the Mandarin road, and drove our parties out of Saimatse and Aiyang. After a good deal of fighting, in which both sides suffered severely, our outposts settled down a little south of the places named. It then transpired that General Rennenkampf, with the whole or part of his division of Cossacks and a small body of infantry, was the aggressor. . . . But with regard to his strength and the nature of the fighting which took place no accurate information is obtainable. It may be concluded from the Japanese silence on the subject that they received knocks quite as hard as they delivered. This is the more probable, as Rennenkampf has the reputation of being one of the most enlightened and dashing leaders on the Russian side.

It is therefore not clear whether Kuroki out-manœuvred Keller for the possession of the Motienling positions, or whether they were abandoned to him for strategical reasons which at the present are obscure to us. But this much we do know, that on June 27 these coveted positions fell into the Japanese possession, practically without serious engagement, when the world was expecting them to be disputed by an army of at least 20,000 men.

IV. THE ADVANCE TO LIAUYANG.

In the last chapter we left the Japanese invaders slowly converging on Liauyang by the three main routes from the southern seaboard. While these operations were in progress a fourth force, which had landed at Kerr Bay, Talienwan, and Dalny, was occupying itself with the more or less simple problem of driving the outposts of Stössel's garrison back upon a perimeter, which would allow of a scientific investment of Port Arthur.

The combined naval and military operations which brought about the reduction of this Russian stronghold in the Far East are of such engrossing character that it will be necessary to devote a separate paper to their study. At present we will confine ourselves to a more or less consecutive narrative of what had now become the main operations of the campaign.

The first definite movement in July was on the extreme right, where, as has already been shown, Kuroki had established himself in the famous Motienling Pass. To understand the precise character of the fighting which occurred between this point and Liauyang, it is necessary to make a short study of the *terrain* over which the three Japanese armies would have to pass before they could co-operate against the army which the Trans-Siberian railway was now giving Kuropatkin, and which the latter general was mobilising at Liauyang.

Oku, on the extreme left, was destined to operate on the fringe of the Liau-ho Plain, more or less slavishly following the trend of the railway. Nodzu, in the centre, although he was destined eventually to advance practically upon the same front as Oku, had, before he could effect a complete junction with the left, to traverse the under features of the great mountainous mass which forms the southern geography of Manchuria. But although this country is extremely difficult, yet there are a number of valleys of considerable expanse which, in a rough, uneven manner, converge towards the objective of the Japanese advance.

Kuroki's task on the extreme right was even more difficult than that of Nodzu, since on his front the mountainous masses were of greater frequency and altitude. A reference to Mr Fraser's descriptions of Motienling will convey to the student a fair idea of the nature of this *terrain*.

The mountain-range in which the Motienling Pass is situated runs north and south. Six miles to the west lies another range, similar in character and height, and parallel in direction. Between these two there is a great valley. Lesser valleys, formed by spurs thrown out from the main ranges, intersect the central valley. Through each subsidiary valley tumbles a stream which joins the river flowing along the main valley. It follows that the depression which holds the bed of this river divides the intersecting valleys into two distinct sets, one belonging to the Motienling Range and the other to the opposite range. The Russian forces in occupation of the further range make use of the small valley traversed by the Motienling road. It happens that the spurs thrown out near the Pass radiate fan-wise, with the result that the valleys formed by them converge on the Pass (p. 202).

We have therefore Oku on the right, operating practically on the flat, except when, at stated intervals, spurs and limbs of the mountains stretched "fan-wise" across his front; Nodzu forging ahead through a country fifty per cent more hilly than that in front of Oku; while Kuroki, on the left, finds another fifty per cent in topographical difficulties added to those which have to be surmounted by the army on his left.

It will now be necessary to study the climatic conditions of Southern Manchuria, in order to fully understand the difficulties of campaign which the invaders would be called upon to overcome. The climate of Southern Manchuria may be called extreme. For four months in the winter the whole country is ice-bound, and at periods the cold is so intense as to render, on this account alone, military movements extremely difficult. Mr Alexander Hosie, of the British Consular Service in China, has put on record possibly the best economical description of Manchuria that we have in English. Writing on the climatic influences upon road transport, he says :—

> In the north of Manchuria snow falls to a depth of two or three feet, while in Newchwang it rarely exceeds twelve inches. The summer heat of Manchuria is dry and easily endured, but the winter cold is intense, especially when a north-east wind blows. The rainfall is small, usually averaging about thirteen inches, half of which falls as a rule in the months of July and August. When the country is ice-bound the roads in the interior, bad at their best, are suitable for cart traffic; when it begins to thaw, and during the rainy season, the soft loam of which they are composed becomes a veritable quagmire, wherein animals are frequently suffocated or drowned. Climate, therefore, has a very important influence on the traffic of Manchuria (p. 153).

It will be seen, therefore, that the Japanese had not been able to make the fullest use of the period of "fair going" between the hardening after the thaw and the first burst of periodical rainfall. Two months would elapse before the tracks in the valley hardened to allow of sufficient bottom for rapid transport and cavalry movement. But at the end of August until the winter set firmly in there would be nearly three months of excellent campaigning season. Although Mr Hosie presents a very dismal prospect during the rainy season for the purpose of military transport, yet this very season brought certain other military advantages, which to some extent discounted the trials of the road.

We in the British army have discovered that for military operations there are few climatic and topographical conditions which are insurmountable. The Japanese also knew this, and they realised that although the rainy season might impede the pace of progress, yet it brought with it the growth of hundreds of thousands of acres of *sorghum* (millet), which, by masking their movements, would be a very considerable compensation for the disadvantages of the season.

We cannot believe that they appraised this advantage to be sufficient to warrant the delay which we have already deplored in the opening of their campaign. But doubtless having realised that the initial opportunity had escaped them, they timed their final concentration to enable them to make full use of this agricultural screen.

There is one more point in the climatic conditions existing in Manchuria which, though it does not come within the scope of the present chapter, is of such great importance, and has been so forcibly brought before our notice subsequently in the campaign, that we may be forgiven for making reference to it here. There is just a short period before the spring thaw becomes absolute which enables a clear-sighted staff to undertake operations necessitating rapidity of movement. The rivers remain frozen, and as such passable for a short time after the winter has broken. The opportunity is short and fleeting, and in their recent operations against Kuropatkin at Mukden the Japanese seized this opportunity.

While discussing these ways and means, it would be well to throw a cursory glance at the transport conditions existing with both armies. For the main part, until the end of September, the Japanese were dependent upon road transport. With the left army, their capture in rolling-stock was only sufficient to run one train on the branch line to Talienwan. As is well known, the Russians employ a broad gauge throughout the whole of their railway system. It therefore behoved the Japanese, as they had not succeeded in capturing sufficient rolling-stock to work the line, to convert the gauge to that existing in their own system, and to import the necessary rolling-stock. No mean undertaking, when it is remembered that such rolling-stock had to be conveyed 500 miles by sea.

It is quite possible, and due consideration should be given to this surmise, in consideration of events which took place last month, that the whole of the Japanese strategy was very much cramped during the first year through lack of railway communication. Nor were the Japanese blind to the fact that in a gigantic struggle of this kind the fortunes of war to a large extent lie upon the knees of the gods. They had to be prepared against adverse circumstances during those months when free egress from the Manchurian coast would be denied to them owing to the ice. In the event of the winter campaign going against them, they might of necessity have to retreat upon Korea; therefore, from the very moment that they first effected a control in the Hermit Kingdom, they pushed forward a railway scheme which would give them at the worst a communication from Fusan to Wiju, and at the best an auxiliary line of communications on the road to Liauyang.

For the time being, however, they were obliged to depend upon local transport to meet the demands of their ever-increasing army in the field. The local conditions in Manchuria were well suited for this task. Mule- and bullock-carts, of a type which long usage had proved the most suitable for surmounting the natural difficulties, could be procured in large quantities. In fact, both armies have been largely dependent upon Chinese carts to maintain the communication between rail-head depots and units in the field. In the case of the Japanese, each unit brought a certain amount of obligatory transport with it, in the shape of light pony-carts, while for the purpose of small-arm ammunition supply, each unit was equipped with a pony-pack train.

The scope of this treatise will not allow a minute examination of this all-important adjunct to military campaigning. But it may be sufficient to show, with regard to the Japanese, that they depended, until their railway was in working order, for their main supplies on locally hired cart-trains, plying for the left and centre armies between five sea bases and the front, while the advance bases distributed by means of a brigade transport brought from Japan.

The Russian system appears to have been much the same, though they possibly depended more than the Japanese upon the local transport for the distribution of their *matériel*. But at all halting-places they developed largely, for the purpose of distribution, the power which efficient railway engineering gave them.

We will now return to the operations. Whether Motienling was abandoned to Kuroki by bad management or design, it is evident that the Russian general speedily came to the conclusion that it would be necessary to repossess it. On July 4 Count Keller, who was commanding on Kuroki's front, made a reconnaissance against the Motienling position. It is almost a pity that he pushed forward only a reconnaissance, as, on that date, the actual position he was feeling for was but thinly held. The Japanese easily checked the reconnaissance; and Kuroki, sagaciously foreseeing that a reconnaissance was only the forerunner of an offensive move against him, strengthened his supports at the foot of the Pass, while maintaining the same appearance of weakness in his outpost line.

Nor had he misjudged his enemy. Count Keller on June 17 developed an attack against him with a division of infantry. Strategically Russia's plan was good, and if Count Keller had developed it a fortnight earlier instead of his reconnaissance, he might have given Kuroki considerable trouble to repossess the passes. As it was, even if strategically sound, tactically the Russian attack was bad. Roughly, the idea was to force the Japanese main position by a night-manœuvre with a brigade attacking from the front. Daylight was intended to find two Russian infantry regiments in possession of the Japanese right flank, and so complete the operation. The night-attack was made; but though it successfully drove in the weak outpost line, it was unmercifully handled by the Japanese brigade in support, while the flank-attack never developed. We will be kind enough to surmise that it lost itself in the mist, which was heavy on the passes that morning.

But it must not be considered that the whole of the Russian and Japanese strategy on the latter's right flank centred absolutely in Motienling: for the moment it was the pivot of the operations, but Rennenkampf was active on Keller's extreme left—so active that his movements rendered abortive the original rider to Kuroki's objective.

We will now turn to the development of the operations on the Japanese extreme left. Having sustained a signal defeat at Tehlitz, it was obvious to Kuropatkin that with the material he had in hand it would be hopeless for the present to contemplate another effort to retrieve the initiative. Tehlitz, Siuyen, and Keller's operations had given him a fairly accurate indication of the strength of the Japanese forces now advancing against him.

He had attempted to crush Oku with 25,000 men, to find that a division from Nodzu's army had joined Oku, and that he had given battle to close on 80,000 men. He had therefore to anticipate that when the Japanese concentration had become absolute, he would be facing anything from 150,000 to 200,000 men. The Japanese stratagem was as obvious as the course it behoved Kuropatkin to employ against it. The Russian Commander-in-Chief therefore set himself to delay the advance of the Japanese from the south until he felt strong enough to throw a heavy force against Kuroki, and thus foil the object of the flank-march from Korea. Having dealt successfully with Kuroki, he would then be free to deal more comprehensively with the Japanese main army.

There are three ways of successfully delaying the advance of a modern army dependent upon a long line of communication, without accepting the risks of a decisive engagement. You can operate against its communications with mounted troops; you can build field-works all along its front at convenient intervals, and deceive it into the belief that it will have to fight a heavy battle to win these entrenchments; and you can also by means of a skilfully commanded rear-guard cause it to expend ammunition.

The season of the year and the pre-harvest growth on the land prevented the Russians from employing the former; but they worked a combination of the two last expedients with some skill and a considerable measure of success. Four positions covering the railway were intrenched between Tehlitz and Liauyang. These were Kaiping, Tashichaou, Haicheng, and An-shan-chan. Before each of these positions the Japanese army halted and reconnoitred for days. At Kaiping, Haicheng, and An-shan-chan they were hoodwinked by the Russian rear-guard into a considerable expenditure of artillery ammunition, and at Tashichaou they underwent the temporary paralysis which during the earlier phases of the war seized each Japanese army in turn after its victories.

We will briefly examine each of these engagements in succession. The distance which separated Kaiping from Tehlitz is about sixty miles, and we find that, when the Russians had fallen back from Tehlitz, twenty-one days elapsed before the Japanese were in touch with them at their next position.

The Russians had intrenched the line of low hills

at the foot of which lies the walled town of Kaiping. These trenches covered an irregular front of about nine miles, and the approaches were rendered more difficult by reason of a river which followed the course of the Russian position four hundred metres to the south of it. On the 8th of July Oku had brought his forces, which now consisted of the 6th, 3rd, and 4th Divisions, on to the rising ground astride of the railway, four thousand metres south of Kaiping.[1] The intervening country was covered with high millet. A reconnaissance during the day showed that the enemy were holding their intrenchments in force. Oku determined to employ his usual tactics and carry the position by a *coup-de-main*. Under cover of darkness he pushed his assaulting infantry down to the river bank, and moved his artillery into position behind him, so that at daybreak he could open a concentrated fire to enable his men to make a passage of the river. The Japanese Staff prided themselves that all the arrangements for this daylight attack were carried out without a hitch.

Precisely as they intended, as soon as it was light enough to see the sights, the massed artillery poured a concentrated fire into the Russian works. This was kept up for half an hour, and then, as no reply was

---

[1] The Japanese 5th Division after Tehlitz had deflected back to Nodzu's line of advance, which was parallel to that of Oku and within co-operating distance.

forthcoming, the infantry waded across the stream and advanced to Kaiping to find that Stackelberg and the Russian rear-guard had evacuated it on the previous evening.

The reports of this action which reached this country at the time stated that the Japanese were in hot pursuit of the retreating enemy: it would seem that in this case, as in many similar, the precise meaning of the phrases employed was lost in translation from the Japanese into English. Presumably Oku reported that he was keeping touch, for there was no pursuit. The Japanese threw out an outpost line five miles north of Kaiping, while the whole force halted there until July 22.

The next defensive position in the Russian line of resistance was at Tashichaou. Here Kuropatkin determined to force a battle. It would be expedient at this juncture, when the Japanese line of communications was steadily lengthening, that he should entice them to expend ammunition, and previous experience had shown him that once they engaged in operations they were extremely lavish in its expenditure. The defences at Tashichaou were of much greater strength and far more elaborate than those of Kaiping.

The Russian rear-guard had fallen back by two roads, and on July 23 the Japanese screen found it in strength at Tashichaou, its right resting on the railway, its left in the hilly country five miles to the east. There seems little doubt that the first day of fighting at Tashichaou brought very little success to Japanese arms. The axiom which predominates in the mind of the Japanese soldier, be he general on the Staff or humble conscript, is, "Find your enemy and smite him." The success of these tactics, which a 'Times' correspondent at the time diagnosed as "sledge-hammer," had eliminated some little of the ordinary caution which was so remarkable in the initial steps of the Japanese campaign. Either Oku was in a desperate hurry to make up for lost time, or he had not realised that it was possible for his enemy to profit by the lessons of the war as bitter experience unfolded them.

Tashichaou was to show the Japanese that the Russians were learning. In comparison to the mere field-works against which the Japanese hitherto had been so successfully hurled, Tashichaou presented a prepared position. The rains had broken, and the "going" in the soft loam was heavy in consequence. As a result, the Japanese infantry outstripped the guns labouring in the sticky morasses, which at this season of the year pass in Manchuria for roads. What did that matter? The Japanese infantry were committed to the assault without artillery preparation. On the first day they failed. Even that magnificent tenacity, which during the past ten months we of the

West in our amazement have learned to admire, could not save them. They were driven back from the assault all along the line, and so complete was the failure on the Japanese right that a cumbrous counter-attack pursued the retreating Japanese infantry to within four hundred metres of the guns which had struggled up to come into action at this critical moment just before sundown.

But the Japanese general has that wonderful reserve of recuperative force to fall back upon. As we reflected in a previous chapter, inability to carry a position, and losses, do not seem to demoralise his infantry; rather they seem to spur them on to greater and even more desperate effort. Where an occidental general might have accepted defeat, the intrepid Oku commenced again. As the sun was setting the Russian positions were subjected to a heavy artillery preparation; the Russian guns made spirited reply, using for the first time in the campaign indirect fire.

When night fell Oku determined to carry the Russian left by night-attack. The assaulting division formed in the high millet, with instructions to undertake and assault at 10 P.M. But already the Russian general considered that he had fulfilled his *rôle*, and while the Japanese infantry were snatching hasty repose before their desperate venture, the Russian right wing was quietly evacuating its position—the smallest possible rear-guard being left to hold the

Japanese when they recommenced battle in the morning. In fact, most of the defences were held by mounted troops.

At 10 P.M. Oku launched his assault against the left of the Russian line of works. Though but a skeleton force held the trenches, the taking of them was a costly affair. The troopers held the three assaulted works stubbornly; their resistance added 500 casualties to Japan's total for the day. Even when they had carried the works, the Japanese did not realise that the Russians had already evacuated, and at daybreak a heavy preparation was opened against the Russians' right, to enable the whole Japanese line to advance to the assault. There was no reply, and it was only when the infantry advanced that the Japanese general discovered that he had been engaged in shelling empty trenches.

On this occasion, as at Kaiping, there was no question of a pursuit; but the occupation of Tashichaou was of immense strategic value to the Japanese. The immediate result of the Russian retirement from Tashichaou railway-junction was the evacuation of Yinkow. This had been prearranged, and took place immediately General Stackelberg fell back with his rear-guard.

The net result of this latest success to the Japanese arms was the possession of a summer sea-base, which for six months in the year would be of inestimable value to the army of invasion. General Oku's corps, which had been joined by Marshal Oyama and his staff for the purpose of directing the entire Japanese operations in the field, halted at Tashichaou until July 31, and then, with the 5th Division in line with it, moved forward on Haicheng, where it was anticipated that Kuropatkin would make a desperate stand. Haicheng is only a day's march north of Tashichaou; but the field-works which the Russians had raised in front of the town looked so ominous that the Japanese army again deployed for battle before it was discovered that the frowning earthworks were empty. It was therefore not until August 3 that General Oku was able to establish his headquarters in the town, and throw out a line of outposts six to eight miles north of this centre. This outpost line remained in close touch with the Russian rearguard, which had established itself at An-shan-chan, twelve to fourteen miles north of Haicheng. The southern Japanese army, which now consisted of Oku's and Nodzu's joint corps, halted in front of Haicheng from August 3 to August 25.

We must now transfer our narrative to Kuroki on the right flank, whose operations from the end of July to the actual decisive engagement at Liauyang furnish alike the most interesting and least understood feature of Oyama's advance. We left Kuroki in possession of the Motienling Pass, after Count Keller had pushed two reconnaissances against him. From July 17 until the end of the month Kuroki had no serious collision with the Russians, except at Chatao, twenty miles north-east of Motienling. To this point Kuroki had detached the 12th Division, to prevent Rennenkampf turning his extreme flank. The 12th Division had been successful in its object, and had forced the Cossack leader to abandon any immediate project he might have entertained against Kuroki's communications. As far as a wide detour threatened, the nature of the country was sufficient safeguard against such a movement.

In the meantime Kuroki had been brought up to strength by drafts from Japan, while his actual fighting-line had been augmented by the two reserve brigades apportioned to him. Count Keller had also been reinforced; possibly he had by the end of July 20,000 men—at least, this is Mr Story's estimate of the strength of the army of the East. Whether this is so or not there is no accurate information; but we surmise that since the loss of Motienling Keller's force was only destined by Kuropatkin to be a delaying force, as road-making preparations in the rear of his army were mere dressings in comparison with those which were put in hand in the immediate rear of the positions selected on the Tang-ho.

From this indication it is legitimate to conclude that it was Kuropatkin's intention to deal a heavy blow at the Japanese right, in the vicinity of the Tang-ho. But we readily allow, in discussing the Russian operations, that we are dependent, to a very large extent, on such circumstantial evidence as disclosed itself after the various engagements had taken place.

For the sake of description we will call the action which Kuroki fought on July 31 the battle of Towan, that being the name of the Manchurian village which lay practically in the centre of the Russian position. As Mr Fraser says—

The position of General Kuroki's army and the opposing Russians is easy to understand. The Japanese occupied the Motienling range and its spurs, the enemy the opposite range. The valley between runs north and south for about thirty miles. The Japanese occupied the whole of the eastern side, overlapping the enemy's front at the southern end. The Russian front was shorter, but indented to overlap the rear position at the end of the northern valley.

The action is not of sufficient significance for us to discuss it in great detail. The Russians were more or less skilfully entrenched on high hills commanding the upward approaches from the valley. As their front was contracted, Kuroki put into practice those tactics with which we have now become familiar in nearly all the land engagements. He used one division and the majority of his artillery against the Russian centre. The 12th Division on the north was detached to turn the Russian left, and the Guards'

Division to the south was destined to make a similar movement against the Russian right. Trusting to his concentrated artillery fire in the centre, Kuroki judged that while his flank movements would be strong enough to prevent the Russians from reinforcing their centre, he would be able to cope with it by direct attack.

It was a manœuvre which, in consideration of the natural and artificial strength of the Russian position, would have hardly found countenance with Western tacticians. But the ferocity and endurance of the Japanese infantry attack had not then been realised. This extraordinary endurance of infantry is probably the most cogent lesson that this great struggle has given us.

By evening the Japanese had driven the Russians from their position, and had again demonstrated that the fundamental excellence of Japanese generalship is their power of making full use of their entire strength. At Towan, Count Keller was able to hold his own against both the attack on his centre and right; but he succumbed to the persistency of the 12th Division making the turning movement against his left, and by evening was in full retreat.

As so little has reached us in this country of description of the formations which this peerless infantry used when advancing to the attack, and as we have in

Mr Fraser the testimony of an eyewitness, we extract the following from him:—

Covered by the guns, they advanced in three long lines, that every now and then were lashed by the enemy's shrapnel. But rushing from cover to cover, they suffered little loss, illustrating to perfection the ability of properly extended infantry, utilising cover, to advance in face of artillery. The Japanese have already realised the importance of thin formation, and, in adopting the South African methods in this respect, they to a great extent discarded those of German and other Continental armies.

In this encounter, during the Russian retreat, Count Keller was killed. Mr Douglas Story speaks of this old pupil and aide-de-camp of Skobeleff's in the most enthusiastic manner:—

A strict disciplinarian, General Keller demanded efficiency in every grade beneath him. To secure it, he made many changes in the regiments of his forces; replaced many of the commanders. At his death he commanded an army effective in every branch, ever ready for combat or fatigue, devoted to its leader. His loss cannot be measured in words (p. 223).

This authority also states that at the time of his death his command numbered some 50,000 men. In spite of the feebleness of his attitude in front of Motienling, we will accept Mr Story's appreciation; but we think that it would have been better for Kuropatkin and Russia's cause if casualty had more thinned out the officers in high command during the earlier phases of the struggle.

Kuroki contented himself with taking and holding the positions he had wrung from the enemy with considerable loss, and we have the record of another of those long and seemingly purposeless delays which mark this phase of the Japanese operations. But from Towan, Kuroki came into co-operative touch with the main army, which was then moving upon Haicheng, and from this date onwards the whole of the Japanese force advancing upon Liauyang could be treated as a whole under the command of Oyama.

With the three Japanese armies thus in line, we now enter upon the decisive phase of the first year's campaign. It will be well, before we follow the victorious Japanese through those blood-stained eleven days which gave them the possession of Liauyang, to study Kuropatkin's position.

Kuropatkin, as we have endeavoured to show, had manœuvred during the past five months to delay the Japanese advance until he should himself be in a position to oppose them with a force with which he could hope to deal them a crushing blow. He had on one occasion attempted the initiative. The results had been disastrous. In the circumstances it was impossible for him to hope to be able to again attempt the initiative until something had been done to arrest the steady and successful forward movement of his enemy.

He had hoped to have been able to delay the

Japanese advance long enough to concentrate at Liauyang a force that would enable him to take the initiative in superior numbers. In default, if the Japanese should succeed in concentrating before he was ready to strike, he would be able to receive their blow from behind his entrenched position, which advantage he computed, in the circumstances, to be worth 100,000 men to him. He knew that his army was the objective of Oyama's advance, just as much as Oyama knew that once Kuropatkin took the initiative the second time his own main force would be the objective of such projected enterprise. Kuropatkin's calculations gave him the necessary striking force by the end of September. Oyama was in a position to attempt his blow a month earlier than this.

Confident in the strength of his fortifications, Kuropatkin was prepared to accept this blow, which he was eminently confident he would be able to parry, and by the end of September even encounter, if his existing forces should not be strong enough to do more than parry.

Various estimates have been given enumerating the strength of these rival armies when they clashed at Liauyang. The most eminent authority in this country has calculated that Kuropatkin was in superior numbers. But as most of these calculations have been made upon a basis which we have already shown in the first instance to have been faulty, we are at liberty to take exception to this estimate. It will be found that the most the Siberian Railway could have supplied gave Kuropatkin a field-army of about 150,000 men and possibly 500 field-guns.

Against this force Oyama was bringing eight regular divisions, augumented with six reserve brigades. The whole of the regular divisions had been brought up to war-strength during the halt before the final advance, therefore it is safe to calculate that the Japanese army, exclusive of the cavalry division, brought 200,000 bayonets and 600 field-pieces and howitzers into the field. But in consideration of the fact that Kuropatkin gave them battle on ground of his own choice and preparation, he had every right, if his challenge were accepted, to be confident as to the result. Here again, the extraordinary powers of the Japanese infantry were to upset the Russian general's theories.

Having so far examined in brief the conditions of the two armies which were now in touch, we will return to the narrative of Kuroki's advance against Kuropatkin's left. Kuropatkin's left consisted of three distinct ranges of hills, which formed the watersheds of the Taitse-ho and Tang-ho. The first position, which was fifteen to twenty miles south-east of Liauyang, covered about ten miles of front. The next position, which was six miles in rear, was the continuation of the main range or spur of hills which stretched down into the Liau-ho Plain, the most westerly limits of which furnished Kuropatkin's first position in opposition to the main advance of Oku's army. Between these first and second parallels lies the Tang-ho, till it suddenly swings north-west to join the Taitse. Behind the line of the Taitse lies the final range of hills, which Kuropatkin hoped as a last resource to use as his main protection for his railway communications north of Liauyang.

On August 25 General Ivanoff, who had succeeded to Keller's command of the so-called Army of the East, was holding a line some ten miles in extent from Taitensu, on the Pekin road, to Hwantsuling, a village five miles north-west of Anping. Ivanoff had five divisions: his right, composed of the 3rd and 6th Divisions of Siberian Sharpshooters, our old friends of the Yalu and Motienling; and his left by the 10th European Army Corps, which was to be seriously blooded for the first time.

The Russian positions were of considerable strength, and the approaches were so difficult that the Japanese found themselves unable to make full use of their field artillery. During the 26th and 27th the Japanese made slow and sure progress, especially in the centre, where the infantry advancing at night carried most of the Russian advanced positions with the bayonet; but on the 26th, when the real Russian works were reached, the intrepid infantry ceased to make headway.

As Kuroki was now working in concert with the rest of the army, and as news had arrived of Oku's successful advance against An-shan-chan, it was imperative that Ivanoff should be driven in at any cost. Although his front had contracted, the nature of the approaches to the positions it defended precluded the usual flank movements which Kuroki had hitherto employed. He therefore decided that the 2nd Division should pierce the Russian centre by night-attack. It seemed to those foreign military experts who witnessed the operations to be one of stupendous risk.

As is usual in Japanese dispositions, the most precipitous and difficult portion of the opposing line was selected for the attack. There was to be no question of supports and reserves: the whole division was launched in the darkness, either to carry the position or to hopelessly fail. It was an operation in which no halfway measure would be of account. This we believe was made clear to every company and section commander. If the 2nd Division failed to carry the position in front of it that night, the whole of Oyama's operations would be prejudiced, perhaps rendered abortive.

The engagement which ensued was sanguinary in the extreme. But in spite of bayonet thrust and magazine fire, in spite of boulders which were poured down upon them, in spite of the almost inaccessible character of the cliff which was selected as the weakest point of resistance, the men of the 10th Army Corps were swept from their trenches; and in spite of desperate endeavours, both that night and the following day, to recapture the position, it still remained in the hands of the gallant Nishi, who knew that his division would never fail him.

We can well imagine Kuropatkin's consternation when he received news of the loss of a position which he must have calculated upon holding against Kuroki until he could deal with that officer's force in his own time.

Ivanoff immediately withdrew to the left bank of the Tang-ho. Curiously enough, Kuroki made no attempt whatever to harass him in the passage of that river, but seemed content in the occupation of Anping. In fact, though the rear-guard of the Russian army fell back in full view of Kuroki's force, no attempt was made even to punish him with artillery fire. But it must be remembered that the weather during this period was wet and stormy, and as Mr Fraser tritely remarks, "The Japanese horses do not take kindly to opportunities, and as they are masters of the batteries and not the gunners, we were doomed to disappointment."

But although Kuropatkin must have had his plan seriously upset by this unexpected evacuation of Tang-ho, yet his left was still adequately and strongly protected by the conformation of the hills enclosing both sides of the valley of the Taitse-ho, and if he had only been more fortunate in the officer whom he sent in command of his reinforcements to Ivanoff, it is probable that he might have secured success instead of disaster against the Japanese right wing.

We must now return to the main attack by Oku's and Nodzu's armies against the line of defences which were protecting Liauyang. It will, of course, be impossible in this treatise to give anything like adequate space to this, the first of three mighty engagements that the land operations have produced; but in outline this battle furnishes a fascinating study.

In the first place, we have the fundamental theory of the occidental upset by oriental handling of occidental patented machinery. At Liauyang the Japanese put their own theories of infantry attack to the real test, and proved them to be right. The ingredients for the mixture were properly devised, but the proportions were not adequate. At Liauyang Oyama and his staff learnt the lessons of modern war, which six months later were to give them the overwhelming victory at Mukden. And yet, in the circumstances, and considering the political pressure which was placed upon Kuropatkin, we cannot think that he was wrong to take the risks of giving them this chance of learning a lesson.

For nearly three weeks the outposts of the Japanese army had been in touch with those of the Russian forces holding An-shan-chan, which position marks the northern limit of Japan's first invasion of Manchuria. On August 25 the army began to advance, and immediately the Russians fell back before it, making just a small pretence of delaying it at An-shan-chan and positions north of that point. This opposition was never meant to be serious, and bad weather rather than Russian resistance delayed Oku and Nodzu for one day.

By the night of August 29 the Japanese outpost line was in touch all along the front with the outposts protecting the positions which Kuropatkin was now determined to defend stubbornly. The first Russian position which brought Oyama's army up short was a range of low hills which lay across the Japanese front, practically east and west, joining, as it were, the railway on the west with the higher mountainous region on the east, where we have been following Kuroki in his operations. This position was about seven miles south of Liauyang.

Taken as a whole, the extent of front that Kuropatkin was holding, now that Kuroki had driven Ivanoff across the Tang-ho, approximated fifteen to twenty miles. The Russian left roughly stood at right angles to the Russian right. That is to say, Kuropatkin's front represented two sides of a triangle, the

K

base of which passed through the town of Liauyang, while the apex was pushed into the mountainous regions which grow up out of the Liau-ho Plain.

Against the southern side of this imaginary triangle Oyama pressed his main attack, while Kuroki had orders to follow up his first success by attempting to turn the most northern angle of the triangle. Both Oku and Nodzu in their march up from the seaboard had experienced very little difficulty in dislodging the detaining forces opposed to them. Oku's experience had been such as to lead him to believe the shock of his infantry assault to be invincible. In the three main engagements of his recent operations—namely, Nanshan, Tehlitz, and Tashichaou—although his infantry had been foiled in their primary endeavours, yet the remaining energy of their onslaught had been so substantial, that in every case they had eventually won through. Learning, therefore, that Kuroki with a single division had been able in a night-attack to carry the key of the first position in the enemy's main line of defence, both Oku and Nodzu determined to hurl their armies upon the positions which confronted them.

The Russian fortifications in front of the main Japanese army furnish an extraordinary example of incomplete engineering skill. In view of the nature of the attack which the Japanese made upon them, they were extraordinarily strong. Judged as positions which could be worked round, they were marvellously weak. The extreme right of Kuropatkin's front rested in the Liau-ho Plain, and had as its protection a cavalry division, which, in the existing state of the country, could only have been used as very inferior infantry. Kuropatkin's right centre was practically unintrenched —the Russian strategists trusting to the natural difficulties of the country, and the effect of massed artillery on the fringe of the plain below.

But it was not Oyama's intention to effect a strategical victory by causing Kuropatkin to evacuate his positions by having his flanks turned: it was his intention to hit him in his positions, and paralyse him by the strength of the blow struck. How much the Japanese hoped to accomplish by these very elementary tactics we do not presume to surmise; but recent events have shown that they realised after Liauyang that the weight of the crushing blow in front is nothing in comparison to a similar blow from behind.

On August 29 the five Japanese divisions which furnished the main army were in line in front of the Russian works. They lay practically east and west, with the left division on the railway. The 5th Division, which was the left of Nodzu's force, had already established itself in certain low under-features leading towards the high hills, which, as has already been shown, the Russian engineers had failed to fortify.

On the night of the 28th the Japanese dug themselves in upon the top of a slight rise which slopes down towards the Russian front. The pickets of both armies were within speaking distance, making the best of the cover which the standing millet gave them. Towards morning the whole of the Japanese artillery was moved into position. Practically it was massed in four groups, dividing the five miles of Russian intrenched hills into four sections. As soon as it was light enough to correct the sights, the Japanese began to search the Russian position with a slow bombardment.

Judged from the Japanese point of view, the Russian front presented a chain of five low hills, averaging something between a hundred and a hundred and fifty feet. At the right was the eminence of Sasanpo, which, surmounted by a Chinese watch-tower, dominated the whole country-side for a distance of five miles. Much of the position was covered with scrub and brushwood. A strip 1500 yards in breadth of the millet had been cut, in order to unmask the immediate approaches. In places a double tier, and sometimes a treble tier, of trench-lines were discovered; and over the left the trace of wire entanglements was visible from the gun-stations.

'The Times,' which has published the only really comprehensive account of this battle which has reached this country, refers to the intrenchments as follows:—

This four and a half miles, however, had had every device known to modern engineers in the matter of earth-works used upon it. Here there were no shallow trenches and death-trap citadels as at Nanshan. Wherever the contour of the position required it, a double tier of trench had been cut into the hillside,—one low down, to give scope to the flat trajectory of the modern rifle, the other higher up, but well below the sky-line. The trenches, which were 4 feet 6 inches deep, and narrow, had had their front carefully turfed, so that it was, at artillery range, almost impossible to distinguish the parapets. Each section of the defence had its covered way, leading to commodious splinter-proofs cut into the reverse of the position. From the foot of the position for 1200 yards along the whole front millet had been cut, while there was no portion of the actual approach to the position that had not been prepared with obstacles. At all the salients these obstacles took the shape of a honeycomb of deep pits below and barbed-wire above.

The Russians answered the morning challenge from the Japanese guns with a brisk artillery reply. None of their guns were visible; but they burst shrapnel with considerable accuracy by means of indirect fire, controlled by observation from the summit of Sasanpo. The Japanese gunners made very little effort to find the opposing gun positions; they contented themselves in searching those sections of the defence in front of them which it would behove the infantry to assault before sundown.

During the morning the infantry pressed down to the fringe of the uncut millet, and here commenced to intrench. Early in the morning it began to rain, and under cover of fitful squalls the Japanese on the extreme left felt for an opening. But at the foot of Sasanpo the Russians had heavily intrenched a walled village. The first effort from the 6th Division to advance against this village was repulsed, and the volume of fire which opened from the Russian right was sufficient indication of the price which would have to be paid before an assault could be pressed home.

Every Japanese brigade is connected with divisional headquarters by field-telephone; likewise each division is connected with army headquarters. The strength of the Russian defence was immediately communicated to the battery commanders, and towards evening a heavy preparation commenced.

Just in the last quarter of an hour of twilight the whole Japanese front leapt up from its trenches in the millet and dashed into the coverless zone in front of it. The Russians had been waiting for this, and the crash of musketry with which the advance was received almost drowned the deeper sounds of the preparation. For perhaps another fifteen minutes this intense volume of battle tumult swept up and down the front, and then everywhere the gallant little infantrymen had been swept back into the millet.

The price of their temerity had been enormous. It would have deterred most commanders from ordering a repetition of the endeavour. But not so with the Japanese. The reinforcements were pushed up to stiffen the line, and the same troops who had been scourged with shrapnel all day and chastised back to cover at evenfall, were ordered to make a night-attack. In the dark, between seven and ten, the front of an army corps advanced to the assault with naked bayonets. By midnight they were back again in their trenches, defeated but not disheartened; and three hours later they were falling in again, to make a third desperate effort just before daylight.

Again they were driven back to the cover of the millet. But on the right Nodzu, employing the same desperate measures, had been able to make headway. Too late the Russians realised their error in trusting to the natural difficulties of the country. Nodzu massed his men upon the hillsides, and defied the efforts of the batteries in the plains to dislodge him. One regiment of the 5th Division had even turned the Russians from the lowest of their trenches on the extreme left. It was an advantage which had been dearly purchased, but it would have been cheap at five times the price. It was this advantage that was pressed in daylight during the 31st, which caused the retirement of the whole Russian line back upon their final positions in front of Liauyang.

But the Russians did not abandon their forward position without a further struggle. The whole position was subjected all through the 31st to a terrific bombardment from 250 pieces of artillery; yet both at nightfall and at 10 P.M. the Japanese infantry were driven back—in places at the bayonet-point—to their hurriedly made trenches in the plain.

Oku was desperate, for the news had reached Oyama that Kuroki was feeling the pressure of the Russian reinforcements which Kuropatkin had sent to Ivanoff. It was not realised then that Kuropatkin had thus transferred his reserves to his left to save himself in retirement. It looked as if Kuroki were about to be crushed for the want of co-operation on the part of the main army.

The last and final assault was ordered for the early morning of September 1. Oku pushed up his last reserve brigade to stiffen his assaulting lines for a final heroic effort. Nobly the battalions breasted the hillside all along the line, to discover that the works were empty, and that after repulsing them in the evening the Russians had fallen back upon Liauyang.

At daybreak it was thought that the battle was over; but the two divisions which were sent forward found that Kuropatkin's army had only fallen back six miles to a second position encircling the south-western approaches of the town. It was impossible to push operations farther that day, since the men were exhausted and the ammunition supply required general replenishment.

We must now leave the main army panting for one day in the plain in front of Liauyang, and expecting on the morrow to brush aside all opposition as they advanced against the ancient capital, and turn to Kuroki on the far right. So far Kuroki's army had been merely moving in touch with the main army. It was now to be called upon to make the great strategical move which we here in the West understood to be the culminating-point in the strategy of the Japanese operations.

On August 30 the 12th Division, which was Kuroki's right division, was detached to push northwards, make the passage of the Taitse, and establish itself at Kwantung, for the purpose of placing itself athwart Kuropatkin's communications. It is difficult, with the story of the battle of Mukden fresh upon us, to animadvert upon this movement. We can only say that, as a strategical move, this decision on the part of the Japanese staff was on a par with the incompetence of General Orloff, who allowed this solitary, unsupported, and detached division to make the passage of the Taitse unopposed, when he was in a position not only to have prevented the crossing, but to have overwhelmed the division while in the act of crossing.

Almost before this false move had been completed, Kuroki realised the risks the 12th Division was running, and he subsequently despatched the 2nd Division to join the 12th north of the Taitse. Even then the Russians practically had Kuroki at their mercy, if the senior officer on the spot had been prepared to act as strenuously as he did two days later. Mr Fraser refers to this chapter in the history of Liauyang as follows:—

The flanking move was now complete, and it only needed daylight of September 1st to inaugurate the attack. But Kuroki's army was divided,—a division, a brigade, and two battalions remaining west of the Tang-ho, whilst two weak divisions were upon the north bank of the Taitse, completely beyond the reach of succour from the forces investing Liauyang. A gap of fifteen miles of rough country, the Tang-ho and the Taitse, separated Kuroki from the rest of the Japanese army. The Russians had thrown away a succession of chances. On the 31st they had the 12th Division wholly at their mercy, but failed to fire a shot. Up to the end of the 31st Kuroki could have retired into the mountains in rear, if the gap had been broken and his force cut off. But once the artillery and baggage had crossed the river he was entirely committed. The Taitse, swift and deep, could only be forded by infantry, and that only here and there. For the retirement of the artillery, the reserve ammunition, the impedimenta of two divisions, there was available only a single slender bridge, which, in the event of an attack by the enemy, must have proved totally inadequate. To those knowing Kuroki's position it seemed inconceivable that the Russians did not swoop down upon him; and hardly less conceivable that Marshal Oyama should have jeopardised so considerable a portion of his forces upon an undertaking that lacked the essential elements of success. The Japanese Commander-in-Chief may have been justified by the knowledge that the Russians permit liberties which an enterprising foe would turn to advantage. But he will find it hard to explain why he took a liberty regardless of consequences at a point where was the crux of the whole situation (p. 312).

But though Kuroki must still have been anxious, even after his 2nd Division crossed the Taitse, yet he knew, and those foreign military observers with him knew also, that his flank movement had failed. Although he was across the Taitse, and his mounted troops were in touch with the Russians at Yentai coal-mines, yet a solid wall of positions lay between him and his objective. These positions were held by an enemy which, if it was not expeditious, was at least up to the present unbeaten. Already he was separated farther than he really liked to be from the main army. Therefore it was impossible for him to continue his movement northward.

To a general of Kuroki's calibre there was but one alternative: this was to attack his enemy in his nearest and strongest positions. The Russians will long have to regret that Kuropatkin himself had not been a witness of Kuroki's endeavour. But the Russian Commander-in-Chief, concerned with his main army, had already despatched reinforcements to his left,—not now with the intention of crushing and annihilating Kuroki, but for the less glorious purpose of holding him, while he withdrew his own army.

The wedge which Nodzu's intrepid infantry had pushed into the Russian centre during the fighting of the 30th and 31st, received simultaneously with the Orloff version from the extreme left, had decided him in his estimate of the progress of the battle. Mishchenko was sent to the west to augment the flank-covering division, while General Grekoff, with a mixed force of Warsaw and Siberian troops, was left to hold the trenches just south of Liauyang.

How well this bluff old cavalry officer fulfilled his charge is now a matter of history. His orders were that he must hold on for forty-eight hours, which would be time sufficient to enable Kuropatkin to clear such baggage and *matériel* as he did not wish to destroy.

Forty-eight hours were his orders, but he held his trenches for over seventy. On the 1st, it is true, Oku and Nodzu only pushed a reconnaissance against him. But so confident was the former general that his troops would be in Liauyang that night, that he issued orders concerning the hour of entry on the following morning. By evening his infantry had been fed and rested, and as soon as it was dusk the 6th and 4th Divisions fixed bayonets to carry the final trenches. The fierce onslaught of 20,000 men was frustrated by the withering sheet of lead poured out from the cover of the trenches. The Japanese fled back to their field-works, and on the morning of the 2nd both Oku and Nodzu settled down to prepare the way with artillery.

With his six batteries Grekoff sullenly gave them back their fire, and during the next twenty-four hours three more desperate infantry assaults were rendered abortive. By this the story of Manjayama had reached headquarters. Kuroki with his tiny force was successful, and yet the Japanese main army was still checked. The necessity for driving in that rear-guard was desperate, and the 'Times' correspondent tells us how, on September 3, Oku set his teeth, and determined to carry the position whatever the cost.

This was evidently a moment for which Oku had been waiting. At last his enemy was shaken: it would be his business to pulverise him. The word was telephoned to the battery commanders. We have already described the awe-striking Japanese artillery preparation; but hitherto we had had nothing, the civilised world had never seen anything, to compare to the final preparation for the advance of the Japanese infantry against the Liauyang field-works. The massed and scattered batteries took the line of Russian resistance in sections. The 250 guns opened first on the Russian settlement. Great columns of dust and smoke rose up from amidst the grey stone buildings, then suddenly out of this whirlwind of bursting shell shot up great lurid tongues of fire. Either the bursting charges of the common shell or the incendiary torches of the retreating Russians, or both, had done their work. The houses, the fodder stocks, the go-downs of the settlement, were in flames. The Japanese gunners redoubled the service of their pieces. The very rocks of Sasanpo quivered with the blasts of ever-recurring discharges. The air shrieked with the rush of high-velocity projectiles. A great dense pall of black smoke went skywards and covered the doomed settlement. It spread upwards and upwards until it hid Liauyang pagoda and all from view, and above it became mottled and chequered with the fleecy burst-puffs of scores of shrapnel. Below this the pall was streaked with splashes of green and yellow and fiery red, as the earth was torn up by the force of the high explosion or the flaming fire of the burning byres cast broadcast by the relentless sequence of accurately calculated discharge. Could the vandalism of war reach such a pass? In one short hour could that modern settlement, with its gardens, its homes, its markets, be reduced to a pile of smoking ruins? Ask of the great red flames that licked along the false sky-line of smoke and dust like the track of a forest fire; ask of the dull reverberation in our ears, which overpowered all the other distant sounds of war! The gutting of the Russian settlements took thirty minutes; . . . then, supported by their miniature mortars, the Japanese infantry moved forward to carry the trenches with the bayonet. It should have been easy now, for no infantry could have remained unshaken; yet the Russian musketry fire rolled out, and for the seventh time during the past five days the men of the 3rd Division were fain to turn their backs against the leaden blast from the Russian trenches. Gallant little men, too much had been asked of them.

Grekoff had done his duty nobly: at dusk that evening the last of his batteries crossed the bridge over the Taitse-ho north of the town, in rear of the last of the baggage-train. By two o'clock in the morning his last battalion gave the engineers the office to destroy the railway-bridge. An hour later the 5th Division carried empty trenches, and occupied the ancient Manchurian capital.

We must now return to Kuroki. As we have already shown, he was determined to break the last line of Russian resistance which kept him from the railway. The front that was held against him covered nearly ten miles. But there was one point near the centre which Kuroki put his finger upon as being the key of the position. This was the small brae known as Manjayama.

On the 31st Kuroki subjected Manjayama to a severe artillery preparation, and then launched the men who, from the Yalu to the present moment, had never failed him, against the position. But it was as futile and as expensive as Oku's subsequent attacks on Grekoff's rear-guard were to be. Three times the glistening line of bayonets advanced to the assault. Three times they were driven back to the cover of their shelter-trenches in the standing millet.

But Kuroki was as grimly determined to achieve his object, regardless of what it might cost in human lives, as Oku had been in all his engagements. That night the Japanese infantry massed in the millet, and as soon as the moon went down a brigade in line swept over the pickets and into the trenches of the coveted position. The carnage on the summit was terrific. For an hour in the darkness Occidental and Oriental wrestled for the prize. Finally the Russians were driven from their stronghold, and when day broke Kuroki was in possession of his point.

But for the time being it was a dear possession, for the arrival of Kuropatkin's reinforcements prevented Kuroki from developing his advantage as quickly as he had hoped. The Russian commander realised the vital importance of this little knoll, and every gun that could be trained upon it was used to prepare the way for the desperate effort that the Russians were to make to regain it.

During the night of the 1st the Russians retook the hill, bayoneting every man of the Japanese battalion that held it. But before this success could be made absolute, two more Japanese battalions delivered a counter-blow equally annihilating in its effect, which left the Japanese in unshaken possession of the hill, despite the desperate efforts which, throughout the 2nd, the Russians made to repossess it.

On the 3rd of September the Russian tenacity began to diminish, and Kuroki was able to develop his operations from the pivot which he had now made secure. But he had never been strong enough from the first, and now it was too late. The diminution of the Russian attacks was due to the fact that the Russian flank army was now relieving Grekoff of his duties of rear-guard.

As has been already shown, on the following day Oyama and the main army were in Liauyang. The

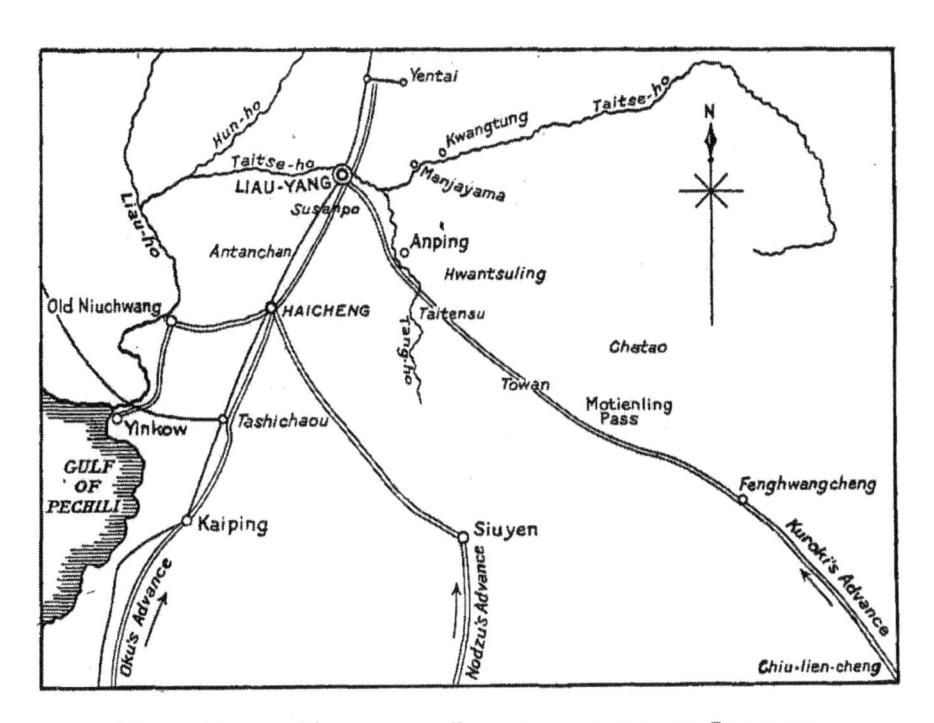

ROUGH SKETCH-MAP OF THE JAPANESE ADVANCE ON LIAUYANG.

great battle for supremacy in Manchuria had been lost and won. Kuropatkin had been defeated; but he had saved his army practically complete, except for 16,000 casualties that the twelve days' battle had cost him. Oyama had beaten his enemy, and had possessed himself of his positions; but he had failed to bring about the result which would save his country from a second year of war. The twelve days' struggle had cost him 30,000 men.

V. PORT ARTHUR.

It is now our intention to turn aside from the main issue of Oyama's advance into Manchuria and to study briefly the conditions which in 1904 centred round Port Arthur. We have already dwelt upon the fundamental strategical error which placed Stössel's garrison at the mercy of the Japanese as soon as the latter were moderately successful. It will not be necessary in this chapter to refer back to these dogmatisms; but we will point out that of itself the actual siege of Port Arthur is more than an incident in the great campaign. When we consider the importance which sea-power has upon all strategy, we must realise the significance both of the effort which was made by Japan to reduce Port Arthur in the shortest possible time, and of the stubborn front shown by the defenders.

In the peculiar circumstances of Russia's position in the Far East, the defenders of Port Arthur were fighting for the only means which could, with any certainty, ultimately turn the balance of success in their country's favour, while the attackers were struggling to succeed with equal knowledge of the value of the naval base, which uninvested would command their own communications.

The whole thesis of the importance of the struggle is to be found in Nogi's simple and manly general order to his troops, made on August the 24th, when it was certain that Russia would despatch an armada to the Far East:—

> SOLDIERS,—The task you are about to undertake is exceedingly important. I may also say that the safety of Japan and the honour of our army depend on the issue of this fight. Think of these things. Overcome all difficulties. Pay the debt every soldier owes to his country. The enemy will resist obstinately. If your commanding officers fall, let their juniors replace them. If these fall, let non-commissioned officers be their substitutes. If the non-commissioned officers fall, let privates succeed them. Whatever obstacles you encounter, fight to your last man.

It is not our object here to trace back the past history of Port Arthur. In our opening chapter we touched upon this point, and we will now proceed to handle the blood-stained narrative which centres round the recent history of this citadel, taking the fortress as the Japanese found it, when on May 28 Nogi first threw out his outposts on the north-eastern end of the Kwangtung promontory.

Since the days of Todleben and Sevastopol, the Russians have always possessed a character for military fortification. And from the moment that they were quietly allowed to possess themselves of Port Arthur, they proceeded to put to its best use this faculty for which they held a European credit.

The defensive works at Port Arthur may, for the purpose of generalisation, be divided into three classes. There were the forts which frowned along Golden Hill and Liau-ti-shan, constructed directly for the purpose of guarding the narrow and difficult fairway into the naval base. There were the main and permanent fortresses which girdled the old and new towns of Port Arthur, and which were destined to be the keep and citadel of the Russians in this limb of their possessions in the Far East.

Besides the permanent forts, there were existing before the outbreak of war certain subsidiary works which were designed, in the event of disaster, to keep at arm's length from the final citadel any hostile force pursuing a land campaign.

What is most remarkable, perhaps, is the natural strength of the country in the immediate environment of the Port. The conformation of the hills which raise themselves proudly round the lagoon which furnishes the inland harbour, seems by nature to have been adapted for the very object of defence. This lagoon is practically encircled by a curtain of saw-topped ridges, which vary in altitude to anything from two hundred to fifteen hundred feet. They stretch away landwards in a mass of succeeding folds and ridges, so that one can almost sympathise with the belief which the Russians held that this, their Far Eastern first-class fortress, was impregnable. The main trace of the inner and permanent works was ready made by the hand of Providence. This is evident, since we find that the Russians selected for their permanent defences practically the same alignment as the Chinese had fortified years before.

These permanent works, intended for land defence, consisted of a chain stretching from Tahke Bay on the west to Ehrlung, due north of the old town of Port Arthur, including Kikwan or Cockscomb Hill, Kinkeeshan, and the Shaoku-shan group. East of the railway and north-east of the new town are Wangti, Antzu-shan, and Itzushan. These were the main defences — permanent as opposed to the subsidiary line beyond them, which in reality, since the war, had been rendered almost as powerful as the fortress they were intended to protect.

To the west, in the subsidiary line of outer fortifications, we have north of Tahke Bay, Wankiatu, Takushan, the Kikwan outer forts, Banjusan due north of Kikwan, and the lesser Ehrlung forts protecting the waterworks. North of Wangti, again, are the powerful lunettes of Sueizeyang and Fort Kuropatkin; to the east of this is the Metre Hill group, covering the powerful redoubts of Panglu-shan; whilst south of the

Metre group we have the now far-famed 203 Metre Hill fort with its buttresses, 110 Metre point and Akasakayama, which has played so great a part not only in the history of this siege, but in the history of the whole war.

The perimeter enclosed by this girdle of subsidiary works averages just about fifteen miles, yet even outside these limits there were further subsidiary works,—to the north, Wolf Hill and the Ehrlung lunettes; and swinging round again to the east, the forts and redans which cover Louisa Bay. To these we will refer subsequently.

The main defences are closed works of enormous strength. Their ditches are completed with caponiers and galleries, and for the most part the escarp and counterscarps are formed by cutting down or blasting into the solid rock. Also, the forts being situated on the tops of high hills, it must always have been difficult for the besiegers to have observed and judged the effect of their breaching operations, even if it were possible for modern artillery to breach such heavy parapets.

In front of these permanent works the Russians, after the outbreak of war, completed three lines of defence. The first we have already described in our account of the battle of Nanshan on the Kinchau Isthmus: eight miles south of this was their second line, which stretched from Ingentsi Bay on the north to Liau-ti-shan on the south-east of the Kwangtung promontory, and consisted of a powerful chain of lunettes and redans. Ten to twelve miles south-east of this line was a third line of defences.

Apart from caponier and gallery, each separate work was protected by *fougasse*, mine, abattis, and entanglement; and in some of the lunettes even fish-torpedoes were found, giving evidence of the infinite resource to which these desperate electricians gave effect when it became evident that the garrison of Port Arthur would have to struggle in hand-grips to preserve their nation's honour.

To hold these mighty lines Stössel had over forty thousand Siberian troops — an army corps behind intrenchments. And such intrenchments! What a stupendous task lay before the Japanese. Yet with the memory of Nanshan before us, and the knowledge of the naval support that Togo would be able to give to the army, there were few who deemed that the task was impossible.

We can now turn to considerations which are of greater import than the mere record of spade, mattock, cement, and mortar. Captain Thuillier, in his excellent work on 'The Principles of Land Defence,' says :—

It is believed that the teaching of all past history, as well as the experience of our last war, alike bore out the opinion that the following are the prime conditions which every defensive work should fulfil :—

1. It should admit of the utmost possible scope for the effective use of the weapons employed by the defenders.

2. Conversely, it should restrict to as great an extent as possible the effect of the attackers' weapons.

These conditions apply equally to all times, and all weapons,—to the days of pikes and broadswords, of bows and arrows, battering-rams and catapults, and to those of magazine rifles and quick-firing guns.[1]

From what we have read and described of the massive strength of these great defensive structures, it would be inferred, if one had not such admirable axioms as the above at one's elbow, that Port Arthur was the veritable impregnable fastness that the Russians themselves believed it to be. But the expert may possibly see in the appearances which most impress the layman the greatest weakness. We have on record the impressions of a very able British Sapper, who, writing in the leading journal with regard to these very fortifications, committed himself to the following opinion :—

My general impression of the half-dozen forts which I passed close to, and others I saw in the distance, was that, though powerful to a degree, they were perched on such elevations as with difficulty to search the ground before them with their fire. An enterprising enemy, it struck me, would find in these declivities, depressions, and valleys quickly becoming dark in

---

[1] The Principles of Land Defence. By Captain H. F. Thuillier, R.E. Longmans & Co., 1902.

the gloaming, many a spot technically termed "dead ground," in which he might mass companies or battalions before leading them onwards.

If a British expert came to this conclusion during a more or less perfunctory visit, how much more likely were the Japanese sappers, some of whom themselves had worked as coolies in the completing of this fortress, to realise their weaknesses and shortcomings.

The final issues of the siege have proved how right is the mental impression left upon that English officer's mind. The very strength of the Russian fortresses proved their undoing, since even though those great keeps towered above the surrounding country, they did not admit of the utmost possible scope for the effective use of the weapons employed by the defenders, nor conversely did they restrict to as great an extent as possible the effect of the attackers' weapons.

In an earlier paper it was shown how, when Oku defeated Stössel's lieutenant at Nanshan, the Japanese 2nd Army pressed the defeated Russians back upon their second line of defence. The three divisions of Oku's army kept touch with the Russian outposts until the first of Nogi's divisions was able to land; then, leaving the 1st Japanese Division, Oku commenced his march north up the Liautung peninsula, on which we have followed him as far as Liauyang.

Nanshan was fought on May 27. The second of Nogi's regular divisions, namely the 9th, did not land in Kwantung until a month later. We make this point here, as it was, in our opinion, over the handling of the Port Arthur investing army and the retention of Oku's two divisions in the Kwantung peninsula that the Japanese made their most far-reaching strategical miscalculation.

But this we have already dealt with in a previous paper, and we will now proceed to examine the incident of the investment and siege of Port Arthur, as far as the materials to hand will allow.

For nearly a month Nogi was not in a position to do more than keep touch with Stössel's outposts, and during this period we have now the familiar picture of the two armies, fully intrenched, almost within pistol-shot of each other. The Russians held the line which included Hsitau-shan and Kenshan. Both of these latter positions are hills of considerable height, standing up from the plain, much after the manner of the kopjes in South Africa. In fact, in the whole group of hills which furnish Kwantung there is to be found a considerable similarity to many landscapes in Natal and the Transvaal, now familiar to the British army.

On June 26 Nogi was finally reinforced, so that his strength was brought up to three divisions, which made him in the matter of numbers well superior to the Port Arthur garrison. The same day that his latest reinforcements arrived. Nogi issued orders for the attack of Hsitau-shan and Kenshan. On the following morning a division marched against each position, and in spite of its strength the former hill was carried by noon, by the same troops that had stormed the centre at Nanshan.

The glacis of Kenshan, however, was difficult and steep in the extreme. The Japanese divisional general, who had only at his disposal mountain guns with which to prepare his advance, delayed longer than the divisional general on his right, with the result that just as he commenced his assault his troops came under a searching fire from the guns of certain of the Russian gunboats which had slipped out from Port Arthur. These vessels successfully checked the infantry until they themselves were driven back to their shelter by a portion of Togo's fleet.

This little interlude delayed the advance, but not for long. About four in the afternoon a regiment of Japanese infantry was loosed against the steep glacis, and though two Siberian regiments held the work, and the assaulters had to pass over a prepared minefield, by sundown the Rising Sun was waving over the table-land, while the Siberian regiments were in full retreat to the south.

This was a very significant engagement, and observers at the time realised that everything that had been said in praise of the Japanese infantrymen was justified. They also realised that in view of an assault by such infantry as these, no one had a right to link the word impregnable to the frowning citadels massed to the south of them. Four battalions of little white-gaitered infantry had driven their enemy, who were at least equal in numbers, out of his prepared position, with a loss of under five per cent. Nogi immediately occupied and intrenched the captured positions.

The Russians realised at once the serious nature of this Japanese success. In the first place, in Kenshan, it wrested from them an observation-post which placed them in complete visual command of the Japanese sea-base and land movements: also, it enabled Nogi to throw up his right to such an extent as to restrict the sea-board on the north of the peninsula, which still remained open for the purpose of supply-running.

General Fock, who at the moment was in command of the Kwantung field army, made three heavy and distinct counter-attacks on July 3 and 4, in the hope of regaining the positions. These counterstrokes were delivered with great gallantry, and the disregard of casualty was equal to that of their adversaries. Eyewitnesses speak of the strange phenomenon of Siberian Rifles advancing across the plain in a solid phalanx to the beat of drum and with colours flying. What is more remarkable, the Japanese allow that these dense columns of charging infantrymen succeeded in getting in places to within six hundred yards of the magazines that were pumping nickel into them.

By day and night Fock endeavoured to carry out Stössel's instructions that he should retake the positions at any cost. On the night of July 3 his infantry actually made their way into the Japanese trenches, and for the first time in a war which was soon to be prolific with similar instances, the men armed with weapons that kill at three thousand metres destroyed each other with bayonets. For an hour the Russians remained in possession of the regained trenches, to be driven out at last by the Japanese reserves.

When his third counter-stroke failed, Fock gave up all hope of driving Nogi back upon the narrow isthmus of Nanshan, and fell back to the second line of subsidiary works protecting Port Arthur from the land side—that is, the line from Liau-ti-shan to Ingentsi Bay. For the moment Nogi was not in a position to follow up his success. The Japanese supply services were beginning to fail, and the executive was feeling the strain of four armies based on the sea; moreover, the time that would be required for the purpose of clearing the port of Dalny of the hostile mine-fields had not entered into the calculations of the Japanese War Department.

Matters were not running very smoothly just at this period, but early in July the sailors managed a fairway between Dalny and the Elliot Group, and towards the middle of the month matters began to improve—so much so that Nogi's reserve battalions arrived, together with the howitzers and a sufficient supply of war material to allow him to renew his advance.

On July 26 Nogi set his army in motion, with the object of driving the Russians in from their advanced works. He was now fully mobilised both in men and artillery to enable him to undertake, if successful, the investment of the Russian garrison. If he could force them back from their present position, their next line would be the semi-permanent works subsidiary to the main trace.

Near the centre of the Russian line, and practically due north of the Tiger's Tail, stood Wolf Hill fort. It was this that Nogi had selected as the objective of his attack, and against this work his massed artillery opened. After a sharp, though severe, bombardment on the 26th, the Japanese were committed to an assault.

We have had many striking instances in the campaign of the Japanese attempting to carry a position by infantry assault without waiting until it had undergone a sufficient artillery preparation. Tashichaou and Liauyang possibly are the best illustrations of this. The first infantry assault on July 26 was a similar failure. The gallant little men went through to the foot of the steep hills which they were called upon to climb, and then came to a standstill; the divisional generals, realising that more preparation was necessary, stood fast while the gunners swept and tore the bevelled edges of the Russian works with a continuous stream of shrapnel and common shell which must have proved a revelation to the Siberian riflemen subjected to it.

It would appear that this struggle for Stössel's second line presented a foretaste of the terrible, horrible carnage which was destined finally to place the story of this siege before all others of its kind. Most frightful tales of the carnage are given, which, though they prove little in the consecutive narrative of the operations, are of themselves horrible monuments of the degrading minutiæ of modern war,—a minutiæ which the historian is prone to forget in his ordering and shaping of the broader issues of the struggle.

We read of the intrepid infantry of Japan seizing the lower trenches on the Wolf Hill fort. Of the men clinging to the dead ground afforded by a line of *krantz* being lassoed by the Russians from above, and dangled in mid air until they could be conveniently despatched. Of a repetition of the Inkerman story, when, ammunition failing, the combatants resort to the missiles of primitive ages. Of assaults that wither in the open, and are swept back to cover by a "nickel blizzard" that nothing could face or stem. Of a company commander who, motionless, with a handful of his men, lies for hours amongst the shattered *débris* of his command, feigning death until nightfall, and then, instead of selfishly seeking safety under cover of darkness, ultimately makes a lodgment which on the morrow proves the lever to victory.

Of the devotion which was required from each individual rifleman taking part in these assaults we can form a very fair estimate from the following description given by a wounded private, and placed on record by the Japanese in their own pamphlet entitled 'The Russo-Japanese War'[1]:—

On the morning of the 24th, at five, we charged the enemy's fort. No battle is so terrible as an assault on a fort. All the machine-guns on the forts all around fired on us without intermission; half of our men perished before the object of our attack was reached. But we were determined to carry the fort at all costs, and after severe fighting we finally succeeded in capturing it. We had barely occupied it when the Russian forts on the right and left and in our front fired their machine-

---

[1] The Russo-Japanese War. Fully Illustrated. Part V. Kinkodo Publishing Co., Tokio.

guns with increased energy. Our soldiers fell one after another, and our force was shortly reduced to an insignificant number. Moreover, the Russians attacked the battery in great numbers, and we were at last compelled to abandon the fort, which had been occupied after such arduous efforts. During the retreat I was wounded, and fell beside the wire-entanglements, being unable to continue my retreat. I resigned myself to my fate, and wrapped a bandage round my wound. I could not, however, lie at ease, for fear that the Russians might discover me. Happily a hole had been created by the explosion of a shell in the ground some ten yards from where I lay, so I crawled thither and concealed myself in the hole, where there were several Russians killed lying on top of each other. Three or four hours afterwards I felt exceedingly thirsty, but my water-bottle was empty. In searching for water I discovered a pool of blood beneath the dead Russians. No idea of the nature of the liquid entered my brain: I at once scooped up the blood with my hands and drank it.

Once their centre was pierced the Russians fell back in good order, taking their wounded with them to the third defensive line in front of Port Arthur. But General Nogi showed a spirit of military initiative which at this period was generally foreign to Japanese commanders. Though the assaults of the last three days had cost him over 5000 casualties, on the 30th he launched his army against the new positions which the Russians had taken up on the Tai-ho.

The Russian outposts were completely surprised. They retreated, in many cases leaving their arms piled behind them. The consternation of the pickets communicated itself to the troops in the defences, who on the left and centre evacuated before Nogi's advance without firing a shot.

With the exception of Takushan, the most eastern of the Russian defences in this line, the garrison had fallen back on the semi-permanent subsidiary defences of Port Arthur. From this date Fock's command ceased to have that mobility which warranted the character of a field army, and the investment proper of Port Arthur began.

It would be well at this point, before we plunge into the narrative of horrible carnage which prefaced the fall of this fortress, to study a little of the economic conditions existing in each army, in order to bring our reflections into focus with the outside operations which were influencing Nogi's dispositions.

Although operations were progressing so favourably before Port Arthur, both the Japanese naval and war departments could not help feeling a certain degree of anxiety with regard to the course that the campaign was taking. As has already been pointed out, the original outline scheme had considerably miscarried, through influences which, if not altogether unforeseen, had not been fully reckoned upon.

First and foremost, although the Japanese possessed sufficient command of the Far Eastern seas to enable them to carry out their military operations, yet Togo had not succeeded in bringing about a decisive fleet action, or in his alternative scheme of completely sealing the entrance to Port Arthur. Moreover, the mischances of war had reduced the fighting strength of his battle squadron by one-third. Thus, while in the Far Eastern waters he possessed a superiority in armoured cruisers and torpedo craft, he was inferior to the existing Russian battleship power.

But his moral supremacy was such, that even with his four remaining battleships he could hope, if the Russian admiral would give him the opportunity, to hold his own. If it had only rested with the Russian Pacific Squadron, the Japanese after six months' experience might well have dwelt secure. But Russia was now threatening with a naval reinforcement from Europe, which, if it arrived in time to join forces with the Russian Pacific Squadron, would be strong enough, even if its fighting value was considerably discounted, to wrest the command of the sea, and with it the fortune of the campaign, from the hardy little Japanese.

Consequently, there devolved upon the army now investing Port Arthur a more important, a more far-reaching, duty than the mere reduction of a hostile citadel. It was essential that the army should do what the navy had been unable to do —namely, destroy or capture the Pacific Squadron as it lay under the shelter of the Port Arthur batteries, and thus set Togo free to deal with the reinforcement that, it was now announced, was sailing from the Baltic.

Also, and in considering the difficulties which were rising up against the Japanese General Staff, and which they could not then have hoped to overcome as happily as they have overcome them, the following must not be lost sight of. The Siberian railway had proved of a military value far in excess of the assessment made for it both in European and Japanese military estimates. While Kuropatkin had been delaying and trifling with the Japanese armies of invasion, he had succeeded in concentrating at Liauyang a force which, if it was not sufficient for the purpose of reattempting the initiative, was at least so nearly equal to that which Oyama could bring against it that the hope of complete and paralysing success could not at this period have entered into the Japanese calculations.

The most they could have hoped to do was to defeat Kuropatkin. To do more than this they required the four divisions which, with their reserve brigades, were now detained in the Kwantung promontory. It was these considerations which made it imperative that this vaunted Russian stronghold must be reduced. It was these considerations that allowed Nogi to sacrifice his infantry in battalions in order to achieve the desired end.

We will now turn to the internal state of the fortress itself. Again we are handicapped through a lack of reliable evidence. But there seems reason to believe that the supplies, both military and otherwise, were ample. This we know, that a very large trade both by junk and steamer was entered upon by speculators from the Pe-chili and Shan-tung coast-lines.

That the garrison felt the stress of war there could be no doubt, but that it was reduced at any period to an absolute state of exhaustion there is no reason to believe. The defences were thorough, and consequently the effect of shell-fire could not have been overwhelming within the main *enceinte*; and, as all those who have experienced the trying ordeal of a siege will know, the moral effect of shell-fire lessens with experience.

Apparently—and this has been the cry throughout the whole campaign, whether on sea or land—the Russian garrison lacked most in the matter of leadership. But when a body of men are gathered together with the one determination of self-preservation, and it is found that the existing leaders are unworthy of the confidence placed in them, it has ever been observed that somewhere in the company a man will appear who, by superiority in intellect and moral courage, either directly or indirectly ultimately usurps a definite control.

Such was the case in Port Arthur. Stössel, though he may have possessed many excellent qualities, was not of hard enough stuff to carry through without support. In the moment of emergency the best officers will come to the front, and we find in the ill-fated Kondrachenko the heart and soul of the splendid defence which the Port Arthur garrison made against perhaps the most scientific, persistent, and vicious siege that, in the history of war, has ever been pressed against a beleaguered garrison.

Until the unlucky shell entered the casemate in which Kondrachenko was issuing his orders, the garrison of Port Arthur showed a front which rendered the advent of the Baltic Fleet a menace not altogether chimerical. But once he was gone, the whole fabric seemed to wither, and within a very few days the permanent *enceinte* was pierced. We have then the pathetic incident of a surrendered garrison. It is difficult, of course, to understand the Russian attitude at any time; and as we have said before, we have little in the way of evidence either from the lines of the besieged or besiegers. But until the death of Kondrachenko the spirit was probably much as we find it described in 'The Yellow War,' "resigned and determined."

These were doubtless the circumstances which induced Nogi to make the desperate efforts which built up the tradition in his army of "bloody August." At the beginning of August the Port Arthur siege-train had been landed at Dalny and conveyed to the lines of the left division. We have shown how on July 28, while the rest of the Russian line was forced back, the garrison of Fort Takushan maintained its ground.

Takushan is practically an outpost in advance of the outer Kinkeeshan forts. It commanded a considerable front, and by doing so was a constant thorn in the besiegers' side, since the gunners on its summit were able to follow every movement in the outpost line of the 11th Division.

As soon as the siege-train arrived it was brought into the position that had been prepared for it in front of Takushan, and on August 7 the heavy artillery opened their maiden fire upon it. To show how precipitate are the Japanese conceptions of attack against a defended position, the siege artillery only opened fire at four in the afternoon, and three hours later the infantry were streaming up the nullahs, fissures, and waterways which steal down the faces of nearly all these Kwantung hills.

Nowhere do we find an adequate description of the desperate fighting which gave the Japanese the possession of Takushan. The position was fully prepared, from the crown-works on the main crest to the lunettes at the foot of the glacis. A triple line of barbed-wire entanglements encircled the base, while batteries of machine-guns swept the approaches. It was a case in which the divisional general chose to preface his assault with a venture by a forlorn hope.

Fifty men were selected from six companies of the Marugame Regiment. These three hundred were launched in the dusk against this wellnigh impregnable position. It proved a veritable forlorn hope. The three hundred were annihilated. Then followed a section of sappers to clear the entanglements which the few half-demented survivors from the forlorn hope reported as being the cause of their undoing. These men perished miserably before the wire-clippers had cut a third of this scientific abattis.

It was, however, a case of not accepting failure until culminative failure produced success. By midnight the wounded men who could still crawl from strand to strand in the entanglements had cut a passage, and, in spite of a ceaseless fire from machine-guns, the 22nd and 10th Brigades drove the Russians out of their works at the point of the bayonet before daybreak.

Takushan, and its complementary fortress Shakushan, was a serious loss to the garrison. They had hoped to save it: having lost it through the singular intrepidity of the Japanese infantry, they endeavoured, on the following day, to recapture it by a heavy counter-attack. Again their gunboats coming out from the roadstead gave them help, but it was no use—Takushan was lost. Realising that indirect fire from Takushan might find his squadron as it lay at anchor in the harbour, Admiral Witgeft immediately entered upon that desperate sortie which was the last nail but one in the coffin of Russia's Pacific Squadron.

The outposts of Nogi's army were now facing the extreme northern outworks of the Port Arthur subsidiary works. On the east, now that they were masters of Takushan and Shakushan, their advance was arrested by the powerful forts east and west,— Panlungshan, and the two similar outworks on the slopes of Kikwanshan. Before they could pierce the main *enceinte* from the north, they had to grapple with a further chain of semi-permanent outworks—namely, Fort Kuropatkin and the Sueizeyang group. That the reader may form some conception of the task which Nogi set his assaulting infantry, we will quote 'The Times' expert's description of the Sueizeyang works:—

Two lunettes or flanked redans, each in plan forming the equal sides of an isosceles triangle, with shorter perpendiculars at their unjoined ends, were constructed. Deep moats, in which were built bomb-proof shelters roofed with steel plates covered with earth, surrounded them. In front, connecting the apices of the lunettes, which measured 30 yards across their open bases, was a vast crown-work; ...

the parapets or walls were of earth not less than 25 feet thick. Behind these, baulks of timbers, iron-plates, &c., covered with many feet of earth, constituted shelters safe from fire for the garrison. This great work was defended by no fewer than two field-guns, two mortars, three quick-firing guns, and four machine-guns, disposed in the west and east lunette.

Completing the chain, to the south-west of these works lie the Metre group of outworks, one on 174 Metre Hill and the other on the far-famed 203 Metre eminence.

Prompted by the success which had marked the earlier assaults, and realising that every day which kept his army of first-line troops from the north was of significance in Oyama's campaign, General Nogi determined to make a desperate effort to reduce Port Arthur before the end of August, trusting to the magnificent *élan* of his men rather than to the prescribed occidental methods of approach to a first-class fortress, hitherto unprepared and unassailed. Once again the wisdom of the West was proved superior to the heroic confidence of the East, and the week ending August 24, covering as it does Nogi's premature attack, is, as far as the Japanese are concerned, the most tragic in the campaign.

On August 19 the first army, directed by General Matsumura, moved out against the 174 Metre range, to the left of Sueizeyang. There was no guile in the dispositions for the attack. The battalions selected to make the assault were just hurled at the positions. On the left of Matsumura, Baron Oshima, with the 9th Division, made a similar assault, his right brigade casting itself against Fort Kuropatkin, and his left up the nullahs which converged upon the crown-works of Panlungshan, the northern Ehrlungshan-Kikwanshan outworks.[1] On their left again came the 11th Division, which had the least success of the three first divisions of Nogi's command.

One can imagine the terrible scenes which this week's fighting witnessed. Most of the Japanese assaults were still delivered by night, but, since August, divisional generals found the defences and entanglements so intricate, and the commanding fire so accurate, under the beams of star-shell and searchlights, that the advantages of darkness were minimised by the disadvantages. Subsequently nearly all of the assaults were carried out by day.

The scope of this treatise will not allow of a minute study of these terrible operations which cost the Japanese nearly 20,000 casualties, and which only resulted in the permanent occupation of Panlungshan —a possession which, though of vital importance, for nearly six weeks cost the Japanese in its retention over 100 casualties a-day.

The story of the magnificent courage of the Japanese infantry—how, breaking time after time in face of

[1] Japanese name—Banjushan.

fearful odds, they re-formed—must be told in a more complete history of the operations. But though we must perforce eschew the detail, yet there are incidents for which space can be made. Every devilish device that modern science could contribute to the defence works was employed by the subtle Russian sappers. The wire entanglements were electrified for miles, dealing death, upon touch, to the eager pioneers who sought to clear a way for the desperate infantry behind them. In places the fire zones were so impassable that the sappers who sought to cleave entanglements had to be provided with light steel shields as well as non-conductive gloves. Hand grenades, loaded with a high explosive, were extensively used by both sides. The Japanese forlorn-hopes went into action with two, three, and four of these infernal implements hanging round their necks, until it was found that a premature burst might so communicate itself as to annihilate a battalion more thoroughly than could the enemy. Primitive mortars fashioned from bamboo were substituted, which, with a range of fifty yards, flung these diabolical missiles into the trenches in advance of the assaulting infantry.

But Port Arthur, unprepared by artillery bombardment and unapproached by sap, was not to be carried by escalade. Even in those sections where, using every ingenious device, such as spar-torpedoes for

NOGI CHANGES HIS TACTICS. 189

destroying the death-charged entanglements, the infantry were able to gain a foothold, even in Fort Kuropatkin, and subsequently in the famous 203 Metre Hill, the Japanese heroism proved abortive. Russian shrapnel and counter-attack turned the Japanese out, so that at the end of the sixth day Nogi's army fell back panting from all it had attempted, except from the Panlungshan secondary works, and in carrying these the 7th Regiment, which went into action 2700 strong, was reduced to 208 bayonets.

A grisly tale with a dramatic sequel, which already has cost Russia and Japan almost a million of men. Port Arthur was not yet to fall to the fiery onslaught of Japanese escalade, and the telegram on August 21 went to the War Department in Tokio which informed Oyama that he must operate against Kuropatkin without counting upon the 100,000 men with Nogi at Port Arthur.

Nogi now set himself to sap up to the works which he desired to carry. For once the teaching of the decadent occidental had been right. The spade, the mattock, and the large-calibre howitzer are the prime implements in the reduction of a first-class modern fortress, notwithstanding the fact that the besieging general commands incomparable infantry.

Hitherto, for artillery support, Nogi had depended upon his field-artillery, howitzers, and the 4·7 and

SIEGE OPERATIONS.

6-inch guns of the Naval Brigade. Now the legitimate siege-train was demanded, together with guns of large calibre from the coast defences in Japan. These latter, 11-inch howitzers, arrived at Dalny on September 14, and were in action from October 1.

After August 26, the investment of Port Arthur settled down to the monotony of siege operations; while the Japanese toiled with a very stubborn soil to push parallel after parallel up towards Port Arthur's subsidiary line of defences. For a month the besiegers gave themselves up almost entirely to the spade and platforms. The besieged did not bear this steady menace mildly. Shot for shot, heavy Oboukhoff and Krupp gave back the Japanese preparations; while sortie upon sortie delayed and impeded the work in trench and parallel.

But by the 19th of September the Japanese had broken sufficient ground to again put into practice the tactics in which they excel. Parallels had been pushed up to within assaulting distance of Fort Kuropatkin, the Sueizeyang lunettes, and the forts south-east of 174 Metre Hill. The 1st Division had been stiffened by the arrival of large drafts from the Second Reserve and the 1st Kobe (Reserve) Brigade, and in co-operation with the 3rd Division it was to attempt the assault of the outworks to the Russian perimeter, while the 11th Division demonstrated against the Ehrlungshan fort.

Fort Kuropatkin and the Sueizeyang group were carried on the second day (20th) with heavy losses, and Nogi stood possessed of the garrison's main water intake; but Matsumura with the intrepid 1st Division had not the same good fortune. He selected to assault 203 Metre Hill and its complementary peak, Namaokayama. Both hills had considerable crown-defences, and the Russians had placed batteries of heavy guns in each. But the main advantage that the Japanese would reap from the possession of the 203 Metre range was that from its reverse slope they would be able to render the old town, roadstead, and docks untenable.

Success was, however, not yet to come. Matsumura launched his fifteen battalions against the Russian works. After a bitter struggle his troops occupied Namaokayama, and secured a foothold on 203 Metre Hill. In fact, on the night of September 21 it was reported that the whole position was held. But, as one of the most moving writers from the front has said—

> The first line of the defence was taken. It had cost much in the taking, but this was trifling to the cost of holding it... What the bayonets had not been able to do shrapnel quickly accomplished. The Japanese officers tried to find cover for

their men, but there was no hiding from that pitiless rain of lead, and in a quarter of an hour the captured trenches were three times as full of Japanese casualties as they had held Russians.[1]

At daybreak the Russian gunners had concentrated every available gun they could bring to bear on the reverse of their lost work, and had literally swept the Japanese out of it. General Yamamoto, commanding the 1st Brigade, was killed, and the gallant 1st Division left three thousand men on the slopes of Metre Hill and another thousand on the glacis of Fort Kuropatkin.

After the heavy losses and ill-success at the Metre range, Nogi and his engineer advisers came to the conclusion that 203 Metre Hill was too well supported from the citadels behind it to be the real stepping-stone to success. It was therefore determined to transfer the active operations to the eastern face of the perimeter, and to drill and burrow into the great rock-masses at the foot of the Cockscomb forts.

The rest of the brilliant story must be told in few words. The sappers set themselves to sap right up to the counterscarps of the outer works. Slowly, with infinite pains and infinite loss, fort after fort was torn from Stössel's grasp: Hachimokeyama and

---

[1] The Yellow War. By "O." William Blackwood & Sons, Edinburgh and London.

North Ehrlungshan on October 16; the trenches and redoubts on the Ehrlungshan glacis ten days later; and on November 4 the glacis-crests of Ehrlungshan, Sungshushan, and E. Kikwanshan were reached, and the caponiers within many of the ditches destroyed. But in the meantime the Baltic Fleet has left Libau, and another fifty thousand men have reached Kuropatkin in the north. Although the Russians were unsuccessful on the Sha-ho, yet Oyama's force suffered almost as heavily. If Kuropatkin is to be crippled completely, the investing army should no longer be in Kwantung.

We have now come to the closing scene in this terrible and yet magnificent drama. Generals Kodama and Fukushima, the reputed mainsprings of the Japanese General Staff, had come down from the north to help Nogi with their professional advice, and doubtless to press upon him the urgency of Japan's present necessity. The Russian Pacific Squadron must be destroyed before either it leaves the harbour, and in despairing effort damages Togo's remaining strength, or the arrival of the reinforcement from the Baltic changes the balance of power in the China seas.

Again the calculating brain of the great Nogi was concentrated upon the Metre range. The possession of Namaokayama had given him the command of the western roadstead, and his fire from this point had driven the Russian ships, like a flock of sheep in a hurdle angle, into the inner and eastern basin. Here they were practically immune from his fire. But 203 Metre Hill would lay the inner basin open to a bombardment which nothing in this world could sustain, much less such a vulnerable quantity as ships.

The Metre range was to be taken. Circumstances also had somewhat changed since August. Then the gallant 1st Division had been asked to advance across the open with little help from parallel and covered way. It had been a desperate measure without due precaution and under inadequate preparation. Now it was different, and as a counter-balance to the time the Russians had had to improve the position there existed the three months' loss of *morale* under the severe strain of the unsuccessful defence of secondary works. A 'Times' correspondent gives the best minute description of the Russian position that we can find :—

Royusan—to employ a term which includes both the 203 Metre and the 210 Metre peaks—is very steep: on its west front, about two-thirds of the way up, the rocks buttress out, causing a sheer drop of about 30 to 40 feet. It is possible to climb up this, but the feat is not an easy one. Above this natural obstruction comes the first of the artificial ones, in the form of a broad trench running completely round the hostile front of the mountain. This was the first of the positions held by the infantry. On the crest there are numerous trenches and cross passages dug fairly deep and made of sandbags.

THE PREPARATION.

This position is also flanked by Akasakayama, still in the possession of the garrison.

It was determined that new troops shonld be utilised in this assault, which it was intended should be final as far as the subsidiary works were concerned. The 7th Division under General Osaka had just arrived from Japan. It was the last of the thirteen territorial divisions to leave Japan, and the strapping sons of the northern island were dying to emulate the deeds of their brothers.

To General Saito, the senior brigadier, was assigned the tactical direction of the assault. The whole of November 27 was given up to artillery preparation. It was no apology this time. The infantry were not to be turned loose upon the hillside. The parallels had been pushed up as near as possible to the objective, and giant howitzers throwing six thousand pounds in a battery salvo were in position. Something of the full extent of the inferno this preparation must have been we can gather from the too brief description which 'The Yellow War' gives us:—

But there are other scenes and sounds which dispel as an illusion the suggestion of a peaceful working day. The still winter air quivers and vibrates as the huge watershed in the west catches and hurls back in deafening reverberation a continuous din of war. Just watch that nearest crest-line for a moment. Flash after flash gleams out against the embevelled top; great geysers of snow and *debris*-dust spurt skywards to swell the lowering yellow cloud drifting sullenly along the valley. . . . Look down in the parallels below. Your ear squirms to the laboured whir of enormous shells as they displace the frosty air.

On the 28th Saito is prepared to develop the dispositions he has made. The men of Hakadate and sappers are crowding the advanced parallels. They are loosed against the south-west corner of the hill—the 210 Metre point. Eleven companies of little karki-coated riflemen struggle upwards in face of a devastating fire. By three in the afternoon 150 men have made a lodgment, and cling desperately to a mean summit of the under-feature.

At the same time two battalions essay the assault of Akasakayama, the flanking fortress. With all the *élan* of fresh, unblooded troops they debouch bravely from the parallels. Then the full shock of the defence opens upon them. For a time they battle manfully against the blizzard of rifle-fire and shrapnel; and then the terrific slaughter quenches the *élan*, and they are driven back to the shelter of the trenches.

By nightfall the maiden effort of the 7th Division had failed. The little group of stalwarts were driven in from 210 Metre point. Its loss was fatal to the major assault worming its way up the main face of 203, and on the 29th all the infantry that had escaped the carnage attendant alike on success and failure were back in the trenches.

The 29th was given up to recalculation. As has been noticeable throughout these stupendous operations, at the moment when failure seemed to face the efforts of the whole, some small insignificant unit would, in a manner inexplicable, score a tiny advantage upon which it became possible to build success on the very crest-line of failure. On the morning of November 30 a handful of infantry, holding an under-feature-knoll on the face of 210 Metre point, suddenly pushed on to the summit and surprised the wearied Russians there. The Japanese made no Spion Kop errors: sappers with sand-bags were ready, and immediately the crest was seized it was hurriedly intrenched. Again Saito was in possession of a firing-line to support his main assault

But open assault was impracticable still. Again recourse was made to the sapper, and during the night of the 30th the engineers commenced a rough sand-bagged covered-way at right angles from the advanced parallel running up the face of 203 Metre Hill. On the 1st of December it was determined to make a general final assault. The assaulting columns had been reinforced, and the men were filing along the covered-ways into the parallels, when suddenly, without warning, two detachments holding the advance positions on the face of "203," seized with panic, broke cover and came pouring back to the shelters in the plain.

Again had a postponement to be made. But all the time the 11-inch howitzers, the naval guns, and the siege-train were casting ton after ton of metal into the stubborn and devoted defenders. The glacis-approach was a veritable shambles. During the 2nd, 3rd, and 4th the giant engines of war in rear were allowed to do their work. And right well they did it, for on December 5, when, at 2 P.M., Saito launched eight battalions against the position, they climbed into the devastated Russian works with comparative ease. The garrison had shot its bolt. We cannot proceed to the miserable sequel without one more reference to the work we last quoted, which alone gives us any appreciable idea of the ghastly nature of modern war. 'The Yellow War' describes the captured position in the following sentences :—

Only those who have seen an *abattoir* in a Chicago packing-house can form the least conception of the spectacle. Upon the summit of the highest level of the works the morning rays of the wintry sun caught the white and scarlet of Japan's symbolic flag. On the bunting scarlet predominates, and thus it was on this war-scarred crest. The virgin snow was stamped out, and in the slush and *débris* that remained, scarlet—the life's blood of hundreds—predominated. By that strange perversity which rules our moral code, the work of brutal killing had barely ceased before the softer touch of human resolve had commenced its charitable operations. The surgeons and their orderlies were hard at work. They waded into the shambles and handed up the living when it was possible to separate them from the dead.

What it cost Japan to finally carry 203 Metre Hill is not exactly known. But the 7th Division had over 7000 casualties alone within a week of its arrival at the seat of war. Yet it was worth it, for within a week the 11-inch howitzers were in position, and Togo able to report "the destruction of almost the whole of the enemy's fleet in these waters." This miserable end to a magnificent squadron we have already commented upon in the chapter devoted to the study of the naval strategy. A few words will now suffice to bring the melancholy story of Port Arthur to a close.

On December 28 that incomparable force, the Japanese Sappers, had tunnelled from the glacis-crest of Ehrlungshan beneath the scarp of the main work. A ton of dynamite will accomplish much. The revetted parapet crumbled away, and before the garrison could recover from the stunning effect of this gigantic explosion or be reinforced, the men of the 11th Division and the Kobe Reserves were into the breach and had the main *enceinte* of Port Arthur pierced. Three days later Sungshushan, a complementary defence to Ehrlungshan, was carried in a similar manner, and on the following day Stössel opened negotiations for the surrender of his trust. On January 2nd Port Arthur capitulated to General Nogi's army after a fine resistance which lasted 155 days. The siege is perhaps most remarkable for the extraordinary, disgusting, and selfish cowardice of the officers of the Pacific Squadron. The fortitude and gallantry of the garrison is only eclipsed by the magnificent military energy of the Imperial Japanese Third Army.

VI. ROJDESTVENSKY'S ARMADA.

It must have been obvious to the most casual observer that if there were one weak link in the chain of Japan's armour that caused apprehension in the War Department at Tokio, it was the possibility of Russian naval reinforcement from Europe. The Japanese are not the people to demonstrate their apprehensions, any more than we find them giving publicity to their future military intentions; but it is possible to trace through the history of the past eighteen months many signal indications that, much as it was fashionable in this country to scoff at Russia's activity in the Baltic, yet the sage Japanese strategists never looked upon the menace as chimerical.

We know that in January 1904 the presence of the *Oslabia* and *Aurora* in the Red Sea precipitated the termination of diplomatic relations between the two belligerents. We have already traced the history of the titanic efforts which were deliberately undertaken by the Japanese, regardless of expenditure in blood and treasure, upon the knowledge that Rojdestvensky's squadron was a real factor. And during Rojdestvensky's stay in French-Chinese waters we have had evidence of the first indignant ebullition of Japanese feeling that the war has brought forth. This, in our reasoning, is very significant.

Since the commencement of the campaign the neutrality of China has been infringed by both belligerents with considerable freedom,—in fact, as far as the whole campaign is concerned, the question of China's neutrality hardly seems to have been a distinguishable factor at all. But although there has been so extensive an infringement of the so-called considerations of neutrals, yet it was not until the lay populace of Japan actually realised that, even at the eleventh hour, it might be possible for their enemies to turn the tables upon them, that they gave the smallest evidence of relaxing their power of self-control.

We have known for many months past, that from the very commencement the Japanese War Departments have entertained similar anxieties to those which subsequently agitated the Japanese press. But, for reasons which it is not necessary to discuss here, they held their peace until they were in a position to finally verify the conflicting information with regard to the finding of the Russian squadron.

There were many in this country (and in dealing with matters naval we only refer to the opinion of experts) who openly stated that Rojdestvensky's squadron would never reach Far Eastern waters. As has already been shown in this treatise, when Rojdestvensky sailed from the Baltic the Russian Pacific Squadron still existed, though blockade-bound. There seemed to the experts who judged of the campaign with external knowledge a reasonable chance that the Port Arthur garrison might keep the investing Japanese at arm's-length until this succour from Europe arrived.

With so much at stake, it was a legitimate surmise that an effort was being made to save the remnants of the magnificent squadron which had been the mainstay of Russia's bullying policy towards Japan.

There was the school of experts who would not allow that the Baltic Squadron was ever intended to do more than furnish a pretence at a diversion. There were some who even suggested that the Russian Admiralty were simple-minded enough to believe that, by suddenly producing a Russian squadron in the Indian Ocean, they would succeed in drawing off the greater portion of the Japanese fleet from the Yellow Sea, and thus enable the immured vessels to break away. Then there was a third school who, believing the primed press reports from the Baltic littoral, maintained that the Russian ships were not seaworthy.

To crown all these arguments came the crucial moment of the Dogger Bank incident, which, it was argued by many, was a deliberate and predesigned attempt to embroil Europe in Russia's Far Eastern trouble. This last expression of opinion will bear subsequent analysis. There was, however, reason to support all these speculations, and each in turn lent colour to the many purposely promulgated stories of unserviceable weapons, plates, and machinery.

But we ourselves, having given careful study to all the published matter with regard to the Baltic Fleet that we have been able to discover, are forced back to our original belief—which was that, after the loss of the *Petropavlovsk* and Makaroff, the Russian Admiralty believed that the Pacific Squadron was doomed: that no effort they could make, however strenuous, would be of sufficient character to enable them to save the residue of their Far Eastern warships from destruction.

We are borne out in this theory by the following statement in Captain Klado's extraordinary Essays on the Russian Navy.[1] He quotes from the report by Admiral Skrydloff, written, subsequent to the loss of the *Petropavlovsk*, in April of last year. The extract which concerns us at the moment runs as follows:—

> Our success at sea must principally depend on the squadron leaving the Baltic, which consequently ought to be stronger than that portion of the Japanese fleet with which it would be

---

[1] The Russian Navy of the Russo-Japanese War. By Captain Klado of the Russian Imperial Navy. Hurst & Blackett.

faced. It is, therefore, essential that due regard should be had to the character of this squadron at the time of its departure, as well as that of its arrival at the seat of war. That arrival will have very different results, according as to whether it takes place before or after the fall of Port Arthur.

We can readily understand from Klado's book alone, if it were not for other evidence, that the character of the Baltic Fleet as it was then found when Skrydloff penned his despatch was not of sufficient stability to warrant the hope that the officer appointed to its command would ever be able to arrive in Japanese waters before the reduction of Port Arthur and the consequent destruction or loss of the "remainder" of the Pacific Squadron. This being the case, the whole scope, nature, and condition of Rojdestvensky's plan of operations ignored Port Arthur.

We do not profess to know any more of this plan of operations than the public which has had access to the same information as ourselves. But we believe that a study of the Russian movements and procedure, from the start to their appearance off the coast of Annam, support these contentions, and it certainly is worthy of attention, since, whether Rojdestvensky was successful or not, the passage of his armada from Europe to the Far East is one of the most complex and interesting incidents unfolded in the naval history of the world.

Two points seem to stand out with considerable

clearness with regard to the original inception of the mission of the Baltic Fleet and with its subsequent despatch. It would appear that when, at the outbreak of war, it was first deemed necessary to despatch ships from the Baltic, the calculations were based upon the assumption that a reinforcement was required for the Pacific Squadron.

In spite of Skrydloff's despatch and other as important warnings, the work of preparation was proceeded with, on its original instructions, until Rojdestvensky was ready to start. Then we get the evidence of the want of unity between the various executive departments in St Petersburg which has been the ruin of the whole Russian cause. Rojdestvensky found himself about to be pushed off in command of what should have been the main naval menace to Japan, but which was really only intended by the Russian bureaucracy to be a reinforcement to a squadron which was now practically non-existent.

Rojdestvensky, though he knew that the task he had undertaken was stupendous, felt that by remaining at sea, if only the effete machinery in St Petersburg would put forward its best effort, he would maintain his character of aggression, while at the same time he improved the value of his *personnel*, and enabled the dockyards at Revel and the Neva to bring him up to that strength which would give him sufficient preponderance to seek with confidence a trial of strength with the Japanese Fleet.

But his fear seemed to be that once having sailed from the Baltic, the authorities at St Petersburg would leave him as he had been designed, a mere reinforcement, instead of supplementing his fleet with every ship that the dockyard hands could man and turn out seaworthy.

No one can hope to adequately probe the machinations of an intelligent Russian's mind, any more than he would aspire to pick the brains of a Japanese diplomatist. But we have a shrewd suspicion that much of the attitude which Rojdestvensky displayed after the Dogger Bank incident was intended not as a deliberate insult to this country, but as a demonstration of necessity to the Departments he had left behind him.

The relationship between Klado and Rojdestvensky is quite transparent. Klado was landed at Vigo, not as hostage, scapegoat, or witness, but with the deliberate intention that he should use the Dogger Bank incident as a foundation upon which to build a campaign of agitation sufficiently sensational to rivet public attention upon the last desperate chance of Russia's Navy. It seems pitiful that an admiral commanding the forlorn-hope of a nation of so many millions should have to take recourse to such measures. But in the history of modern kingdoms is there anything comparable with the present condition of Russia in every stage and class?

It was a day full of grave national import for Russia, when on the 13th of August 1904 Admiral Rojdestvensky hoisted his flag on the *Kniaz-Suvaroff*, then lying at Libau. In the person of this admiral, and in his squadron of fourteen war vessels, centred the last hopes of Russia. What does history know of this admiral, in whose hands the Czar was placing the destiny of his Empire? Contrary to the precedents existing in the sister service, Rojdestvensky is a comparatively young man,—that is, he is well under sixty. When passing through the Russian naval schools, he specialised in marine artillery. As a lieutenant he served during the Turko-Russian War in 1877-78, under Baronof, on board the *Vesta*, and is credited by his own countrymen with having given evidence during this campaign of pre-eminence rarely met with in one so young.

Latterly—that is to say, since the Dogger Bank incident—we have seen published in this country derogatory statements concerning the character which Rojdestvensky earned during this campaign. But although it is quite possible that published tradition has over-estimated the prowess of the little *Vesta* and her crew, we find that it will be equally just to discount the uncomplimentary reflections which have recently seen the light: anyway, shortly after the close of the Turkish campaign, Rojdestvensky, decorated and promoted, found an appointment to his liking in instructing the Bulgarians in river navigation. But it was as attaché to the Russian Embassy in London that the full merit of Rojdestvensky's capacity was realised by sailors in this country.

In 1894, after a very considerable experience throughout Europe, the present Commander-in-Chief commenced his association with Admiral Alexieff. He accompanied that notable to the Pacific, when the Vice-Admiral flew his flag from the mast-head of the *Vladimir Monomakh*. This commission in the Far East covered the Japanese-Chinese war. After having commanded the guardship *Pervéniets* for some months, Captain Rojdestvensky returned home to undertake a succession of staff appointments, until in 1903 we find that he succeeded Avellane as head of the general staff of the navy. Consequently we must estimate the admiral in a very different category to the libertines, Starck and Prince Ukhtomsky.

We would ask the reader just to consider the stupendous nature of the task which lay in front of the Russian admiral, before admitting an opinion based either upon sentiment or indignation. In the first place, to understand the true position—it being given that Rojdestvensky himself had abandoned all hope of material help from the Russian vessels still in the

Pacific—it is necessary to estimate the force to which he would find himself opposed.

The Japanese, with a candour which is irreproachable, after Port Arthur published an official list of their naval losses. This included a first-class battleship, two second-class cruisers, and various smaller and more or less obsolete or unimportant craft. In comparison with Russia's losses, those sustained by the Japanese were infinitesimal. But although we respect the candour of the Japanese Naval Department, yet at the time it was impossible to be certain that the list included the entire tonnage which had been rendered unserviceable by war.

Although it had been hinted in various quarters that the Japanese had lost two battleships in the Russian mine-fields, yet a writer in 'Blackwood's Magazine' was the first to make an authoritative statement on the subject. This writer's information came from two independent sources which curiously dovetailed. It therefore had to be calculated at this period that Togo had under his command four first-class battleships, eight armoured cruisers, eighteen protected cruisers, ten unprotected cruisers, and anything between eighty and a hundred torpedo craft. At the time the Japanese official statement showed five battleships, but by an addition of the registered displacements of the ships of this type published by the Japanese, it was impossible to make five first-class vessels fit into the total,—an indiscretion in publicity unusual in the Japanese Admiralty.

The inference therefore was, that the battleship total had been arrived at by the inclusion of one or another of the coast-defence battleships. To oppose this fleet Rojdestvensky, when he sailed from the Baltic, had under his command seven battleships, one armoured cruiser, and five protected cruisers. Each of the rival fleets, therefore, had its own disparity. In the matter of battleships the Russians were superior both in gun-power and numbers; but leaving out their superiority in torpedo craft, the Japanese appeared to possess all the rest of the points.

To sum up, naval opinion placed great faith in the swift Japanese armoured cruisers. Collectively, Togo's fleet was superior in homogeneity, pace, total gun-power, *morale*, and, most important, strategical position. Viewed in this light, we can well understand the character of the mission which Rojdestvensky entrusted to Captain Klado. With all the moral, material, and strategical advantages against him, Rojdestvensky could only hope to arrive at a successful issue to his venture by superiority of gun-power in first-line ships or act of God. Pace and numbers were with his adversary.

Therefore it was obvious, and it was obvious to every thinking man for months before the event, there was no intention of a dash to the Far East for the purpose of attempting to raise the blockade of the Pacific Squadron. But rather, when assured that a supplementary and even a third squadron would be despatched to reinforce him, Rojdestvensky settled upon a plan which would enable him to arrive in Chinese waters with as powerful a fleet as Russia at the moment was capable of mobilising. To some degree the ridicule and the sarcasms of the British press served his purpose, for, slavishly swallowed, each gutter report that Russia's money turned loose upon the world helped to mask the Admiral's real condition and objective.

Whether the Naval Intelligence Department of Japan was similarly hoodwinked we are not in the position to know, but, judging from the fact that all Japanese naval authorities expressed apprehension of Russia's naval resources, we would suggest that they have not been as easily duped as the British reading public.

It was unfortunate, no doubt, that Rojdestvensky's squadron was not sufficiently advanced to enable him to make the effort for Port Arthur in time; unfortunate that the working out of his coal and supply scheme allowed Togo a respite to repair the damages of nine months' war: but it were better that the Japanese should have these advantages than that the Russian squadron should arrive in Japanese waters destitute of coal and the various ways and means that Rojdestvensky had either to bring with him or organise in advance.

On October 15 the Baltic Fleet hove up its anchors and steamed away from Libau. On the 17th it anchored off the Danish coast and picked up its Danish pilots, together with the fantastic story of hostile torpedo craft in the North Sea. On the following day it passed through the Great Belt, and on October 20 commenced its voyage down the North Sea. Rojdestvensky had broken up his fleet into four divisions, and two flotillas of destroyers. The first Battleship Squadron was under the Commander-in-Chief, the second was flying the flag of Rear-Admiral Felkersham, the Cruiser Division was commanded by Rear-Admiral Enquist, while Captain Radlof controlled the Military Transport Division.

On the night of the 21st-22nd, two of the Admiral's divisions ran amuck on the Dogger Bank. It is not our intention to devote a great space to this deplorable incident. In our opinion there are only two ways of satisfactorily explaining this extraordinary occurrence. Either the Russian Admiral believed implicity the fable of the Japanese torpedo-boats, or a deliberate and inhuman attack was made upon our defenceless fishermen.

If the Admiral believed the fable, then we can understand the reasons which prompted him to steer a false course. If he did not believe it, and arrived off the Dogger Bank by accident, then his seamanship was so indifferent that it could never have got him out to the Far East.

We would prefer to think that the first surmise is the correct one, but the Russians look upon the ethics of human existence from a standpoint so different to our own that the wellbeing of half a dozen fisher-folk would not deter a strong official from developing his scheme over their corpses.

Rojdestvensky and his associates felt that they could afford to take no risks: if necessary, they must be prepared to brand the existence of their squadron into the minds of the executive left behind in Russia; otherwise, once they were clear of the Baltic, they would not have the backing which alone would make their perilous enterprise successful. It seems callous, beastly, and dreadful, but we must always remember that the Baltic Fleet was then, as it was to the end, playing for a desperate stake.

We will pass from the incident, leaving the wave of public indignation which swept across this country, and the curiously constituted Commission, for other pens to analyse. But we cannot pass over the delicate moments of last October when the Press in this country clamoured for the blood of the guilty even unto the very gates of Vigo, Rojdestvensky's city of refuge after the outrage.

We had a week of intense excitement, culminating

with an oration from the Prime Minister which seemed to indicate that the full measure of national endurance had been reached. Then followed a fall from "blood heat" to "zero." So much so, that the sitting of the International Court of Inquiry became an affair of but passing interest, and the country never troubled to search for the cause of the Prime Minister's change of front.

It had had its fit of heroics, it had been able to expand its chest for one half-day after the Southampton speech, therefore it never troubled about the small significant suggestion made on the morrow by the French ambassador,—a suggestion which killed the heroics on the Prime Minister's lips, and fed the Spanish cables with sober cipher messages to the Admiral of the Mediterranean Fleet.

England was just reminded that once the International Court of Inquiry was agreed upon, the Dogger Bank incident as an affair for reprisals was closed; that henceforth the Russian Fleet anchored off Vigo was an active agent in the Far Eastern problem, and as such, if molested by a second Power, would place France within the range of her treaty obligations.

The indiscretions of Ministers are many: they must be, since they have many masters to serve. But it is not often that, after a year of "hedging" policy, they engage in an oratory diametrically opposed to the most intimate interests of their prevailing policy. Neither belligerent had reason to be best pleased at the development of the Anglo-French *entente cordiale*, but Russia had cause to view it with dismay. The endeavour to destroy it was within an ace of succeeding, thanks to the influence of sensation-mongering journalism on the Cabinet.

Be that as it may, for the moment the lowering storm-clouds were rent in two, and though the thunder of the dissipated tempest continued to rumble, yet for the time being policy had triumphed over the indiscretions bred of the nation's newly-developed disease of sensation-lust. On the 28th of October, leaving four officers behind, including the redoubtable Captain Klado, the Baltic Fleet steamed away from the Spanish coast.

On October 29 Rojdestvensky's fleet began to arrive at Tangier. Here it was to divide. The Battle Squadron was destined to round the Cape of Good Hope in its voyage to the Far East, while the Cruiser Division, under Felkersham, took the Suez Canal route to the appointed rendezvous east of Africa.

Whatever route Rojdestvensky might choose after he made the Indian Ocean, the Baltic Squadron had over 15,000 miles to cover before it could make Vladivostok. Felkersham's Squadron—taking the Chagoo Islands, as was thought at the time, as being the most likely place of rendezvous — had 2000 less.

Therefore it was within the pale of possibility, though not of probability, that Rojdestvensky's armada should arrive in Japanese waters early in January if it never delayed, was coaled expeditiously, and steamed twelve knots.

As we have demonstrated that such expedition never entered into the Admiral's calculations, there is no need to speculate upon means of a procedure that would have consumed 10,000 tons of coal daily. As it is, under more economic conditions the fleet exhausted anything between 16,000 and 20,000 tons per thousand miles. It were therefore absurd to have imagined that a dash to Port Arthur was ever seriously contemplated last October, and there is no profit in laboriously following in minute detail the voyages of the various units of the fleet to their half-way house.

On November 5 the Russian fleets left Tangier. Five days later we hear of Felkersham at Suda Bay, and on the 12th Rojdestvensky is coaling at Dakar, the French position at Cape Verde. Rojdestvensky, who by this had given evidence that he was not hurrying, did not leave Dakar until the 16th.

On the following day the first of the supplementary reinforcements for which Captain Klado had been agitating left Libau. This division consisted of the protected cruisers *Oleg* and *Jemtchug*, the converted cruisers *Rion* and *Dnieper*, and five destroyers. This division was commanded by Captain Botrovosky.

On the 24th of November Felkersham is at Port Said, while two days later we had evidence of Rojdestvensky's interpretation of his licence under the Franco-Russian Alliance by the arrival of the Russian Battleship Squadron at Gaboon. On November 27 Felkersham leaves Suez, and on the 2nd of December he is signalled as passing Perim, thus going safely through the zone which Captain Klado, in his most Anglophobe mood, believed, in view of British complicity with the Japanese, to be the most dangerous section of the voyage. Three days later he was reported as coaling at the Musha Islands, in the French East African waters.

December 6 finds Rojdestvensky off Great Fish Bay. He is subsequently reported as rounding the Cape of Good Hope; and on the 1st of January, when Stössel is negotiating the surrender of Port Arthur, the Russian fleet, after experiencing very rough weather, anchors off the Ile Sainte Marie, Madagascar. The concentration of the Russian fleets was practically effected, for on the 3rd of January Felkersham was reported from Passandova Bay, in the north of the French island.

Here, then, was Rojdestvensky's haven. As had already been shown, he had no intention to dissipate the few chances he possessed by rash haste and unschemed venture. The northern coast-line of Madagascar furnishes several excellent anchorages. In fact, British Sound or Diego Suarez is one of the finest anchorages in South African waters. Here, practically under the security of French guns, Rojdestvensky would await the result of the Klado campaign, engaging in the meantime in the very necessary task of bringing the *personnel* of his fleet up to standard.

The school of naval experts who had estimated the Russian venture as a pure demonstration, now openly congratulated themselves upon their perspicacity. Their impressions were endorsed by various statements claiming that no arrangement had been made for coaling the fleet on the continuance of its voyage to the Far East. French correspondents who gained access to the Russian admiral repeated the familiar story of worthless material and untrustworthy machinery.

In reality, we discover quite another impression was formed by the British expert who had occasion to find himself in North Madagascar at that period. The Russian vessels were systematically exercised in gunnery and steam tactics, while the fouling, of which so much had been made in this country, was considerably reduced by the application of a special diving contrivance designed for this contingency.

But even while this country generally was still scouting the idea that Rojdestvensky had serious intent in his demonstration against Japan, the Japanese themselves were beginning to show the uneasiness which the Russian admiral's deliberate movements were causing the directors of naval intelligence in Tokio. For the first time since the war began, the Japanese press opened an agitation with regard to the traffic in this country in Cardiff coal. During this period the Japanese press furnished a very significant and instructive study.

On January 10 Captain Botrovosky entered the Canal with Rojdestvensky's reinforcements, and for several days we had in this country practically no naval news beyond reports of Botrovosky at Jibutil, and the same old hackneyed depreciations of Rojdestvensky from Nossi Bé. Of the Japanese navy we had next to no information. But the Admiralty here knew that the Japanese had instituted a very comprehensive network of naval intelligence throughout the Malay Archipelago. On January 25 it was reported from Tokio that a Special Service Squadron had been formed, with an unknown mission. Twenty days later a telegram dated from Kure stated that Admiral Togo had left that port for an unknown destination.

Except for two official statements, which brought the Pescadores, and the port of Kelung in the northeast of Formosa, within the zone of naval operations, the world was vouchsafed very little other news with regard to the Japanese navy. It might be said that the public was unable to furnish Rojdestvensky with any information of movements at all. In fact, the one or two statements which were promulgated with regard to Japan were obviously made with intent to deceive. It must be remembered that the Japanese had every opportunity to keep their movements secret. Whatever flying bases they had established in the Formosa seas were certain to be distant from the ordinary trade-routes, and for the rest the Japanese controlled the whole cable service.

We are, of course, not in a position to know what information at this period may have reached Rojdestvensky, but it will easily be appreciated that, no matter how much money the Russians may have spent in naval intelligence in these waters, their facilities for acquiring, disseminating, and suppressing information did not compare with those of their enemy.

But while Rojdestvensky had been dawdling round the coast of Africa, the Baltic shipyards had been at work to enable the Admiralty to prepare the Third Squadron for the Far East. This squadron, with the exception of the first-class battleship *Slava*, included the majority of vessels for which Klado had agitated before he commenced to urge defiance of the Treaty of Berlin.

This second reinforcement, which left Libau on February 15, was under the command of Rear-

Admiral Nebogatoff, and consisted of the battleship *Emperor Nicholas I.*, the three ocean-going ironclads, *Admiral Seniavin, Admiral Oushakoff,* and *General Admiral Apraxine,* the cruiser *Vladimir Monomakh,* with colliers, transports, tugs, and a repairing ship.

On March 9 the skipper of a vessel which had been coaling the Russian fleet at Nossi Bé arrived in Durban, and gratuitously informed the first news scavenger that the units of the Russian Fleet were so covered with seaweed that he did not think it would be possible for them to proceed. This was followed on March 13, the day which marked the arrival of Nebogatoff at Suda Bay, by a statement from our communicative friend, the late Russian Minister in Washington, that Rojdestvensky was recalled to Russia. Previous to this several of the Russian colliers had cleared from Nossi Bé for Delagoa and Batavia.

The next definite news which we had of Rojdestvensky came from the steamer *Dart*, which arrived at Durban from Rangoon, and reported that it had passed a fleet of thirty warships and a large number of colliers 250 miles north-east of Madagascar. It is now known that Rojdestvensky relinquished the hospitality of the French waters on March 16, just about the same day as Nebogatoff was entering the Canal.

Immediately it was definitely known that the

Russian fleet had sailed, there came from every direction information purporting to announce the course which it was steering. It was authoritatively stated from many centres that Rojdestvensky had been recalled. Others maintained that he was steering for the Sunda Straits; but beyond the report from a liner on the Ceylon-Aden run, that it had passed a mysterious fleet of ships of war at night, to all intents and purposes the Russian Main Squadron had disappeared into the great void of the Indian Ocean.

The next naval intelligence which reached this country reported Japanese converted cruisers at various points in the Malay Archipelago. There was also a statement that a squadron of Japanese line-of-battle ships had been sighted near Singapore. We can only imagine that if this squadron really consisted of battleships, they had made the northern entrance of the Straits of Malacca with the express purpose of being sighted and identified. But we have had experience that the average mariner reports anything that he sights in warship trim as being a battleship; and it was far from probable that Togo should have sent his main force so far south as Singapore.

On April 2 Nebogatoff anchored at Jibutil, and, in accordance with the now established precedent, took in his coal within the range of the French guns. By this time those naval experts who were responsible for giving the country information as to Russian movements were beginning to look anxiously for the reappearance of Rojdestvensky. It seemed fairly certain now that he need not be expected off Cape Town, and anxious eyes were turned towards the Asiatic Archipelago, especially in the direction of the Sunda Straits, by reason of the arrival at Batavia of several colliers suspected of Russian freights.

On April 7, however, the situation as far as the Baltic Fleet was concerned was cleared up, for at 1 P.M. that day the steamer *Tara* sighted forty-seven Russian sail off One Fathom Bank, in the Straits of Malacca.

Rojdestvensky had for the present completely thrown off the mask. There was no subtlety, no concealment in his movement. He chose to arrive in Far Eastern waters by the most direct trade-route. His fleet was reported intact, and having passed through the Straits it disappeared, steering a north-easterly course. On April 11 the P. and O. liner *Nubia* sighted Rojdestvensky's armada 100 miles south-east of Cape St James. It was still on the same course. Contemporary information reported Japanese scouts to be in touch with the Russian cruisers. Consequently it was anticipated in many quarters that Rojdestvensky, without waiting for Nebogatoff, felt himself strong enough to push through the Formosa Channel in spite of any opposition that Togo might bring against him. By many, therefore, a fleet action was considered imminent.

But the Russian admiral had very different plans. On April 13 he brought his fleet to anchor in Kamranh Bay, one of the many anchorages on the coast-line of the province of Annam. Here again he would be under the shadow of the protection afforded by French neutrality. Here, therefore, he would coal, refit, re-provision, and await the arrival of Nebogatoff and his substantial reinforcement.

This was the last straw: the whole Japanese press, inspired, no doubt, from official sources, rose up in indignant protest. From their standpoint they had right; and after sufficient delay to enable Rojdestvensky to refit, the French admiral at Saigon requested the Russians to depart. Rojdestvensky courteously assented, and removed to an anchorage a little farther up the coast.

We hear of him next at Hon-Kohe Bay on the 25th of April. As has now been definitely demonstrated, the construction which is placed upon neutrality observances by the various Powers is elastic to a degree. The situation in the Far East became so involved that it was almost ludicrous. Rojdestvensky, with an immense armada, established himself in the waters of his country's ally. Japan, arguing very rightly that such hospitality as Rojdestvensky was receiving exceeded the licence allowed to belligerents, remonstrated with acrimony. France requests Rojdestvensky to withdraw, and backs her demand with endorsement from the Tsar and her infinitesimal naval strength in Chinese waters. Rojdestvensky promises to heed the request, but fails to act. What is the next move?

Allies are not going to break off negotiations on such a score. We sympathise with Japan; but as long as the law of neutrality and the law of nations is such a debatable problem, we fail to see what redress, other than by her own strong right hand, was open to her.

In the meantime Rojdestvensky had taken in his stores and coal, and, what is more important, had been joined by his reinforcement. On the 1st of May Rojdestvensky was reported to be in an anchorage south of Hainan; three days later Nebogatoff was passing through the Straits of Malacca, having taken twenty-nine days from Jibutil, and coaled twice. In all probability the junction of the two fleets took place at the Paracel Islands, which, giving his fleet an average of ten knots, Nebogatoff would have reached on May 9. The only news from the Japanese side was the statement of a cargo-boat arriving in Shanghai, that it passed a large

Japanese squadron in the Straits of Tsushima on the 26th of April.

It will be well at this juncture to study the strength of the rival fleets. For this purpose we will borrow from Sir Cyprian Bridge's excellent treatise on the war.[1]

RUSSIAN.			JAPANESE.		
Battleships.	Knots.	Heavy Guns.	Battleships.	Knots.	Heavy Guns.
Kniaz-Suvaroff	18	4 (12-in.)	Mikasa	18	4 (12-in.)
Orel	18	4 "	Asahi	18	4 "
Imperator Alexander III.	18	4 "	Shikishima	18	4 "
Borodino	18	4 "	Fugi	19	4 "
Osliabia	18	4 (10-in.)	Chin-yen	14	4 "
Sissoi Veliki	16	4 (12-in.)			
Navarin	16	4 "			
Imperator Nicholas I.	14	2 12"; 4 9"			
Admiral Oushakoff	16	4 (9-in.)			
Admiral Seniavin	16	4 "			
General Admiral Apraxine	15	3 (10-in.)			

From the tables we now publish it will be seen that, while the Russians held their opponents in the matter of battleships, they were sadly out-classed by the Japanese fleet in all other essentials. It must be remembered that a comparative table of gun power is only an indication of the calculable value of a fighting fleet as estimated by the weight of metal it can hurl against a possible adversary. The precise destructive value of this weight depends greatly upon the condition of the vessel upon which it is

[1] The Naval Annual, 1905. Edited by T. A. Brassey. Griffin.

RUSSIAN.			JAPANESE.		
	Knots.	Over 6-in. guns.		Knots.	Over 6-in. guns.
Armoured vessels—			*Armoured vessels—*		
Admiral Nakhimoff	18	...	Nisshin	20	1 10″; 2 8″
Dmitri Donskoi	15	...	Kasuga	20	4 8″
Vladimir Monomakh *	13	...	Idzumo	22	4 ″
			Iwate	21	4 ″
			Tokiwa	22	4 ″
			Asama	22	4 ″
			Azuma	21	4 ″
			Yakumo	20	4 ″
Protected cruisers		5	*Protected cruisers*		18
Small cruisers		0	*Small cruisers*		8
Converted cruisers		12	*Converted cruisers*		10 (?)
Torpedo-boat destroyers		13	*Torpedo-boat destroyers*		25 (?)
			Torpedo craft (1st and 2nd class)		67 (?)
Displacement of armoured vessels		102,068 tons	*Displacement of armoured vessels*		134,576 tons
Gun power		26 12″; 8 10″; 12 9″; 13 8″	*Gun power*		20 12″; 1 10″; 30 8″

* We have omitted the *Gromoboi, Rossia, Bogatyr*, and the Vladivostok torpedo craft.

[It is rather difficult to arrive at the exact armaments, as all the authorities vary. According to a correspondent of 'The Times,' Captain Klado has published the following estimate: Total tonnages of the armoured ships are—Japanese, 144,000; Russian, including the Vladivostok division, 120,000. Of 12-in. guns the Russians had 26 and the Japanese 24. The 10-in. guns comprise 15 Russian and 1 Japanese; the 8-in. 18 Russian and 37 Japanese. Of smaller calibre weapons the Japanese had nearly twice as many as the Russians.]

mounted. Thus, though we can diminish the percentage we would allow for gun power in several of the Russian battleships owing to their antiquity, we cannot yet appraise the relative value of the similar armament on Japanese armoured cruisers.

We have not sufficient evidence to judge of the results when both belligerents had cruisers in the line on August 10. But although there could be no concealment with regard to the strength of the

Russian fleet, it seemed possible that the ebullition of feeling in Japan over the alleged breach of neutrality covered a suspicion of naval losses which have been concealed as ably as was the fate of the *Yashima*.

But even if this had been the case, and the Russian admiral was aware of these losses, they were not so serious as to greatly affect the Japanese chances of success.

Of course, the final issue of all titanic struggles must lie upon the knees of the gods; but Togo had so many advantages in naval essentials that it was impossible to conceive any other issue except the one which, as allies, we desired.

VII. THE OVERTHROW OF THE ARMADA.

THE sanguinary encounter in the Straits of Tsushima, which culminated in the practical annihilation of Rojdestvensky's armada by the 29th of May, may be reckoned the deciding issue of the great struggle. It is possible that it is the greatest action that has, or ever will be, decided upon the water. Few people in this country realised the far-reaching effect of the issues that were involved. Few people, even now, appreciate what this final triumph of the Oriental over the Occidental means to the peoples of the East. It is the herald of a new awakening, the scope and limitations of which are not within the ken of the wisest.

It has not yet been possible to discover the deductions which governed Rojdestvensky after he left Chinese waters, or inspired the course of action which he pursued after he sighted the island of Quelpart.

Instead of reconnoitring the Tsushima Straits from some temporary anchorage, the Russian admiral elected to follow the almost puerile course of steaming at once into confined Japanese waters.

There could only be two reasons for this course: either Rojdestvensky imagined that he had eluded a portion of the Japanese fleet and left it behind him in the Formosa Straits; or he was so confident in the main fighting strength of the battleship and the inferiority of the torpedo, that he was prepared to meet and fight Togo without taking into consideration strategical or geographical considerations.

It cannot be that he had only sufficient coal to take him to Vladivostok, since it is definitely reported that Russian agents had made coaling arrangements farther north along the Chinese coast. These arrangements, however, may be now claimed as strategic counter-moves, made for the purpose of covering up the trail. Not that we believe that a false move like that would have deceived such an astute strategist as Admiral Togo.

It is our impression that Rojdestvensky had abandoned as impracticable the only sound course which lay open to him, and had selected to hazard everything upon a fleet action. Possibly, while he was waiting on the coast of Annam, it may have been borne in upon him that the coal and supply question would take too long to perfect; or he may have received information which left him the sole choice to employ tactics which we cannot but condemn.

It is now tolerably certain that Rojdestvensky

remained off the coast of Annam until May 12. This date would have given Nebogatoff just time to coal and make any necessary repairs after his voyage across the Indian Ocean. Whatever may have been Admiral Rojdestvensky's faults as a sailor, it must be allowed that, after he sailed from the coast of Annam, he successfully lost his fleet as far as European information was concerned.

A general impression prevailed in this country that he would steer the Pacific course and avoid the narrow seas of Southern Japan: all experts agreed that the Formosa Channel would not be attempted. And the only information of a reliable nature that reached the coast-line towns of China between May 12, when a fleet was reported to be at sea off the Three Kings, and May 20, when fifty ships were sighted by the s.s. *Oscar II.* off Batan Island in the Bashee Channel, was to the effect that forty-three colliers had been counted at anchor off Nahbe, and that a portion of Rojdestvensky's fleet had coaled in a bay on the coast of Hainan.

The news brought by the s.s. *Oscar II.* was doubtless correct, but it is quite likely that the vessels coaling off Hainan were a portion of the auxiliary cruiser squadron, which squadron, there is no doubt, the Russian admiral hoped might serve to some extent as a decoy, when for military reasons it became necessary to detach it from the fighting fleet.

In the meantime Admiral Togo kept his whole fleet in the secure harbours of his home waters. It was no secret that the bulk of the Japanese naval strength was lying in the Korean Straits, as we find the fact reported two or three times from different sources between April 12 and May 24. We have not the slightest doubt that the Russian information was good enough to inform Rojdestvensky of this fact.

A single glance at the map, and a small amount of labour spent in making measurements with a pair of dividers, will apprise even the most unlearned that, provided there was no fear of the Russians being able to establish any temporary or flying base in the vicinity of Oyama's sea communications, Togo could not have done better than to have awaited the course of events in the harbours in the Korean Straits. With the means of observation and information at his command, he was master of the situation whichever route the Russian admiral might select in an attempt to reach Vladivostok. And even in reaching Vladivostok, supposing that thick weather had caused the Japanese observation to fail, the hopes for the Russian success were not materially heightened.

The general belief still obtained that the Russians were heading for La Perouse, when on May 26 Europe was electrified by the information that a Russian squadron had appeared off Wusung. The units thus reported proved, however, to be our friends the converted cruisers. But a liner which was making the passage from Nagasaki to Shanghai reported having passed two Russian second-class cruisers. This information was all that was vouchsafed on Saturday night the 27th of May.

Every one interested in this titanic struggle went to bed on that Saturday night convinced that the next twenty-four hours would produce information of a naval shock unparalleled in the history of the seas. Nor had they miscalculated, but there were very very few who could have judged of the terrific nature of the issues which were settled in Japanese waters, or could have imagined that by Monday morning the proud fleet which had sailed in October from the Baltic, flaunting all and sundry that came in its way, should have suffered complete annihilation. It was a sequel the like of which not even the most sanguine had anticipated. As we pointed out in a previous chapter, we had no reason to fear for the final success of the Japanese on sea, but even we never anticipated that Admiral Togo would be able to bring his fighting fleet back to its anchorages in Japan practically complete in all its units.

The actual course that the Russians steered after they left the coast of Batan is not quite certain, but it is probable that once the fleet was clear of Formosa it headed for Quelpart. The information which has reached this country with regard to this epoch-mark-ing battle up to the present has not been sufficiently elucidative to eradicate a certain amount of presumption from any description that we may attempt of the great battle. But there seems to be an impression amongst certain interviewed Japanese naval officers that the Russian armada changed its course after sighting the Liau-kiau group, with the express object of deluding Togo into the belief that the passage northward was a mere feint. We doubt if this be true.

But we rather lean to the view that once Rojdestvensky had made Quelpart, he found that the coast of Korea was shrouded in fog. Quelpart having given him his bearing, he determined to force the Korean Straits, Togo or no Togo, fog or no fog, sea or no sea. From the standpoint of pure heroics it was doubtless a fine resolve, but in the interests of the 15,000 souls on board his fleet, and in the matter of the sacred necessity to his country, it is hardly the manœuvre that we would have suggested.

Rojdestvensky no doubt regulated his course so as to make the peak on Quelpart Island by daybreak on the 27th, or he may have cruised in the vicinity since the afternoon of the 26th. As Quelpart on the map is about one hundred and twenty miles west of Tsushima, twelve hours at ten knots would have brought Rojdestvensky into action just about the hour given in Togo's official report.

Once the Russian admiral had determined to force the Straits, there were three passages open to him. Korea is separated from Japan by barely one hundred miles of water. Two groups of islands help to bridge this narrow channel. These groups are Tsushima to the north and Ikishima to the south. Consequently there were three channels in these Korean Straits which were open to Rojdestvensky: Broughton Channel north of Tsushima, Oriental Channel separating Tsushima from Ikishima, and the ordinary trade channel between Ikishima and the mainland, which latter, in the circumstances, was naturally out of the question.

A glance at the coast-line which encloses these channels is sufficient to demonstrate the terrible risks which were undertaken by the Russian fleet in its paucity in cruisers and torpedo craft. Both coast-lines furnish innumerable anchorages, and the passage being controlled by the observation posts on the two central groups of islands, it would be impossible to imagine a more effective sea area for torpedo tactics. Apparently in the morning the mists were heavy enough to conceal Togo's fleet. Two divisions of this fleet were lying in the vicinity of the Broughton Channel, in two of the many anchorages in the Masampo Archipelago.

It is possible to picture in the mind's eye the impressive spectacle of the great Russian armada heading directly for Japan's territorial waters on that beautiful but fateful morning. All accounts agree that the weather was fine, though a strong breeze from the south-east had raised a heavy sea. The warmer winds from the south caused the usual spring mists to envelop the horizon to the north-west, indicating the coast-line of Korea and all the dangers in lurking destroyers it might conceal. Due north, Mount Auckland raised itself, a yellow and white peak, clear of the shroud of vapour which enveloped the lower cliff-line of Quelpart. As the sun rose, the colour of the seas changed from dull grey to blue.

In the midst of all this crispness of spring atmosphere and beauty of scene, the Baltic Fleet, the last hope of Russia in the Far East, was steaming to its doom. With his two squadrons in line ahead steering parallel courses, the battleships to port and the cruisers to starboard, with the transports and repair ships between the lines, Rojdestvensky set his teeth and steered for Tsushima, the great bluff clump of sentinel rock which was the "switch-board" of all Togo's intelligence.

Never before in the history of sea warfare had necessity dictated a simpler stratagem. But it was a majestic sight. The imagination can conjure up the picture. The two parallel columns of dead-black-painted battleships, eleven of them, weather-stained and smoke-begrimed, conforming to the direction of the *Kniaz-Suvaroff*; followed by the three squat coast-defence ships, wallowing in uncertain alignment in the troughs of the heavy seas. Half a mile to starboard the ancient armoured cruisers followed in the wake of the *Admiral Nakhimoff*, making with difficulty, though tide and sea were with them, the ten knots which kept them abreast of the flagship. Behind them the more modern and smaller protected cruisers, kicking and plunging in the lumpy sea, as if protesting at the little flutter of bunting from the *Kniaz-Suvaroff*, which kept them churning their propellers behind three obsolete iron coffins when they should have been patrolling the passage now looming up in front of them.

Majestically, with the morning sun to its back, the armada ploughed eastwards. About seven o'clock the cruiser squadron was able to make out on its starboard beam the outline of a warship disentangling itself from the horizon mist. Its three funnels proclaimed the newcomer to be of the *Idzumo* class, and the *Vladimir Monomakh*, which was steaming third in the Russian line, was ordered to deal with the intruder. These two vessels exchanged the first shots of the great battle of Tsushima; but the Japanese cruiser had not yet come to fight,—she stayed long enough to finally satisfy herself as to the formation, course, and exact composition of Rojdestvensky's fleet, and then disappeared back into the mists out of which she had come, transmitting information to the admiral as she went.

Togo could not have wished for other information. Rojdestvensky was playing absolutely into his hands. Cables were slipped, and by ten o'clock the Japanese fleet was at sea. The crisis for which they had been waiting and preparing for the last three months was at hand, and the three main squadrons, under the command of Admirals Togo, Kamimura, and Kata-oka respectively, shaped their courses to their appointed stations.

It had been evident to the commander of the *Idzumo* that Admiral Rojdestvensky was steering for the Straits to the south of Tsushima. The main point in Togo's stratagem was to allow his adversary into the Japan Sea, and there, by virtue of his own superior speed, to intern him, and then destroy him at his own convenience. The Japanese entered into the struggle with every confidence. They had the self-reliance built up of the knowledge that they had already destroyed one Russian fleet superior to their own in tonnage and numbers, they had all the advantages of pace and position, and every one of their heavy guns had been replaced.

Precisely at eleven o'clock the Japanese Third Squadron in the following order, the *Kasuga*, *Niitaka*, *Chitose*, and the *Tsushima*, appeared on the port bow of the Russian Battle Squadron. As they manœuvred on this flank the Russian admiral possibly anticipated that the object of their manœuvre was to cut off the transports and impedimenta squadron; he therefore ordered the *Nicholas I.* and *Sissoi Veliki* to attend to Kata-oka's cruisers. A little long-range firing from the Russian Second Battle Squadron, and the protected cruisers sheered off.

Almost immediately, having passed the Straits of Tsushima, the Russian admiral slightly changed his formation, still keeping his battleships in parallel columns in line ahead. Then the flag-ship changed direction to the north-west. The most serious phase of his adventurous voyage was now to commence.

By this time the fog had considerably lifted, so that when the Russian flag-ship altered her course the look-out was able to distinguish on the port beam those smudges on the horizon which mark the position of a fleet of warships under full steam. Twenty minutes or so of suspense, and then every ship in the Russian line knew that they must fight a fleet action before they made port again.

One by one the smudges became concrete, until they developed into Togo's main fighting force, consisting of four battleships and eight armoured cruisers. Although we have studied all the accounts that have so far reached this country of this battle, the translation of Togo's included, yet there is considerable uncertainty as to the actual manœuvring which brought the rival battle squadrons into range. However, there is no uncertainty as to the fact that, as the wind had freshened, Togo with his superior steaming power was able to do pretty well what he liked with the Russians.

Between 1 and 1.15 [1] the battle squadron, consisting of the *Mikasa, Shikishima, Fuji,* and *Asahi,* in line ahead, was steering to the north-east, making a parallel course with the port Russian squadron, which had the *Osliabia* in the van. The armoured cruisers, however, were steering so as to maintain the broadside strength of the Japanese line of battle. The Third Squadron in two subdivisions was manœuvring in order to strike the rear of the Russian line. It was evident that Togo need have no fear of separating from his protected cruisers on the actual battle area, since the Russians had not the steam power to take advantage of any division of Togo's forces. The Third Squadron, under Kata-oka, again appearing to the north, this time on the Russians' port beam, illustrated the calm confidence of Japan's commander.

Somewhere between half-past one and two the Japanese flag-ship put over her helm and steered across the bows of the leading ships of the parallel columns. The action was commenced by the *Kniaz-Suvaroff* at 9000 yards; but this distance was rapidly

[1] Japanese and Russian times vary.

decreased to 6000 when the four Japanese battleships concentrated the whole of their 12-inch fire on the Russian flag-ship.

She made a lovely mark for the expert Japanese gunners. Now she no longer had the sea with her: she and her consorts are said to have heeled over in the heavy water-way to such an extent that much of the Japanese shell-fire was able to hit them below the armoured belt. Moreover, by this manœuvre, as the sun was now dropping towards the west, Togo's gunners had the light behind them, while the Russians found it in their eyes. The Russians tried manfully to master this rain of fire which the Japanese poured upon the van of their column; but though they changed direction, the superior speed of their opponents defeated their elementary efforts at steam tactics.

Manœuvre as they would, they remained exposed to a tornado of 8-inch shells from Kamimura's squadron which raked them fore and aft. This squadron, recking little of the theory which prohibits armoured cruisers from taking their place in the line, steamed in to closer ranges and speedily made the injury in the *Osliabia* from which she presently sank.

All accounts agree that the shell-fire during this opening hour was simply terrific. It must also have been extremely accurate, since half-a-dozen ships were on fire at the same time, and Togo subsequently reports that the smoke from the burning vessels was so dense that his gunners lost their targets. It is certain that, no matter what happened afterwards, the fate of the Russian fleet was decided during this first hour. Gunnery won the victory, the torpedo simply completed it.

It would also seem that by three o'clock the Russians were completely cut off from the Tsushima Straits, and were in the course of being raked by the Japanese squadron of battleships recrossing their bows in line ahead, and the armoured cruisers in similar formation passing under their sterns.

The Japanese gunners, who apparently made three hits to the Russian one, during the first hour concentrated the whole of the fire of each squadron on Rojdestvensky's most powerful units. By half-past two Rojdestvensky's flag-ship had to leave the line, surrendering the van to the *Borodino*. Half an hour afterwards the *Osliabia*, which had been "trailing like a wounded duck," turned turtle and sank.

The beginning of the disaster had arrived. Already the Russian commander-in-chief had been badly wounded, and was transferred to the destroyer on which he was subsequently captured. The whole of the thinking staff went with him, though it is difficult to follow the train of thought which induced these staff officers to consider it their duty to transfer with him. Admiral Felkersham had been killed in his conning-tower during the first quarter of an hour of the engagement; and even while the unfortunate flagship was repairing its damages and transferring its valiant staff, the Japanese third cruiser division was in amongst the Russian impedimenta squadron sinking store-ships and colliers.

From the moment that the *Kniaz-Suvaroff* sheered out of her alignment, the day was destined to end in a *débacle*; it remained with Togo and his subordinates to show how great this *débacle* was to be. It is impossible, as we sit still in this country and read the reports of this fearful example of the penalty which competence is able to exact over incompetence, to realise the true horror and the fearful significance of the scene in the Korean Straits towards evening on May 27. All sting had passed from the uncertain Russian fire. On this the third occasion the Japanese were not likely to make the mistake of running short of ammunition. Rather, they had sacrificed coal to the means which was to make their victory absolute.

Apparently the Russians had broken up between five and six in the afternoon, and this allowed the Japanese to single out the most important units and devastate them till they sank.

The story is too awful for cold-blooded speculation. We are moved to horror when a submarine sinks with its complement of ten or fifteen men. What, then, must be our feelings when we consider that here, in the Japan Sea, Russian ships were sinking in every direction with their complements of 400 to 700 seamen?—that those who had escaped the terrible torment of gun-shot units were drowning in hundreds in an angry sea, in spite of the extraordinary humane efforts which the victorious enemy made to save them? There is no contemporary writing that could adequately reproduce the meaning of this ghastly tale. We on this side cannot attempt it.

But although the Russians were desperately beaten, they were still at sundown making reply to the sustained Japanese onslaught. For a period the Russian battleships had manœuvred in the hope of shielding their helpless flag-ship, and when the *Kniaz-Suvaroff*'s steering gear had been repaired the *Borodino* made an effort to bring some semblance of order into the wavering Russian line.

As its sure consequence this action brought a concentrated fire from the Japanese, until the murk of burning warships brought temporary relief as mingling with the mist it formed a screen. A few minutes past seven in the evening the *Borodino*, a shattered, smoking wreck, sank to join the *Osliabia* at the bottom.

As the sun dipped below the horizon, Togo made the signal for which his younger officers had been gasping. His many torpedo-destroyer flotillas waiting in leash were now loosed to complete the devastation which the guns of the battle fleet had made possible. But this did not mean that the pursuit by the Japanese fleet was to cease. Far from it. Togo, leaving his third division to open a path for the destroyers by a continued bombardment throughout the night, sought to find the main remnant which had disappeared in the shadow of its own smoke. It seemed as if Providence approved of this terrible retribution, for the sea, which in the morning had been so rough that it had made it almost impossible for torpedo craft to manœuvre, had now smoothed down, with the result that the conditions of attack were all in favour of the spiteful little craft.

There is no doubt that, while during the closing hours of Saturday the ships of the fast diminishing Russian fleet clung together for mutual support, as soon as night fell, under the gentle persuasion of fifty torpedo-boats, the residue of the great armada broke up, scattered, and sought to struggle away from a situation that promised only death or ignoble capture.

It probably never will be possible to follow in detail the individual history of each of those fierce torpedo attacks; probably we shall never know for certain if any one of them had greater success than the increase of the *morale* which the Japanese navy had established. But the sequel on the morrow is piteous in the extreme. It naturally has no parallel, and we doubt if past history could show a scene quite so pathetic as the surrender of Admiral Nebogatoff and the residue of his squadron off Liancourt Rocks.

Not that we grudge the Japanese the prizes which thus became theirs, but we cannot help thinking that the captain of the *Admiral Oushakoff*[1] played a better part than his comrades. At least, such are the traditions existing in our own navy, and we know what traditions exist in that of Japan.

It would appear that Admiral Togo desisted from his night bombardment about midnight, and thereupon his squadron steamed north in the darkness to his given rendezvous, with the object of placing itself across the Russian line of advance to Vladivostok as the situation declared itself at daybreak. There is very little detail descriptive of what happened during the early hours of Sunday morning with regard to the actual fighting, but it seems evident that there was really little fighting to be done after the torpedo-boats had finished with the residue of the Russian fleet.

The *Sissoi Veliki*, *Admiral Nakhimoff*, and the *Vladimir Monomakh* were discovered in a sinking condition in the vicinity of Tsushima in the morning. The *Navarin* was torpedoed during the night, and the *Svietlana* was sunk in Chekuten Bay by the *Niitaka*

[1] This officer sank his ship by opening the sea-cocks.

and *Otowa*. The *Kniaz-Suvaroff* and *Alexander III.* had gone to the bottom in the night: whether this was the result of shell-fire or torpedo attack is not known.

It is also certain that some time in the morning of Sunday the main portion of the Japanese fleet discovered at the Liancourt Rocks, 200 miles from Tsushima, a group of Russian survivors consisting of the battleships *Nicholas I.* and *Orel*, the coast-defence ships *Admirals Seniavin* and *Apraxine*, and the cruiser *Izumrud*. The latter, making good use of her speed, for the moment escaped, to be wrecked in Vladimir Bay; but the officers of the ships under the command of Admiral Nebogatoff, as soon as the Japanese opened fire, took the miserable course of surrendering their vessels. An admirable protest against this conduct is found in the action of the captain of the coast-defence ship *Oushakoff*, who, rather than surrender, sank his vessel in deep water under the Japanese guns, and trusted to the magnanimity of the enemy to save himself and his crew.

The most extraordinary reflection with regard to the description of this battle is that, while we can report nothing but disaster and death to the Russian units, the Japanese effected this magnificent end at what may be considered a trifling loss. From the admiral's official reports it would appear that in the course of the action only three torpedo craft were sunk, and that the total casualties from shell and other causes did not exceed 800 men. That he should thus have been able to annihilate his enemy and maintain his fleet throughout seaworthy is a tribute to the superiority of the Japanese as sailors, gunners, and strategists on the sea which will admit of no argument.

What argument can there be when one has to deal with the concrete fact that Togo, without addition to his original tonnage, has destroyed in fifteen months two sea-going Russian fleets, both of which were on paper superior to his own? Perhaps the most pathetic incident in the whole of the miserable chapter is to be found in the arrival of the little *Almaz* at Vladivostok. The scene has been well described by an eye-witness—the scene of wild enthusiasm which heralded the entry into the Russian port of this war-scarred messenger. Her advent naturally portended to those who had been buoyed by hope the speedy arrival of a victorious Russian fleet. What a different tale the little *Almaz* had to tell! It was in naval history what the arrival of Dr Brydon was to the garrison of Jellalabad.

The residue of the Baltic Fleet, under Admiral Enquist, struggled into Manila Bay some six or seven days after the battle. This little remnant was formed from among the only Russian ships that could steam: it consisted of the *Aurora, Jemchug*, and *Oleg*. These three cruisers, not being in a seaworthy state and able to proceed without dockyard repairs, were interned. Thus, out of the whole fighting strength of the Baltic Fleet one cruiser and one torpedo-boat destroyer alone remain in Russian waters.[1]

[1] Russia lost during the war — sunk, captured, or interned — fifteen battleships, three coast-defence ships, six armoured cruisers, eight protected cruisers, and quite a fleet of torpedo-boats, destroyers, and auxiliaries. Japan lost in battle—three destroyers, and by accident or mine two battleships, two protected cruisers, one coast-defence ship, three gunboats, and three or four destroyers.

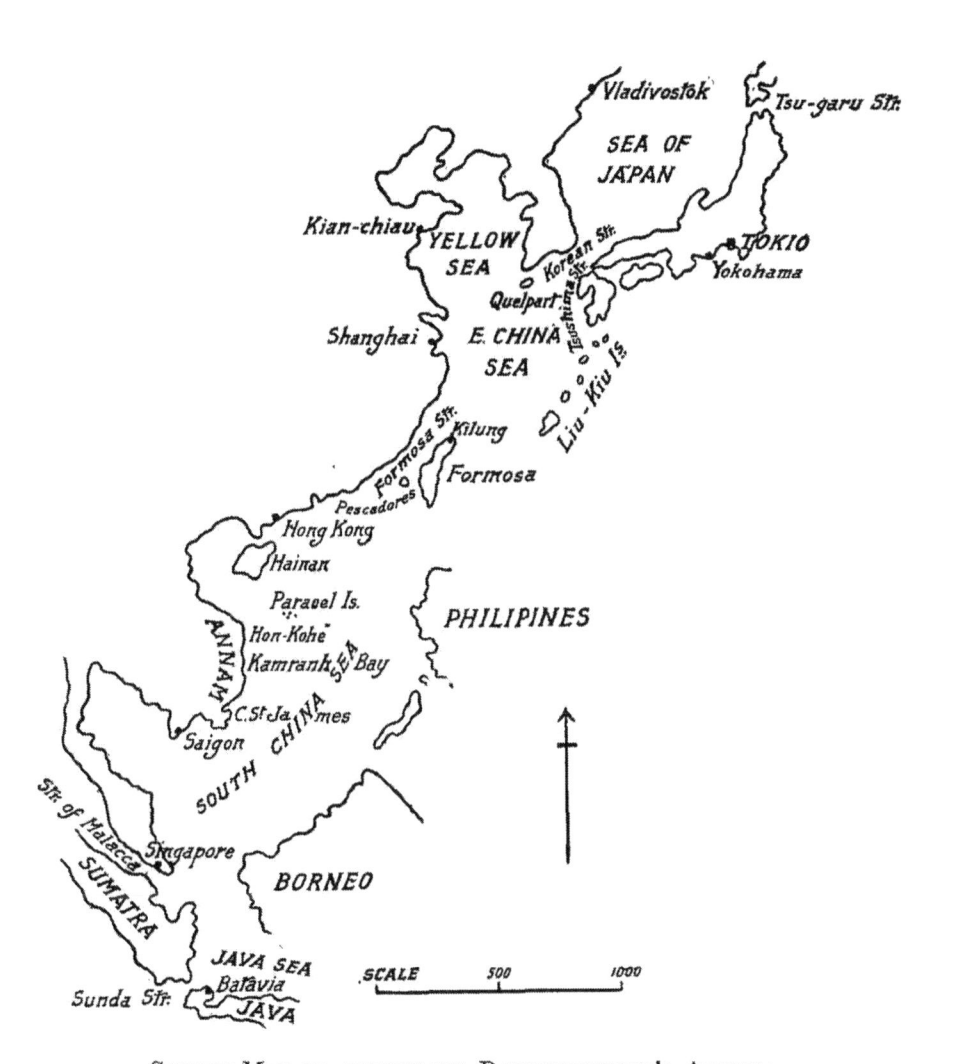

SKETCH-MAP TO ILLUSTRATE ROJDESTVENSKY'S ARMADA.

VIII. THE BATTLE ON THE SHA-HO.

IN a previous chapter we left the Russian army in the act of extricating itself from its position at Liauyang, which ancient Manchu town the victorious Japanese had entered in the early hours of the 4th of September. All day through the 5th of September, judging from the telegraphic reports which reached this country, it looked as if Kuroki was in a position to throw himself across the Russian line of retreat, and thus turn what had been a hard-earned success into a decisive victory.

But, as we have already shown in our previous description of this battle, the enveloping force which Kuroki had at his command was not of sufficient strength and mobility to enable it to press inwards the steel line of massive rearguard which Kuropatkin concentrated at Yentai for the purpose of covering the withdrawal of his army.

As far as can be judged from contemporary accounts of this the first great land battle of the campaign, there were other causes besides the weakness of Kuroki's enveloping force which rendered it necessary for Oyama to halt the persevering battalions which had snatched victory from a situation which at one time seemed wellnigh impossible. Contemporary observers report that the week's fighting had so perilously reduced the reserves, both in artillery and small-arm ammunition, that it would have been unwise to have risked an immediate engagement for fear that the Russian rearguard, too closely pressed, might turn and counter with success.

Also, so our information goes, the Japanese infantry had undertaken and accomplished a task which in its completion left them practically exhausted. At least this is the reasoning of those contemporary observers who have supplied reports to the authorities at home.

It now behoves us to follow the course of the campaign as it unfolded itself during the last weeks of the fighting season. Kuroki's strategical pursuit was stopped on September 6, whether by design or necessity we must leave it to the Japanese to declare when they finally give us the inward history of their campaign. This enabled Kuropatkin to concentrate his beaten army at Mukden. A portion of his force, in anticipation of a Japanese pursuit, had already been transferred early in September to Tie-ling, a position which Kuropatkin was even then preparing on the Chai-ho, forty miles north-east of Mukden.

About the same time that Kuropatkin's precautionary rearguard reached Tie-ling, the head of the 2nd European Army Corps, which had just arrived from European Russia and concentrated at Harbin, also arrived at Tie-ling. As the Yentai rearguard had fallen back to the Sha-ho practically unopposed, and as advices from the front showed Kuropatkin that the Japanese for the time being had finished with the initiative, the general exodus was checked, and Kuropatkin set himself to re-form and reconstruct his fighting force upon the line of the Sha-ho, a small tributary of the Liau-ho, about twelve miles south of the city.

It is evident that Kuropatkin had timed his original concentration in order to be able to take the initiative from his defensive position at Liauyang about the 15th of September. Oyama had forestalled him in his intention. But the immediate result was that Kuropatkin was able to replenish his Liauyang losses and his expenditure in ammunition almost at once. Before the battle of Liauyang had commenced a reinforcement from Europe, consisting of 80,000 men, was already south of Lake Baikal. In fact, the advance-guard of this force had taken part in the fighting round Yentai coal-mines.

Upon this fresh nucleus Kuropatkin rallied his beaten battalions, and by dint of great effort reconstructed, out of the chaos which naturally followed upon so rapid a withdrawal as that from Liauyang, a field army with which he felt confident enough to comply with the orders of the Grand Ducal party in St Petersburg.

These latter, under the signature of the Czar, now commanded him to take the initiative, crush the Japanese, and relieve Port Arthur before it should be too late. By the Emperor's ukase the army of the Far East was divided on September 25 into two parts,— the first to be commanded by Kuropatkin in person, and the second by the veteran Gripenberg, in whose military capacity all Russia pinned great faith.

At the end of September, when Kuropatkin was putting final touches into his scheme of a magnificent advance, the rival armies were practically in touch twenty-five miles south of Mukden. The Japanese line from right to left was in the same order of distribution as it had been since the armies had landed on the seaboard. That is, Kuroki was holding the extreme right, his exposed flank being at Pên-hsi-hu on the Taitse-ho; Nodzu held the country in the vicinity of the Yentai coal-mines; Oku kept the line abreast of the railway, with his exposed left practically on the Hun-ho, the interval being maintained by the Cavalry Division.

Roughly calculated, the Japanese front extended over thirty-five miles. The Russian line lay in a great loop from Hsin-min-ting on the extreme right to

Hua-ling on the east; but the intrenched front was much less, and consisted in this position only of such light field-works as the advanced troops had thrown up to secure the supports behind the line of outposts.

Even at this distance it is rather hard to assess accurately the numbers on both sides; but as near as we have been able to judge by a study of such returns as have reached us, Kuropatkin for the purpose of his offensive was able to dispose of about 25,000 cavalry, 222,000 infantry, and 900 guns. This army Kuropatkin divided into three columns, the left of which was to carry out a comprehensive turning movement on the Japanese right against Kuroki at Pên-hsi-hu.

This column, from which the main results were expected, was under Stackelberg. Virtually it was the Siberian Sharpshooter Corps, composed of Samsonoff's and Rennenkampf's sharpshooters and riflemen.

The centre column, which was to move at the foot of the mountains *viâ* Feng-chia-pu under Bilderling, consisted of the 4th, 5th, 10th, and 17th Army Corps, or such residue of them as could be brigaded. The right column, which was the one under the Russian Commander-in-Chief's personal direction, was composed almost entirely of the Western troops which had during the last two months arrived from Russia. Few of these troops had hitherto been blooded.

From his whole force Kuropatkin had withdrawn six of his best divisions for the purpose of furnishing a central reserve. To oppose this force Oyama had at his disposal very nearly equal numbers: he might have been somewhat inferior in the matter of cavalry and artillery, but it is certain that in the matter of infantry he had a slight preponderance.

A glance at the map will make Kuropatkin's objective fairly obvious. He intended that his right and centre columns, operating on a front of little more than ten miles' length, with his central reserve of six divisions, should be sufficient, if not to overthrow Oku's force and Nodzu's left, at least to be strong enough to necessitate their bringing up their reserves to hold their positions. This result being effected, he trusted that his proved and seasoned Siberian troops, even though they had been seasoned in defeat, would be able to turn Kuroki at Pên-hsi-hu, and operate along the valley of the Taitse-ho just as far as the Japanese retirement invited defeat.

There was nothing unreasonable in the plan. It failed for two cardinal reasons—the first being the fact that the Japanese proved the better troops; the second, that the Russian system of operations did not allow the officer in command of the right army to benefit from the undoubted initial success which Samsonoff gained at Pên-hsi-hu.

But although we do not find it within us to eulogise the military perspicacity which prompted Kuropatkin's grandiloquent order of the day, published on October 2, in which he declared that the Russian Manchurian Army was now strong enough to begin its forward movement, yet we feel that Kuropatkin had at the moment some reason to be sanguine.

On September 26 the circum-Baikal Railway had been opened, making a very considerable difference to the rapidity with which supplies and reinforcements reached him from his rear. He had information from Europe which confirmed him in the belief that although his army had to retreat in front of the Japanese at Liauyang, yet it retreated before an enemy absolutely exhausted with the efforts it had made: moreover, Continental information had heaped praise upon him and his army. Also, his troops, though beaten, had recovered their composure and enthusiasm with a rapidity which lent colour to the Russian belief that but one more effort was required in order to settle finally this "impertinent race of yellow men."

It must be presumed that at this time Kuropatkin had no means of knowing that the Japanese had made every arrangement to meet the severe casualty list which Liauyang cost them; that even while the torches were being applied to the funeral biers, seasoned reserves, men who were doing a Manchurian campaign for the second time, were marching up the sodden roads between the port of debarkation and Haicheng: nor could he have known that by a single stroke of the pen the Japanese had recalled to the colours those veterans who had already passed into the territorial army, making all and sundry liable for foreign service for the space of seventeen and a half years.

Kuropatkin may have congratulated himself upon Prince Khilkoff's energy and the completion of the circum-Baikal Railway, but the additional rapidity of transport ensured was but a flea-bite beside the expansive measures which within three months would double the number of the men with Oyama at the front.

Also, Kuropatkin had reason to congratulate himself because not only was the "going" better, but for the most part the millet, which had masked Oyama's dispositions, had now been harvested. There would be less uncertainty, less mystery about the action which he proposed to fight. He had no fear now in putting the plan to the test, and he reckoned that Stackelberg's experienced Siberians would be more than a match in the hills for Kuroki's thinned and weary ranks.

It will be obvious to the most cursory of students that Kuropatkin's plan stood to win or lose by the success of Stackelberg's column against Kuroki's right. The main body of the Russian column, which was to effect the great strategical result on Kuroki's right, was cantoned in the vicinity of Fu-chin-tang; its outposts were held by Samsonoff's Siberian Cossack Division, while to the left was Rennenkampf's division, consisting of eleven battalions and ten sotnias of Zaibaikal Cossacks. The outposts were actually holding the Kao-tu, Chi-tao, and Wang-fu Passes.

The Japanese were holding the Wan-yu-pu-tzu Pass as an advanced post. This pass appeared to the Russians to be of great strategic value, and also of considerable strength. It was Stackelberg's intention to use it as a stepping-stone to the occupation of Pên-hsi-hu, the key of the whole position in the west.

On October 6 Stackelberg began his advance to the south. He had subdivided his command into three columns, the right of which, passing through Chi-tao-ling, moved directly upon Wan-yu-pu-tzu; the centre, moving through Wan-fu-ling and Hua-ling, made Yu-niu-min its objective; while the third column, marching over the high passes of Kao-tu and Wang-fu, halted as a reserve at Sun-tu-tsui-tzu.

The observation of the Japanese position at Wan-yu-pu-tzu apparently delayed Samsonoff twenty-four hours. He could not make up his mind whether he should essay upon an attack. The Japanese decided for him, for on the 8th of October they evacuated the position and retired to Tu-min-ling. Samsonoff, therefore, changed the direction of his march south and bivouacked that night at Yu-niu-min; while a portion of his force crossed to the south of the Taitse-ho.

Even at this date Pên-hsi-hu was held as little more than an outpost, and if Samsonoff had shown any enterprise at all he could have possessed himself of the whole position, for on the night of the 9th the Russian advance-guard of the 13th Siberian Rifle Brigade drove in all the Japanese outposts. But the Russians had been too slow; and all through the day of the 9th, though the Japanese had been driven from the mountain range of which Hua-ling is the centre, yet Kuroki had sufficient reinforcements to enable them to hold the corresponding ridge which stretched from Tu-min-ling to Pên-hsi-hu.

But even though Kuroki had reinforced his outposts, the position was still critical; for General Lubavin, with five sotnias of Zaibaikal Cossacks, had practically turned the position south of Pên-hsi-hu by establishing himself, on October 10, on the Japanese rear to the south of the Taitse-ho. This outflanking attack was pushed with sufficient vigour by the Russians to enable them to seize a position from which they opened rifle fire on the Japanese pontoon bridge and the rear of the Japanese trenches covering Pên-hsi-hu from the east to the north-east.

We can well imagine how Lubavin, ensconced in this position, must have hungered for the infantry reinforcements for which through Samsonoff he vainly called to Stackelberg and Rennenkampf. They were not forthcoming, and Kuroki, pushing reserve after reserve up to the front, steadily bore back the little force, which at one period completely turned his flank.

By October 12 Samsonoff's Cossacks had been chased back again to the north of the Taitse-ho. But although the action which centred in the valley of the Taitse-ho is probably the most important phase of the operations, yet it must not be thought that the action of the Sha-ho was confined to battling in this enclosed country. The fresh troops from Europe, with flags flying and drums beating, advanced in a steady stream down the railway to batter themselves to a standstill against Oku's masses. The centre army likewise pushed down in its endeavour to dislodge Kuroki's left and Nodzu's right from the line they had taken up covering Yentai.

On the 9th and 10th there was severe fighting along the whole line. The centre army had some success, for crossing the Sha-ho in serried masses they forced in the Japanese outposts along the river connecting with Wan-yu-pu-tzu, and dislodged the brigade of Nodzu's infantry which was holding the highlands Hai-ma-teng and Sun-mu-pu. In fact, the Russian impetus on this front was so great that on the night of the 9th Bilderling's outposts were within five miles of the coal-mines at Huan-pu.

On the night of the 9th, therefore, there was a sufficient element of success covering the whole of the fighting which warranted the sanguine reports of a success which reached St Petersburg. The Warsaw battalions had pushed right down to the Yentai railway station, Bilderling's outposts were rifling the pockets of the dead and wounded Japanese that had been left on the field, and Samsonoff on the extreme left was lamp-signalling all the night for the infantry support which either incompetence or jealousy denied him.

But the morning of the 10th was to produce a situation destined to sweep aside in twenty-four hours the fond hopes which had been raised in the Russian capital of a successful issue to this their supreme effort. Oyama and his Council, sitting within short reach of the switch-board which gave them communication with every important unit in the command, found that although in places it had been necessary for his advanced line to fall back in order to correct the whole battle alignment, yet his troops, together with the latest arrived reserves, were now in a position to hold and ward off the most vigorous of the Russian assaults.

Moreover, the Russians had been four days on the move, and the very force of their energetic attacks had enfeebled them. Oyama and his advisers determined to undertake the most hazardous operation in war. They decided that very night to change from the active defensive to the offensive, and to carry the initiative all along the line into the Russian positions. Hitherto the fighting had been severe, and in places even critical; now it was to become desperate and bloody.

On the night of the 10th the Japanese centre,—those bold battalions of Nodzu's which had won the outer ring for Oyama at Liauyang, and which again in the future were to be the troops which decided the fate of Kuropatkin as a general on the sanguinary field at Mukden,—released from the leash, hurled themselves against the high ground which formed the key of the Russian central position, five miles north-east of the Yentai coal-mines.

Meanwhile Oku, who never flinched from a task requiring the utmost endurance from his men and the most awful sacrifices, precipitated his almost superhuman battalions against the intrenchments covering the Yentai Station. For twenty-four hours, again and again, were these fierce onslaughts made. Time after time they failed, even as they had failed at Sa-san-po, Ham-a-tan, and Tasitchiaou. The flat tops of the ridges were blasted away by the concentrated vigour of a hundred pieces, till at last, after a desperate hand-to-hand conflict with the bayonet, the Russians were driven from their hold, leaving eleven guns and one hundred and fifty prisoners behind them.

The number of the prisoners was just one-tenth of the number of maimed and motionless Russian figures lying on the slopes, and one-twentieth of the little kaki-coated heroes who proved definitely on those blood-sodden slopes that the bayonet is not yet obsolete. Moreover, Oku had got his left division round, and was threatening Kuropatkin's Western conscripts from the direction of the Hun-ho.

Sympathisers and theorists on the Continent had pinned their faith in these new troops from European Russia. And for fresh troops they fulfilled their promise well, for in spite of the fact that Oku got his left division practically round them from the direction of the Hun-ho, and in spite of the fact that under his concentrated fire he hurled assault after assault on them with his wonted and indefatigable vigour, yet they stood, and stood well, suffering decimation until the morning of the 12th, when they showed signs of wavering. Then the Russian centre began to give definitely. It was the same old story of Japanese perseverance. They had worn the Russian resistance threadbare.

On the extreme right, that is to say at Pên-hsi-hu, matters had mended for the Japanese. Originally occupied by a brigade, the position had now been reinforced until it held 20,000 men, which made it secure against the threatened danger. This being so, ten squadrons of Japanese reserve cavalry were able to cross to the north bank of the Taitse-ho at Men-chia-pu, and coming in upon the Russian infantry at Yu-niu-mu, they swept them back with dismounted rifle-fire.

On the night of the 12th, therefore, the result of the battle was assured. Stackelberg's operations had failed, and the most advanced vantage-points that his mounted troops had seized had been wrested from him. Not only was Pên-hsi-hu now so strongly held that it would have been futile to have directed further operations against it, but the Japanese themselves had taken the offensive, and, instead of halting, were steadily driving the Russians back to the line of the river-way.

On the 13th the weather had changed, and heavy wind, rain, and thunder storms swept across the dismal battlefield. Decisive operations were impossible, but throughout the day there was an incessant roar as the rival armies ground iron and lead into each other. With the line of the river at his back, which this very storm would probably swell so that it became unfordable, and with roads knee-deep in morass, Kuropatkin realised that his gigantic operations, that his extreme effort, had failed. Fearing lest he should already have hung on too long, early in the afternoon of the 13th he gave the order for his own column and that of his left to fall back and take up a line on the Sha-ho.

A general retreat began,—Stackelberg on the 14th falling back to the mountains by the original road of his advance. The retirement was slow, and for the next three days the Japanese struggled to turn it into a rout. But for many reasons, the chief of which was probably the state of the roads, together with the exhaustion bred of eight days' stubborn fighting, the Japanese were unable to effect a signal disaster upon their enemy, other than the enormous losses which the retirement entailed. The Russians threw themselves doggedly into their prepared trenches to the north of the Sha-ho, and realising his position, and knowing that Kuropatkin still had untouched six fresh divisions in reserve, and was daily receiving reinforcements from the north, Oyama stopped the pursuit and threw out his outposts along the line of the Sha-ho. But his orders had not circulated in time to prevent General Yamada's Division from crossing the Sha-ho. This force was cut off and overwhelmed by the Russians, losing fourteen guns and a large number of prisoners.

Thus ended the battle of the Sha-ho, which, in point of numbers engaged, the area over which the operations took place, and the issues involved, is probably, with the exception of the subsequent battle of Mukden, the most famous of all time. In actual casualties it cost the Russians 47,000 officers and men: they also lost thirty-five field-guns and a proportionate amount of stores and ammunition. The Japanese casualties in one of the three armies engaged was 16,000. If we add 20,000 to this number to cover the losses in the two remaining army corps, we shall probably approximate the numbers which the success cost them—36,000 officers and men and fourteen guns.

We have given the reason which, to the ordinary student, will seem the most natural for Oyama's decision to halt on the south bank of the Sha-ho; but although we give this, we do not depart from the suspicion that the Japanese were governed in their action by ulterior motives, and that the far-sighted General Staff halted the army short of Mukden for the same reason as they had desisted from pursuit six weeks previously after the success of Liauyang.

They had beaten their enemy a second time, but they were not yet prepared to crush him. It would require another six months and developments elsewhere before Japan would be able to oppose the Russian Commander-in-Chief in Manchuria with an army sufficiently superior in numbers to crush him. The Japanese General Staff knew as well as everybody else that it was only by numbers they could hope to annihilate.

For the second time that summer there had commenced at Mukden a frenzied evacuation. The treasure-chests of the Russo-Chinese Bank were hurriedly moved up towards Tie-ling, and the majority of merchants and non-combatants had already started to leave the Manchurian capital, when again the Japanese magnanimity in pursuit declared itself.

Oyama had decided that Mukden should remain Kuropatkin's headquarters during the stagnant months of the winter campaign. Already the nights were beginning to bring a suspicion of winter. The midday sun was losing its strength, there was a bite in the midnight air. After a few slight and unimportant skirmishes, both armies, with their outposts almost meeting, settled down to watch each other throughout the drier months of a snow-locked Manchurian winter, and to prepare themselves against such opportunities as the coming spring might bring.

The two armies settled down to winter quarters on opposite sides of the Sha-ho. The Japanese naturally extended their left towards the Hun-ho; but it is evident that they preferred the fringe of low hills which border the great plain of Mukden to the open steppe in which the Russians were now forced to canton. For the present all suggestions for active operations on an extensive scale were at an end.

Both armies had to prepare against a common enemy more terrible than Skoda shrapnel and Shimosi bursting charges.

In a month, or six weeks at the latest, the Manchurian winter would be upon them. Neither army could afford to await its coming unprepared. Beyond extending to the left and securing their foothold in the hills on their right, the Japanese practically left the Russians alone. In short, so pacific did the outposts become, that each opposing group invented signals by which they established local armistices for purposes of camp economies.

A bucket shown above a parapet intimated that the occupants wished to draw water from the ice-holes in the frozen surface of the river which separated them. At these ice-holes the unarmed reliefs often met and exchanged small courtesies. But apart from the clothing and housing of these two great armies, the commanders on both sides were engaged in planning the future of the campaign.

In the light of subsequent events, we now know that Oyama, as he sat gloating over the countless spirals of smoke which picked out the Russian bivouacs from the winding-sheet of glistening snow on Mukden's plain, was calculating to bring three more armies into line with the three with which he had won the battles of Liauyang and the Sha-ho, to enable him not merely to defeat the Russians but to engulf them in irretrievable disaster. Nogi's four divisions in front of Port Arthur by spring would have accomplished their task.

During those early winter months contemporary writers in Japan commented upon the extraordinary fact that although the whole of Japan's organised striking arm had been transferred to Manchuria, yet Japan had never before seemed so full of soldiers. The new service regulations were in active effect, and Hasegawa's and Kawamura's armies, three months mobilised, were waiting for the transports.

Nor were the Russians idle. In spite of assurances to the contrary, Prince Khilkoff was maintaining his daily service of twelve trains, and pouring a continuous supply of reinforcements into Kuropatkin's base. This reinforcement had been so successful that a further shuffle in the commands was found necessary. The Army of the East was divided into three commands. These were placed under Koulbars, Gripenberg, and Bilderling,—Kuropatkin, with Sakharoff as his chief of the staff, remaining in chief command. The huge quantities of supplies and munitions and the wonderful network of light railway which fell into the Japanese hands after the battle of Mukden, furnish eloquent evidence of the manner in which the Russians prepared against the spring campaign.

But of that unity of purpose which alone can weld

the departments of a great army into a scientific working machine we find little evidence in the Russian lines. All authorities agree that the intervals in those peaceful months of warlike preparation were filled in with bickerings, petty jealousies, and often open mutiny amongst the directing heads. These disagreements were even of so grave a character that it is reported that Gripenberg would tear Kuropatkin's messages into pieces and fling them in the face of the messenger who presented them; while Koulbars, in disagreement with the chief of the staff, found outlet to his annoyance by soundly boxing that officer's ears.

But with the Japanese how different! Their unity of purpose and fixed idea was sufficient to eradicate even the jealousy of the sister services. In the common cause the rivalries of Army and Navy were relegated to absolute abeyance. The lesson of this great struggle from beginning to end had been that of moral superiority.

But in spite of the internal bickerings in his army, there is no doubt that Kuropatkin held the view that he would be able to again take the initiative as soon as the weather and the reinforcements were favourable, and the raids which he countenanced in the month of January are consistent with this theory. Gripenberg, on the other hand, held the opinion which has now been definitely disproved, that the Russian soldier would prove more than a match for his adversary as soon as the snow was frozen hard on the ground. Why this should be we never could understand, for even Southern Japan is a rigorous climate in winter, and the habit of the Siberian Russian has always been to avoid the rigours of outdoor life during winter months.

Before Mukden, the main theatre of the war, we had little to attract our attention during November and December 1904. There were other and more absorbing interests elsewhere. Port Arthur, the impregnable, was beginning to quiver in the grasp of the intrepid Nogi, while Rojdestvensky was sounding for a suitable rendezvous on the East Coast of Africa.

Little attention, therefore, was given to the monotonous Agency reports from Oku's and Kuroki's fronts detailing spasmodic bombardments, or to Kuropatkin's stilted narrative of the heroic efforts of his Volunteer *chasseurs*. Occasional howitzer shots and the wrangles of outposts were mere *hors d'œuvre* to a reading public, which during the past year had acquired a taste for the strong meat of pitched battles.

Consequently there was a mild recrudescence of interest in the Far East when it was reported that on January 1st an enterprising Russian officer's patrol had insinuated itself between An-shan-chan and Hai-cheng, and destroyed quite a creditable distance of

Japanese permanent way. Wiseacres of pro-Russian proclivity shook their heads, and said that " the world would now see " that Kuropatkin was about to make the scientific effort they had so long promised that he would make, and which we ourselves, until he failed at Hei-kou-tai, believed that he could command.

This theory was strengthened when ten days later Mishchenko's Raid was reported independently from Ku-pang-tsu. The officer's patrol had been but a feeler. Mishchenko's operations were to be a serious attack. In spite of the opportunities which attended this raid, the story has not been well told. The best authority, the correspondent of an American journal who accompanied the force, did not make much use of his opportunity. It is certain, however, that for a considerable period Mishchenko broke the boundaries of the belligerents' self-imposed neutrality. Roughly, the story of the adventure, which reads more like the American Civil War than anything we have hitherto had in the story of the campaign, is the following.

Mishchenko concentrated his force on January 6 and 7 at Pai-chi-pu, on the railway, twenty miles south of Hsin-min-ting. He had a mounted force of about 6000, with several batteries of Cossack artillery. Poor as the American correspondent's description is as military evidence, yet he has penned a moving picture of the night-march which brought the raiders down to San-sha-ho, below the point where the Hun-ho flows into the Liau-ho. One can picture this great horde of semi-savage soldiery muffled in their dirty furs and skins,—the shaggy, ungroomed ponies moving silently, except for an occasional cough, over the hard surface of glistening snow,—the stiff, bitter night-air subduing most local sounds, yet intensifying the creak of uneasy leathers and the clang of metal trappings.

We, who have no experience, can form no estimate of the terrors of frost and cold that the raiders had to endure. However, it is not allowed to us to follow the story of this raid in all its detail. It must suffice to say that on January 10 Mishchenko crossed to the left bank of the frozen Liau-ho, and on the following day divided his command into four flying columns. Each of these columns had a definite objective. Two were directed against old Niu-chwang and Niu-kia-tun, both of which places were immense Japanese supply depots: the remaining two columns were directed against the Japanese railway communication between An-shan-chan and Haicheng. From this point the raid did not fulfil its promise. Time had been wasted somewhere, and the Japanese, who were completely surprised on the 10th, were "wise" to the course of events on the 11th. The supply depot at Niu-chwang was destroyed, and temporary damage effected on the railway, but by January 12 all the flying columns had concentrated again and were in retreat to the Liau-ho, for the most part fighting a rear-guard action with the pursuing Japanese.

For ten days the story of Manchuria was again shrouded in its impenetrable veil of winter ice and snow. But for Kuropatkin's fitful cables of the prowess of his *chasseurs* very little news reached this country. Nor was there much interest in the far north, since the public were still busy counting the loss and gain in the surrender of Port Arthur and the quality of Stössel as a general.

But towards the middle of January the small voice of a French journalist in St Petersburg was able to make itself heard with the announcement that Kuropatkin was on the point of again attempting aggressive operations. Since the Sha-ho he had been reinforced by between 50,000 and 60,000 men, which brought his available striking force up to the respectable total of 250,000 men. Even with these numbers he was inferior to Oyama. Kuropatkin may or may not have known this at the time. But he knew that Stössel's surrender had released Nogi with the equivalent of 100,000 seasoned troops, who were already on the way to join the Army of the North.

We have pointed out already in this paper that the Japanese had thrown their left out towards the river Hun. Their left was now composed of Nogi with his troops from the Liau-tung Peninsula. It consisted of a line of fortified villages on the Hsin-min-ting-Liauyang road, where it crosses the plain enclosed by the Sha-ho and Hun-ho rivers. Against this left Gripenberg's corps was suddenly set in motion. On January 25 the bulk of this corps was suddenly concentrated at Chang-tan, north of the Hun, and twenty-five miles south-west of Mukden, from whence Gripenberg was to make his maiden effort. His force consisted of nearly 80,000 men, with 300 guns, for the most part composed of what was then considered to be the flower of Kuropatkin's army, namely, the 8th and 10th Corps.

IX. THE BATTLE OF HEI-KOU-TAI.

On Monday, January 23, the whole civilised world was horrified with the story of the slaughter of innocent Russian petitioners in front of the Winter Palace and in the streets of St Petersburg. This terrible occurrence, so unexpected in its advent and so far-reaching in its effects, may be signalised as the first real and definite internal demonstration that Russia was the least successful belligerent in the great struggle in the Far East.

There had already been indications that the country, internally writhing, was struggling to express its dissatisfaction in a policy which had brought upon it the present tribulation; was resenting the grip of war taxation, relentless in its greed for money and manhood. There had been naval riots at Sebastopol; mobilisation difficulties; and even a mysterious affair at the blessing of the Neva.

Each of these, judged in the sequence of events, might well have been classed as the protest of an unwilling people. But on January 22 the climax was reached. From that day the struggle in the Far East became an unpopular and disastrous war, forced upon a discontented and powerless people for the purpose of justifying a foreign policy in which the nation as a whole had no sympathy.

But although we allow this now, it is more than probable that if there had been no war—if the people of Russia had not felt the flail of disaster and the pinch of war privation—they would have acquiesced willingly and enthusiastically in the expansion of their empire in the East. And even if the war had been successful there would have been few Russian mouths opened against the Grand Ducal campaign of aggrandisement. This is only natural; for it has to be a great policy, and a magnificent, that will stand the strain of unsuccessful war.

The working heads of the bureaucracy in Russia were well aware of all this. Therefore, when Kuropatkin's crowning effort in the autumn was turned into a miserable defeat on the Sha-ho, every effort was made on the part of the Russian Government to reinforce the army in the field, so that by the spring it might be able to stem the course of Japan's success and to turn defeat into victory. Their ears were not deaf to the grumbles of dissatisfaction which reached them from every corner of the empire. Wherever they had mobilised for sea or land, the secret reports were the same. Libau, Revel, Odessa, Sebastopol,

Warsaw, Kieff, Tiflis, Irkutsk—all had their festering sore. The fall of Port Arthur, the vaunted fortress of the Far East, intensified the spreading waves of popular distrust. Unless victory came quickly, it was certain that the gatherings would come to a head—therefore a supreme effort was made.

Lord Brooke,[1] who, in the matter of military data, seems to be the most reliable of all the correspondents who accepted the hospitality of the Russian Staff, says in his book that "by the 19th of December, exactly two months after the battle of Sha-ho, 85,000 reservists without impedimenta had been received, and fresh troops were coming from Europe in an endless stream." According to this authority, the Russian army by the middle of December was as strong as it had been before it undertook the battle of the Sha-ho; while a month later the same authority estimated that the force under General Kuropatkin was some 400,000 strong, and had about 2000 guns.

All stores had been replenished, and the branch railway lines from Mukden to the Sha-ho were finished. In short, all the arrangements for the battle were complete. Ever since the beginning of January St Petersburg had been urging Kuropatkin to let slip no opportunity which might be turned into a victory. The staff of St Petersburg still clung

---

[1] An Eye-Witness in Manchuria. By Lord Brooke, Reuter's Correspondent. London: Eveleigh Nash. 1905.

to the heresy that the Russian soldier held a superiority over his enemy during a Manchurian winter. They viewed the various indications of internal unrest with apprehension, and, little recking the many circumstances of supply and system which governed his actions, continued to urge Kuropatkin to take the initiative. When, however, the whole country boiled over after the disgraceful tyranny demonstrated on that Sunday in St Petersburg, the authorities were desperate. They ceased to urge the General in the field, but deliberately ordered him at once to save the situation at home, either by the salve of a great victory or the counter-irritant of another desperate disaster.

Just as these demands came the season softened a little. A wave of wintry mildness swept across the Manchurian plains. To all intents and purposes Kuropatkin was ready. He had only been waiting on the weather. The opportunity had arrived. The Russians were now holding an extremely long front; Kuropatkin's left was thrown back in the hilly country forming the watershed of the Sha-ho, in order to cover Fu-shun from a flank attack. His centre practically followed the line of the Sha-ho as far as the railway. From Lu-sheng-pu the line of the Russian defence curved backwards towards the Hun-ho at Chan-tan-ho-nan. The Russian right rested on the plain of the Liau-ho, somewhere on the Hsin-min-ting road. This flank was watched by a cavalry division under Mishchenko and Kosobosky. In all, this was a front of sixty to seventy miles.

It must not be imagined that the Sha-ho was a military obstacle. It was neither deep nor fast enough, except when in heavy flood, to be reckoned as a barrier. At the present season, frozen hard, it indicated the line of country which commended itself to Kuropatkin's sappers as defensible. The 2nd Manchurian Army, which was now commanded by Gripenberg, held the plain between the Hun-ho and the railway. Koulbars commanded the centre, while the 1st Manchurian Army, consisting of the Siberian Army Corps, held Kuropatkin's eastern front in the hills under the command of Linievitch, the veteran commander during the Boxer trouble, who had recently been brought to Mukden from commanding the garrison at Vladivostok.

The Japanese positions to a very considerable extent conformed to those of the Russian. In fact, in many places the outposts were so close together that it was possible from the Russian lines to see the smoke from the cigarettes of the Japanese off-duty pickets. But behind the parallel chains of fortified positions which kept these two armies in touch, two industrious and independent principalities seemed to have sprung up. The Russians showed great mechanical skill in connecting up the wings of their great army with light railroads, telephones, and all scientific means of inter-communication. To a great extent the Japanese did the same, but they were also careful to prepare a second and even a third line of defence within an easy distance of their front, so that if the great army of brave men which Kuropatkin was concentrating in front of them should, by force of numbers, be able to drive them from the first line, the Russians, spent and halting from the effort which had given them success, would find that no less an effort was required to make good the Japanese second line, and, in sequence, the third.

The Russians, too, had prepared against misadventure, but their position was forty miles to the rear of Mukden, and was designed rather to arrest disaster than to form a *point d'appui* for a violent counterstroke. This difference in military appreciation was fully demonstrated during the battles of Hei-kou-tai and Mukden.

There are several indications which tend to show that Kuropatkin at Mukden still believed that although the Japanese-bred soldier might be better than the mujik in the hills, yet his own grey-coated regiments would defeat the diminutive Oriental upon the plain. From the very commencement of the campaign, so far as he could judge, the Japanese had always made for the highest hill-tops in order to give effect to their turning movements. Reflecting upon the very painful experience which he had bought, the Russian General no doubt came to the conclusion that the Japanese had shunned the plain because they felt their inferiority on the level. This thought was set fast in his mind when he designed the abortive operations at Hei-kou-tai, and after that disaster it was this belief which caused him to mass 20,000 of his reserves at Fu-shun as a counterpoise to the combined movement which he apprehended Kawamura and Kuroki would make against his left flank.

It must be allowed, however, that the development of the final closure of the battle of Hei-kou-tai is an enigma even to this moment. The military student can understand the object of Gripenberg's original movement,—his desire to turn the Japanese on the flank on which he believed their military resistance to be the weakest. One can even understand his selecting European troops, for the most part unblooded, to engage upon this enterprise over the frozen plains. Also, it is easy to understand why, as a matter of precaution, the well-tried 1st Siberian Army Corps under General Stackelberg was withdrawn from the left, and sent to stiffen the new phalanxes from European Russia.

The order which the mutinous and sore-headed Gripenberg claims to have in his possession, in which

Kuropatkin asks him to unmask the situation of the chief masses of the Japanese force beyond the Sha-ho, is also easy of comprehension. But, beyond this point, there is little that the student or historian can unravel or conscientiously understand. There is no doubt, however, that the premises of this attempt against Oyama's flank were, at the outset, conducted with considerable skill — that is to say, they were conducted with secrecy, and secrecy in war is synonymous with skill.

On the night of the 23rd the Russians' second army, consisting of the 8th and 10th Army Corps, plus Stackelberg's Siberians, concentrated between Chang-tan and Tu-ti-fang on the Hsin-min-ting-Liau-yang road, about twenty-five miles south-west of Mukden, and five miles to the rear of the defences on the Hun-ho. The weather still remained favourable, as far as a Manchurian winter can be favourable for military operations.

On the night of the 24th Gripenberg moved his army southwards, and crossed the frozen Hun in two places, at Han-chiao-pu and Chi-tai-tzu. Having made the passage of the river at daybreak, the Russian brigades formed for attack, and were launched against an *échelon* of fortified posts, which furnished the Japanese left. Of these the San-de-pu position was the most important. It is essential that the military reader should at this moment fix in his mind the character of the *terrain* in which the fighting took place. 'The Times' of February 4 has given the following expressive picture :—

San-de-pu, like all the other numerous villages around, is a collection of farmsteads, with a caravanserai for winter travellers. Each farmhouse is surrounded by high walls of sun-dried bricks, well plastered with loam mixed with chopped straw. These walls can be neatly loopholed, are about 3 feet thick, and form a splendid defence against bullets. The houses and farm-buildings have all their windows and doors opening into the large courtyards; the gables and rear walls are very thick, and built of the same materials as the compound walls; with rare exceptions every house is thatched. The military would, however, especially the Japanese, probably cover the thatch very thickly with mud or earth to prevent fire. The roofs are of heavy timbers resting on posts, and thus can support great weights. All buildings are low and one-storeyed. The country round San-de-pu is quite level and open, excepting for the villages and burial-places, where there were groves of trees, which have now largely been burned for fuel. The villages are roughly about two miles apart, and vary from 20 to 100 families. The Russians seem to have been driven over the Hun, which flows at this season beneath ice over 3 feet in thickness, and over which carts weighing, when loaded, five tons, can safely travel, and much heavier loads can be carried if straw or millet stalks are laid over the ice. The Hun flows in this region in a well-defined bed, with steep and often overhanging banks from 15 feet to 20 feet above the level of the ice.

Lord Brooke endorses this view, for he refers to the landscape on this very morning as "a wide flat plain with many villages and a good deal of timber, while low sandy hills diversified the landscape, still in its white mantle of snow."

Although the 1st Siberian Army Corps had been sent as a support to the 2nd European Corps, yet Gripenberg was wise enough to place the seasoned troops in the vanguard, and at daybreak Stackelberg found himself within a mile of the Japanese villages, with instructions to attack at once. He immediately threw in the 1st and 9th Divisions, while the attacking line of the 8th and 10th Army Corps deployed on his left.

On the right of our old friends the Siberians, it looked as if a great dark mantle were being enrolled over the wide expanse of spotless snow. This movement was due to the deployment of the two Cossack divisions which were working on Gripenberg's right, and which had orders to push straight through to the Hsin-min-ting-Liauyang road.

What a wonderful panorama must have presented itself to those who were privileged to witness this gigantic struggle! To a very considerable extent this sudden debouching of huge Russian columns from beyond their left came as a surprise to the Japanese. Even before the heads of the great grey columns of Russian infantry shook out into advance-guards, the Japanese outposts were falling back hurriedly upon the intrenched villages. Rapidly over the frozen snow the Russian attack developed:

there was yet no need for guns to unlimber,—the weight of surprise and numbers swept through village after village which the Japanese had held as outposts. Here and there there would be a little desperate fighting in Chinese courtyard and Manchu tomb, but for the time being the resistance was as a drop in the ocean, and the overwhelming and annihilating of these isolated groups of staunch Japanese outposts whetted the lust for victory which successive defeats had not yet extinguished in Stackelberg's inimitable Siberians.

As the red sun forced its way up through the grey winter atmosphere, the crackle and crash of musketry on the left of the Siberians told how the Kharkov and Odessa reservists were being blooded: on the far right, too, the cavalry were meeting with success. A jubilant staff officer canters up with the information that Mishchenko's swashbucklers have captured a whole company of Japanese infantry, and a squadron is marching them back to Chang-tan. Then, above the wicked ring of the bursting shrapnel and the steady detonation of the field-guns in action on the Hun-ho, comes the dull reverberating boom from the north. The turning movement has been successful. Koulbars in the centre and Linievitch on the far left are co-operating. At last the great white Czar's inexorable will is to be exercised upon the armies of the yellow race.

The peaceful calm of a snow-wrapt winter morning has disappeared. For the moment the season is nothing, and the grey-coated thousands swallow up walled village after village, leaving behind them a dismal wreck of human frames, a miserable pattern on the virgin snow. Then the enemy began in earnest to shell the heads of the many Russian attacking columns. It seemed that the head of the attack had pushed itself into a semicircle of live artillery. So rapid and accurate was the shrapnel fire that the effect of the attacking columns was instantaneous. The *élan* died out from the advance. Masses of grey-coated infantrymen heaped and teemed upon the snowy reverses of the sand-dunes, or jostled in thousands behind such cover as the walls of captured villages would vouchsafe them.

Then, for the first time, the commanders of corps realised that although they had turned the first line in the Japanese defence and were now advancing directly upon the left rear of the principal flank defences, yet they had miscalculated. They had been ignorant of the second line of defences. They had simply "butted in," to use an eloquent Americanism, between two held parallels, and now had neither the information nor the direction to grapple with a situation the success or failure of which depended upon the active co-operation of Kuropatkin's centre and left, or a magnificent effort on the part of the

Cossack divisions on Gripenberg's right. We now know that the three succeeding days brought no realisation of the elements essential to success. On the night of January 25, although in the detail of fierce fighting there was no diminution of the struggle, yet all chance of success was gone.

Space will not allow us to fill in detail step by step all the rigorous attacks and counter-attacks which marked Gripenberg's desperate efforts to seize some point in the Japanese *échelon* which would give the necessary leverage to turn his attention upon the Japanese second line of defence, which he now discovered followed the course of the Shili-ho. The Russian divisions had pushed up to within striking distance of the walled villages of San-de-pu and Hei-kou-tai, which were the two main keys which prevented the actual turning of the Japanese first line of defence, facing the Hun-ho and Sha-ho rivers. Here the Russian infantry were brought up sharply to the halt.

Both villages, and especially San-de-pu, had been placed into a perfect state of preparation. The 33rd Regiment of Siberian Rifles flung itself out into the assaulting line, and staggered up into the blaze of magazine and machine-gun fire which the Japanese brought to bear upon it from their skilfully prepared defences. The gallant effort was made with success against the lesser citadel, but failed in front of San-de-pu. With this failure came the night. Now there was no question of a snug and comfortable *zemlianke*.[1]

During the night of January 25 the Japanese were sufficiently conversant with the Russian intentions to make the necessary precautions to turn the initial success on their left into a disaster. The advance divisions of the new reserves had arrived, and even before Gripenberg established his advance, this army was allotted to the left flank of Oyama's front. The regular reserves held in hand at Liau-yang were immediately marched up to the line of the Shili-ho. They were in position on January 26.

San-de-pu was holding its own. The longer that the Russians halted, the more decisive, complete, and overwhelming would be the Japanese counter-stroke when it was struck. We have many sketchy accounts of the desperate efforts with which the 33rd and 34th Siberian Rifle Regiments toiled to make good the footing which was gained in the outskirts of San-de-pu. On the 26th the Russian artillery was massed against the defences in the village: it was hoped that the rain of shrapnel would so wear down the defenders that by evening

---

[1] *Zemlianke* is the Russian term for underground shelters, in which practically the whole army was housed during the inactivity of trench life. Each *zemlianke* generally held from eight to sixteen men. Lord Brooke describes them as having "earthen floors and sides covered with mud. However cold it was outside, it was always beautifully warm in these dug-outs."

NINTH DIVISION ANNIHILATED. 291

Stackelberg's infantry might be able to struggle into possession of the coveted position. In this futile attempt Stackelberg's 9th Division was practically annihilated. Again had the wretched Russian troops, now almost starved, to lie out and face the intense rigour of a Manchurian winter.

The weather had changed, and all through the day the 9th Division had advanced to death and annihilation in the teeth of a blinding snowstorm. Only those who have experienced an Arctic winter can realise what it must be to lie out in a wind against which no blanket, sheepskin, or fur is proof.[1] For the strong and healthy it was awful; what then must have been the state of the many thousands of poor wretches who had been struck down in the snow, whom no ambulance could reach, no doctor succour? Imagination will not reproduce the horrors of such a situation.

On the 28th Gripenberg to some extent made progress—that is, he forced the Japanese from the high ground to the south of San-de-pu, and practically isolated the village which the Japanese had held so stubbornly. But as long as San-de-pu held firm, the moment must arrive when Oyama would be able to loose his war-dogs in counter-attack.

Also on this day it must have occurred to the

[1] It is officially stated that the thermometer on the occasion of the San-de-pu fighting was ten degrees below freezing.

veteran Gripenberg that something was very wrong in the management of the whole Russian army. Beyond the fitful boom of an occasional gun fired from the Russian centre, there was no evidence of Koulbars having moved a finger to aid him. The moment would soon now be passed when co-operation could help him, and we can imagine the urgent messages that he despatched to the Commander-in-Chief begging and praying that he would carry out his part of the contract.

Of the evasive answers which he received we have as yet no knowledge. But this we know, that by the evening of the 28th the Japanese, in desperate array, launched battalion after battalion against Hei-kou-tai. The moment was ripe to turn the Russian effort into disaster, and Kodama threw his veterans in sledge-hammer attack against Hei-kou-tai. All through the night the desperate assaults were continued; time after time the head of each attacking line was swept away by the sleet of Russian fire poured into it. But the men were not to be denied, and at nine o'clock on the morning of the 29th a mass of half-demented infantrymen, climbing over the dead bodies of their comrades, planted the Rising Sun above the highest gable in the village.

The moment of disaster had arrived. Hei-kou-tai lost, Gripenberg ordered his army to retire, and Oyama launched his 30,000 fresh reserves in pursuit.

Worn, emaciated, and beaten, the fine European troops in whom St Petersburg had placed such faith, and who six days before had proudly crossed the frozen Hun and advanced to the attack with all the panoply of medieval war, were now hurled back across the ice—a broken and defeated rabble.

St Petersburg and the Grand Ducal party had asked for a victory or a counter-irritant. Far be it from us to say that a victory was ever within their reach, but a counter-irritant was easily found,—how easily even we in Europe did not then realise.

It is difficult to sum up the results of this terrible battle in the snow. We have already shown how practically one Russian division was annihilated in front of San-de-pu; the Japanese losses, before they were able to reoccupy Hei-kou-tai, were simply enormous; but neither of these compare in any way to the terrible scene of slaughter which was enacted in the final retreat of the Russians back to Chang-tan. A portion of Oku's army pursued them to the Hun-ho, and having reached this point the Japanese, probably from reasons of caution, stayed their hand.

It was estimated at the time in telegraphic despatches that the Russian losses between January 25 and January 29 were just over 10,000 officers and men. The casualties, taking into consideration the atmospheric conditions under which this action was fought, were enormous, less than 50 per cent of the wounded being retrieved from the field of battle. It will therefore not be an ungenerous estimate to hazard 20,000 as the actual losses in the futile endeavour to turn the Japanese line at San-de-pu. A heavy price indeed to pay for a political counter-irritant. The Japanese themselves allowed that they had 7000 casualties. Leaving a margin to cover the deductions of the military secrets bureau, we may estimate that the Japanese losses were just about half of those incurred by the Russians. They had to expend life recklessly to reoccupy Hei-kou-tai, and they also lost a very large amount in the outpost operations of the opening day,—the majority of the Japanese pickets preferring to die at their posts rather than implicate the main line of defence by retiring too rapidly.

Lord Brooke, who was present throughout the whole of this desperate fighting, sums up the effect of the battle in the following suggestive paragraph :—

The battle of San-de-pu had the most deplorable effect on the whole army. The work of three months and more of reorganising the force since the battle of the Sha-ho was almost entirely thrown away. Prior to the defeat of Gripenberg the army had recovered its tone. There were officers, more thoughtful and better informed than the majority, who still had misgivings as to the ability of the Russian army to reverse Liau-yang and the Sha-ho. They did not affect the general spirit. The men, well-clothed and well-fed, cheered by the presence of new comrades, had enjoyed a long rest, and were full of courage. Guns, ammunition, and supplies had arrived in plenty, and confidence in the future was almost universal. Then came San-de-pu with its disastrous ending of over 20,000 casualties; the *morale* of the men gradually weakened, and, worst of all, caused acute dissension in the ranks of the officers. All this had the most depressing effect, and it is beyond question that the defeat of San-de-pu was one of the chief causes of the subsequent rout of the Russians at Mukden.

No analysis that we can make will clearly apportion the blame for the dismal errors in direction which are the chief features of the battle we have just studied.

The actual patent results were the most extraordinary. As soon as Gripenberg had withdrawn his army of shattered battalions across the Hun, he posted into Mukden and flung his resignation at Kuropatkin's head. Not even waiting to have it accepted, he handed in a long ciphered telegram to the Tsar, and, requisitioning a special train, started post haste for Europe.

The wildest rumours were in circulation at St Petersburg, especially when on the following day a confidential aide-de-camp was despatched to the Far East from Tsarskoe Selo, and Gripenberg had instructions to break his journey at Irkutsk.

Even to this moment the whole affair is shrouded with mystery. Gripenberg's story is that he was deserted; that he was left, with his 80,000 men, lone-handed to do battle with the whole of the Japanese army; that by his original night-march he had made an advantage which, if only Kuropatkin and the other officers commanding corps had carried out their obligations, would have resulted in a complete victory.

That is Gripenberg's case: for the rest, everything is conjecture. Some say that Kuropatkin merely ordered a demonstration against the Japanese left, and that Gripenberg brought about a pitched battle contrary to orders. Others attribute the want of cohesion to a breakdown in Kuropatkin's nervous system. It is confidentially said that he was about to order the full development of his whole fighting strength against the Japanese front when he heard of the failure of the Siberian Army Corps. He at once exhibited those failings which were so noticeable in many of our own generals during the earlier months of the South African war: he accepted defeat for his whole force on the fortunes of an infinitesimal portion of it.

This is the nearest solution at the present moment that the student can arrive at. Hei-kou-tai probably furnishes the most curious and disastrous example of disagreement between officers in high command in the field that is to be found in history. But possibly the most striking example of Russian fatalism was the manner in which Kuropatkin's army went back again to ground, just as if an engagement which had reduced its numbers by nearly 10 per cent were a matter of the smallest moment.

Nor did the staff seem to trouble themselves as to what the effect of this demonstration of feebleness would be upon the enemy. They were content to accept defeat just as an ordinary interlude in a long and dreary winter campaign.

One cannot help contrasting this apparent apathy with the state of affairs existing behind the more stubborn line of intrenchments. Although the Japanese showed no activity in countering the small and petty attacks with which Kuropatkin thought he was keeping his enemy occupied and engaged, yet in the meantime they were organising, as secretly and as swiftly as the nature of the season would allow, the onslaught which apparently had been intended ever since they allowed the Russians to winter in Mukden.

As has already been shown, they had increased their army at the front by 50 per cent: whereas at Liau-yang and the Sha-ho Kuropatkin had been called upon to face eight divisions with their reserve complements, he was now required to oppose this same victorious army augmented by seven more divisions, divided into five armies.

Some of the prisoners that Mishchenko had taken during the action at Hei-kou-tai proved conclusively that Nogi's Port Arthur army had reached the front. But over and above this reinforcement by four magnificent divisions on the Japanese left, there was another army in the field which had been spirited away from the shores of Japan with the utmost secrecy. Outside the small circle of military direction, for a long time, the destination of this force was not known. It was given out that it was designed to attack Vladivostok or Saghalin: in reality it was carried to the mouth of the Yalu and marched up by the Mandarin road, past Motienling, until it was necessary for it to strike out and take up its position on the extreme right of Oyama's line. This was the much speculated upon army of Kawamura, consisting of possibly the best fighting material that Oyama had in the field. It was an army of veterans brought to the colours through the new extension of service requisition, which the war had rendered necessary.

X. THE BATTLE OF MUKDEN.

WE left the Russian army quietly settling itself back into its dug-outs, and awaiting such further developments as the season and the Japanese might have in store for it. But although the rank and file moved back into the warm welcome of their underground intrenchments, yet there are certain evidences which show that, in spite of all the various reports to the contrary, Kuropatkin was preparing, if not again to undertake the initiative himself, at least to receive a Japanese attack.

We find mentioned, both in Lord Brooke's interesting work and also in various telegrams to the 'Novoe Vremya,' that the Russian generalissimo late in February ordered his hospitals to be prepared to receive 70,000 casualties over and above those already incurred at Hei-kou-tai.

Japanese sympathisers, who in this country throughout the war have always been anxious to put the very best complexion on everything that emanated from Tokio and the Japanese General Staff, have told us that Kuropatkin and his staff were totally blind and uninformed as to the various preparations which the Japanese were making to open the campaign in the spring.

That the Russians were not able to possess themselves of as complete information with regard to their enemy as the Japanese were able to obtain, we have always been ready to allow; but even after this allowance we think, with regard to the premises to the great battle of Mukden, that Japanese sympathisers have been a little inclined to overestimate the excellence of the Japanese General Staff to the belittlement of their beaten enemy.

For instance, we are confidently informed by some expert military writers that Kuropatkin had no knowledge of the whereabouts of General Nogi's army. Another military writer has told us at great length that this Port Arthur force was successfully screened by a division of cavalry from all intercourse with the outer world while it was preparing to push forward to Hsin-min-ting.

We ourselves are inclined to think that the Japanese plans as they developed were mystifying enough, and that their dispositions, as they brought them to bear upon their enemy at Mukden, were scientific and conclusive enough without crediting them with supernatural energies or powers. That Kuropatkin knew where Nogi's army was by the middle of February is definitely proven by the fact that on February 11 he reported his position to St Petersburg, and that this report was published in several of the Russian papers.

We have quoted this as an instance, because we feel that, in our sympathy to our allies and in the character of that sentiment which we must feel for the successes of the Japanese, many writers have erred on the side of over-enthusiasm, and have thus become partisan. Although Kuropatkin is a beaten soldier, we still maintain that, when an unbiassed analysis of the campaign is procured, it will be found that he is not so totally disgraced as so many writers in this country would have us to believe.

That there were indications of the coming Japanese advance is evident to every student of the campaign. Take, for instance, the affair of the Hsin-kai Bridge on February 11. Here, 160 miles north of Mukden, the Russian permanent way was attacked and cut by a considerable force of Japanese cavalry. This in itself was portent enough, for it was the first time that the Japanese had endeavoured to bring about any considerable enterprise of such a character.

This raid, which reminds us of the Southern cavalry enterprises during the American Civil War, was a really magnificent piece of work. Space will not allow us to give it the attention it deserves, and, as far as we are concerned, it must remain just as it was to the Russians, an indication that some general movement was on foot.

At the end of the last chapter we severely criticised both Kuropatkin and his staff for their want of support during Gripenberg's action. The reason for this criticism is obvious, although even at this date we are not able to do more than surmise the real cause of Kuropatkin's failure. But whatever this cause may have been, it is certain that neither he nor his staff realised how nearly they had achieved a very considerable success. For although we never will believe that the Russians were within measurable distance of a complete tactical success, yet, if they had been able to have forced Oyama to sufficiently weaken his right flank and centre to confront their attack, the season would have slipped by during which the Japanese had calculated to force their great attack,—before the spring thaws had rendered military movement almost impossible.

If Gripenberg's army had been able to maintain its position, or to have effected a further turning of the Japanese left, the battle of Mukden would have been postponed, and possibly would never have taken place. As it was, the Japanese had the merest margin in which to correct the displacement of their elaborate plans which the Gripenberg diversion caused.

But by February 19 everything was ready, and the

Chief of the General Staff, comfortably ensconced near the centre of the great Japanese line, gave the order for possibly the most comprehensive military movement of modern days.

The battle of Mukden is a difficult battle to describe. In the first place, it is a series of different battles, each in itself almost of the magnitude of Waterloo. It would seem to us that the best way to tackle such a subject, which in itself is titanic, and which will probably never be fairly and adequately dealt with, is to give first a brief outline of the positions held by the chief units in the opposing armies, and then to follow the victors in detail from right to left.

Oyama's striking force was divided into five armies. Reading from right to left, on February 19 the positions of these five armies were approximately as follows: Kawamura's army, which, as we have already stated, had been landed somewhere at the mouth of the Yalu, was lying in one of the Ta-ling valleys on the Fu-shun road. Its outposts were in touch with the Russians who were holding Ching-ho-cheng, one of the strong passes in the Ta-ling range. Kawamura's object was to advance upon Fu-shun by the Ma-chun-tun and Ti-ta roads, driving in and defeating the Russian force of Siberian Rifles which, in considerable strength, held these last two positions. Kawamura had the longest and most definite route to follow, consequently, in order that, at the crucial moment, the co-operation of the whole Japanese army might synchronise, it was necessary that he should begin his operations in advance of the others.

Next, on his left, lay Kuroki. He was still lying in the vicinity of Pên-hsi-hu, from which heights Stackelberg had been unable to drive him when he essayed the attempt at the battle of the Sha-ho. The object of Kuroki's advance was to force the great mountain buttresses, which the Russians had covered with defences, lying between the Sha-ho and Ma-chun-tun.

Next, on Kuroki's left, came Nodzu, with the weakest and yet the most efficient army of the five in the field. It was always to Nodzu that some special and crafty object was assigned, and it would appear that, in nearly every one of the great fights, it was Nodzu's army which turned the balance in Japan's favour. It is remarkable that although Japan allowed foreign attachés and correspondents, and their own correspondents, with every other army in the field, yet they refused to allow any one to accompany General Nodzu. The part assigned to Nodzu in this particular battle was, in the first place, to keep the Japanese centre from being broken by any desperate endeavour by the Russians to divide the Japanese army in half; and in the second, when Kuropatkin had finally and fatally distributed the last of his reserves, to force the point of least resistance in the Russian line. Nodzu's headquarters were in the vicinity of Shi-li-ho. His outposts joined at the railway with those of Oku, his old comrade in arms.

To Oku was apportioned a *rôle* almost similar to that destined for Nodzu. Ever since Hei-kou-tai the Russian staff seemed to have conceived that, profiting by the lessons of the battle in the snowstorms, they would on some future occasion be able to force in and destroy Oku. For this purpose they massed against him a very formidable artillery. This manœuvre served the Japanese purpose well, for they also, in this portion of the field, massed a large number of field and heavy batteries.

The object of this decision on the part of the Japanese staff would seem to have been to make the Russians believe that the support to the main attack would follow the railway, and thus keep Kuropatkin from distributing his reserves too early to the strengthening of his threatened flanks. When at last concealment as to the nature of their flank attack was impossible, this same artillery would, by its concentrated fire, be able to prepare for and cover those fierce and desperate infantry assaults which had made Oku's army famous ever since it landed on the Liau-tung peninsula.

There remains one army—namely, that of Nogi.

These veterans from Port Arthur, as fine soldiers as any that ever took the field, had already played a part in the battle of Hei-kou-tai. In this great final effort, however, they were destined to fill the lacuna in the Japanese organisation made by the paucity of its cavalry force. In a word, Nogi was to effect a great enveloping movement on the Russian right flank. For this purpose the army, towards the end of February, disappeared into the great plain west of the Hun-ho.

Some remarkable stories are told by correspondents at the front with regard to the methods which the Japanese employed to disguise and conceal the movements of this Port Arthur army. We have already referred to this subject, and shown, quoting evidence, that the Russian staff were not so much in the dark with regard to this army as these correspondents with the Japanese were led to believe. But that does not matter. We must, therefore, give credence to the statement that the Japanese cavalry was used for the peculiar purpose of screening from view, by surrounding in a complete cordon, this army of over 50,000 men, which was about to carry out an operation which, doubtless, would have been far better conducted if it had been effected by an independent cavalry division.

The ultimate objective of Nogi's army was Hsin-min-ting, the terminus of the Kou-pang-tzu railway.

Geographically, this point was out of the sphere of operations tacitly agreed upon by the combatants, but when the campaign had reached these stupendous proportions this really became a side issue hardly worth noticing. Once Hsin-min-ting was reached, the Russian right was turned.

In our last chapter we gave a description of the country in the vicinity of Hei-kou-tai. This description would do for the whole of the country between Chang-tan and Hsin-ming-ting. This being realised, it is difficult to understand how Nogi's army was able to reach the railway terminus without being opposed.

If ever there was a doubt as to the efficiency of Mishchenko's cavalry and his vaunted Cossacks, it stood confirmed by the successful occupation of Hsin-min-ting by the Port Arthur army. For if, in the whole area of operations, there ever was a *terrain* that was suited to the movements of an independent cavalry division, it was in this particular section.

But, and here the inherent craftiness and military acumen of the Japanese is demonstrated, two events had taken place before Nogi was launched on his dash for Hsin-min-ting, which were calculated to clear the road for him. The first was the advance of Kawamura and Kuroki in the mountains against the Russian left. The second was the arrival of three squadrons of cavalry 160 miles north of Mukden.

The Japanese staff knew their Russian well. They knew that if three squadrons arrived unexpectedly on the railway communications, the numbers of the force would be exaggerated out of all proportion, and that in the general dismay felt for the possible destruction of the railway, which was the main and only artery for the gigantic force collected at Mukden, any menace to its safety would be almost certain to cause the withdrawal of Mishchenko's Cossacks to clear up the situation on the line of communications. And there seems no doubt that this manœuvre had the desired result, for, as will be subsequently shown, Nogi arrived at Hsin-min-ting practically unopposed.

We have not access to the same information concerning the Russian dispositions as we have with regard to our allies, but although there has been a general tendency throughout the whole campaign,— a tendency which the Japanese have not thought it worth while to contradict,—to overstate the Russian numbers, yet we believe that actually at the battle of Mukden the Russian army had reached its highest total. Lord Brooke estimates the Russian strength as being well over 350,000. These numbers to some extent are borne out by the Russian field state, compiled by the Japanese from the evidence of their prisoners after the battle of Mukden.

This estimate, according to 'The Times' correspondent, was as follows: The Russians had three armies—the first under Linievitch, the second under Koulbars, and the third under Bilderling. Under Linievitch were three army corps—the 2nd, 3rd, and 4th—with Rennenkampf's independent corps of Cossacks, making a total of 100 battalions of infantry, 30 batteries of artillery, and 48 sotnias of cavalry. Koulbars had four army corps: the 1st Siberian, the 5th, the 8th, and the 10th, together with the Division of Rifles. His army mustered 144 battalions of infantry and 38 batteries of artillery. Bilderling's command comprised the 1st, the 6th, and the 17th corps—in all, 96 battalions of infantry and 35 batteries of artillery. Then there was a general reserve, consisting of the 16th army corps—32 battalions of infantry, and 12 batteries of artillery. There was Mishchenko's cavalry division, consisting of 96 sotnias and 4 battalions of Za-Amur Border infantry; there were 34 sotnias of Ussuri cavalry, Amur Cossacks, and Orenburg cavalry; and there were finally 36 battalions of horse artillery, mountain-guns, field howitzers, siege-guns, and unattached artillery. The grand total stood: 376 battalions of infantry, 171 batteries of artillery, and 178 sotnias of cavalry,— making numerically about 300,800 rifles, 34,000 gunners (with 1368 guns), and 26,700 sabres, or a grand aggregate of 361,500 of all arms.

Of the disposal of this huge force we have as yet only the broad outline. We know, however, the main division of the three army corps. Bilderling had taken over from Gripenberg and was responsible for the Russian right; Koulbars maintained the centre; and Linievitch opposed Kawamura and Kuroki in the mountains in the east. Rennenkampf prolonged Linievitch's line to the left; and Mishchenko, as we have already shown, was responsible for the open alluvial plains of the Liau-ho and the Hun-ho.

We have therefore in this battle the extraordinary spectacle of very nearly a million of men in action, since we may safely estimate that the Japanese numbers were 25 per cent in advance of those of their opponents.

The first object of the Japanese staff was to confirm Kuropatkin in his belief that the Japanese soldier was not comparable with the Russian in the low country. On February 19 the Japanese army of the extreme right, that is Kawamura's army, all veterans from the Chinese War, broke up its standing camp and threw out two advance-guards to cover the two roads leading directly upon the Russian fortified positions in the Ta-ling range.

The thaw had commenced, but it was not the warm

comfortable change of temperature that we know in our temperate zone. It was a thaw that was slow to beat the efforts of the frost, and as miserable a season for campaigning almost as the dead of winter. But the start had to be made or the ice over the rivers would not hold; and if the ice gave completely, it would be weeks before the surface of the soil would have allowed the pontoon waggons to arrive.

On the 20th and 21st of February, Kawamura's advance-guards drove in the Russian outposts. Then the great serried triple line of works which topped the still snow-driven ridges of Ta-ling stood out grisly and forbidding in front of Kawamura's veterans. As on all previous occasions, the Russian engineers had spared no pains in making their intrenchments as impregnable as the art and science of military engineering would allow. There were the same areas of barbed-wire entanglements, the endless rows of spiked pitfalls, and the many open patches which carried the suspicion of contact mine and other diabolical contrivance. But, grisly as they were, these works had to be carried; and it is curious that a nation so young in the arts of modern warfare should have been able to produce an infantry so dogged, so steadfast, and so persevering, that it was able, by sheer recuperative insistence, to carry obstacles such as infantry had never before been called upon to face.

From February 22 to the end of February 24 Kawamura's veterans were hurling themselves against this triple line of defences. On the 23rd and 24th, to add to the miseries of these desperate soldiers, a blinding blizzard blew down the valley. Even though this almost irresistible force of nature was sweeping in their faces, this inimitable infantry managed, in the midst of desperate carnage, to seize one foothold in the Ta-ling Pass, from which they were able to lever their stubborn, yet less active, enemy. The fighting was Homeric.

We have on record the description of one of these assaults which will stand for nearly every Japanese success. This spectator had the good fortune to be present within a thousand yards of one of these desperate struggles for a hill crest,—a struggle which lasted without intermission for forty-eight hours. Although in the description it may lose much of the fire and animation of the actual event, yet it gives a curiously vivid impression of a class of combat which we ourselves two years ago believed to have become obsolete.

The Japanese were advancing in full daylight to the assault of one of these Ta-ling ridges. Every section of the battalion as it advanced stood out clearly defined, since the blizzard, of which we have spoken, had just covered the ground with a thin fresh veneer of snow. Even though the powdery flakes were still beating in the faces of this intrepid infantry, yet this conspiracy of nature was not altogether an unmixed evil. The carpet of white which swept up the slope they had to face left exposed the triple row of death-traps which the Russian sappers had sunk in the hillside. For a thousand yards there was little cover for the advance. Until it could get well under the slope of the position, where in places the rocks shelved perpendicularly, the assault was absolutely exposed.

But experience, the relentless tutor through eighteen months of war, had taught these men to take their cover with them. Each man had a sandbag on his shoulder, and as each section faced the blaze of infantry fire which opened as they unmasked from cover, they threw the sandbags as a wall in front of them and grovelled behind them for such scant shelter as they gave. And all the while the razor-edge of the position which they sought was swept by a hail of shrapnel which seemed ceaseless in its continuity.

By these means, on the first day, considerable progress was made, and by four in the afternoon the residue of the leading battalion had struggled as far as the wire *chevaux-de-frise*, and had prised and levered the supporting poles of these entanglements from their sockets.

This end accomplished, and the leading battalion had run its course. But the sandbags and the dead bodies of the bearers that it had left behind served as stepping-stones for the next battalion, and by evening this support made good the open as far as the perpendicular rocks and the last forty yards rise before the actual position. It was here that the assault was to stick. Three times during the night were reinforcements pushed up and an endeavour made to rush the summit.

The return of daylight disclosed the countless little heaps of brown bodies half covered with snow,—grim evidence of the ease and completeness with which the Russian defenders had defeated every effort. As bees hang on a honeycomb, so the little Japanese infantry clung to the face of the perpendicular which gave them cover from the merciless rifle-fire which swept down from above. As the watcher lay with his glass glued on the sky-line, he could see the Russian infantrymen raise themselves over the parapet and fire down the slope. Even the pitiless rain of shrapnel did not seem to disconcert them. Their persistence in defence seemed to be as great as that of their enemy in attack.

Presently another section of little fur-clad Japanese would leave the cover of the cliff and gallantly climb upwards. The Russians would rise to meet them, and before half the ascent was made those of the assaulters left standing would face about, break, and rush pell-mell down the hillside. If one such an attack were made that forenoon, twenty sections must have essayed the attempt and failed.

Then, at last, when the whole thing seemed useless, suddenly a corporal and four men made good the ascent to the parapet, and appeared upon the sky-line. The Russians rose to meet them, and there, silhouetted against the winter sky, bayonet crossed bayonet. The long taper weapon of the Muscovite drove the Japanese back, but the interlude of Homeric combat had served its purpose. As the little fur-clad infantrymen sank back with steel-pierced bodies, another section was supporting them. Saved from that pitiless rifle-fire, these latter in their turn appeared upon the sky-line. Section after section poured in behind them. For ten minutes, or perhaps fifteen, the figures bobbed and fluctuated on that crest-line. It was impossible to apportion success or failure.

Instinctively, as it were, there was a lull in the shell-fire. In the immediate vicinity both armies seemed spellbound by the issue being struggled for on that single hill. Then, suddenly, the puffs of shrapnel began to burst again, and the watchers could see the black backs of men firing down the reverse slope of the hill. The Russians had given way. The Ta-ling heights were won by just a score of combats as the one described.

On the night of the 24th Kawamura was able to

telephone to Kuroki that he had made good the passes for Ta-ling. The same day, according to the set scheme, Kuroki had commenced his advance. He had in front of him just as much solid honest hill-fighting as had Kawamura. But, if anything, the Japanese staff had underrated the task in front of their two right armies. They knew that it would take Kawamura some time to reach Ti-ta, but they had not realised to the full extent the possibilities of the Russian resistance. Thus it is we find that from February 24 to the end of the month both these armies were battling their way slowly forward against a constant stubborn resistance, and against almost impregnable positions.

Kuropatkin does not seem to have shown any special apprehension with regard to his left. He seems to have been imbued with the idea that the Japanese main attack would come upon his left. The persistence and the final successes of the Japanese on Ta-ling seemed to confirm this view. For the rest, the remainder of the Japanese lines seemed more or less quiescent. There was no response to his now heavy bombardment upon the positions in front of the Sha-ho, and at that date there had been no compromising reports from either the centre or the left of the Japanese army. It was not till the 27th of February that anything occurred to give Kuropatkin any special line upon which to reframe his dispositions. On the 27th, without warning, the artillery which Oyama had massed in the vicinity of the railway on his centre commenced a heavy bombardment of the Russian batteries, which had been pounding the Japanese centre for the last ten days. The sudden unmasking of large artillery forces on the Japanese centre seemed rather to confirm Kuropatkin in his original view than to perplex him. He had made up his mind that the Japanese main attack would be against Fu-shun.

But the last day of February and the first of March brought a very definite appreciation of the situation with it. Simultaneously Kuropatkin must have received reports, first that, before Kawamura, Linievitch felt himself insecure at Ti-ta and Ma-chun-tun; secondly, that Oku was advancing; and lastly and most significant of all, that the Japanese cavalry had appeared in Hsin-min-ting. Still, so imbued was Kuropatkin with the correctness of his own appreciation of the situation, that he took no notice of the sudden appearance of Japanese cavalry on his right flank; but when he heard that Kawamura was irresistible with Linievitch's present force, he became apprehensive for that flank and immediately entrained his independent reserves to Fu-shun, whither he also transferred his own headquarters.

Once Kuropatkin was committed to the movement of his reserves from Mukden he had played completely into the Japanese plans. Instead of being a mere cavalry demonstration, the appearance of an advanced guard at Hsin-min-ting really meant the overthrow of that flank. As will be seen, each movement of the Japanese had had its relative significance. The advance of Kawamura and Kuroki had not only secured Oyama's right flank, but had attracted the flower and bulk of Kuropatkin's reserve to the opposite flank, from which the decisive Japanese attack was to come. Oku in the centre, under cover of the heavy cannonade which had been opened on February 27, was moving with his right shoulder up in order that Nogi with his Port Arthur veterans should not be left in the air when he finally appeared in definite strength at Hsin-min-ting.

In the meantime our old hero Nodzu was still lying *perdu* behind the batteries which were banging the Russian centre to pieces, ready to seize the first favourable opening which would occur when Nogi's advance had definitely developed. That it was an admirably conceived plan of campaign it would be useless to deny, but it fills the military reader with astonishment that a plan, which was mainly admirable on account of its simplicity, should have been so misunderstood by the Russian staff.

Even if the little *contretemps* at the Hsin-kai bridge had taken Mishchenko up north, there should have been a sufficient Intelligence Department left in

Hsin-min-ting to have foreshadowed the significance of the Nogi movement in time to have prevented Kuropatkin from sending his reserves to protect his left. We do not, at the present moment, pretend to understand Kuropatkin or his plans, as we honestly believe that he failed as a commander in the field, not because he was devoid of military intelligence and the other necessary attributes which go to make a great general, but because he attempted the impossible in endeavouring to maintain in his own hands the command of the vast army concentrated in Manchuria. After mature reflection, it would seem that to this account must be laid the want of co-operation and cohesion which undoubtedly was the main cause of Russia's military collapse.

We have already shown how, at Liau-yang, Kuroki failed to be annihilated because there was no one present on that front amongst the Russian generals who had authority to act; we have likewise shown how miserably Gripenberg's operations petered out for want of co-operation; and here again at Mukden we have a fresh evidence that Kuropatkin's presence was considered essential for the direction of all serious fighting.

But although Nogi followed his cavalry into Hsin-min-ting on March 1, the battle of Mukden was not yet won,—in fact, one might almost say that the battle had only just begun. But it had begun with the balance of advantage in Japan's favour. From March 2 to March 7 the severity of the struggle all along the line of the Russian front was so great and so undecided that it is safe to say that, if the Russians had had any substantial success in any one of the heavy counter-attacks which they hurled against the Japanese centre, it is possible that the great battle would have had to be written off as drawn. During these five days Nogi, on the extreme west, was in a most precarious situation; so much so, that on March 6 he had to send to Oku a supplication for reinforcements, and at that moment Oku was himself so heavily involved that he could not spare a single man.

As soon as he had reached Hsin-min-ting, Nogi threw out his army into fighting formation, and pivoting it on Ta-min-tin, advanced north-east with the object of striking the Mukden-Tieling railway about fifteen miles north of Mukden. On March 2 he moved eight miles; on the following day he still made considerable progress, since the opposition in front of him was not great, so that on March 4 we find that he had covered nearly twenty miles since leaving Hsin-min-ting. This brought him within seven miles of the coveted railway. But often in military operations seven miles are almost as significant as a hundred.

On March 2 Kuropatkin had realised that he had

taken his reserves on a wild-goose chase to Fu-shun, —that the real attack, the real menace, was coming from the west. He immediately trained his independent reserve back to Mukden, and marched it out to foil Nogi's advance. He also, by telegram, brought from Tieling part of the force told off to garrison that strategic point, and also a division of fresh troops which, recently arrived from European Russia, had mobilised at Harbin, and was now on its way down to join the main army at Mukden.

Consequently, March 4 and 7 witnessed the most desperate and sanguinary fighting north-west of Mukden that the campaign was destined ever to see. Nogi's veterans realised that they were struggling for a success which would mean the entire overthrow of the Russian army. Kuropatkin, on the other hand, with his troops, realised that, unless Nogi was hurled back in defeat, the whole toil and trouble of the past ten months would be wasted, and the army enveloped in a disaster which had in it all the elements of a total rout. It would be impossible in this paper to give anything like an adequate account of this fearful struggle on the plain. No report that has so far reached us has done justice to the extraordinary issues in this stupendous *mêlée* north of the Mukden Tombs. A nation's life hung upon the individual fighting value of the opposing soldiery. But of the accounts that have been published, we venture

x

to think that the letter from a Japanese officer to his friends at home, as published in 'The Times,' will in a small way bring before the reader some appreciation of the fearful tension which weighed down all combatants during this titanic struggle.

Writing of these very operations of Nogi's, this officer says: "The 6th was the hottest and worst, and the most savage, of the whole series of the Mukden battles. The Russians held a line from San-sen-ho to Neng-yo-ho, while we ranged ourselves in or about Gyorimbo, which is about four miles west of Mukden station. The doggedness of that Russian advance! Heavy guns and light guns, handy mountain guns and little dynamite guns, all joined in the bombardment of the positions, while the heroic Russian gunners replied shot for shot and shell for shell. Attacks and counter-attacks succeeded each other like the figures on a fairy lantern. We fought with rifles, we fought with bayonets, then with grenades and with shovels and picks, and then with fists. Why, it is no more or less than a gigantic street brawl. One of the battalion commanders was killed and the colonel wounded severely, and one after another the company officers went down. Once when I whistled to the buglers, and the charge was sounded, just barely forty out of a battalion of skirmishers leaped to their feet, and the rest remained still, no cowards, but dead men—dead at their posts. Those who replied to the call had no right to do so: they ought to have been in the ambulances. Though these doings could never be told vividly enough by my pen, and, perhaps, no words could ever do justice to the bravery of the men, Russian and Japanese, and the hardships they endured. The Russians, five or six times our number, charged time after time so resolutely up to our position that some of them actually passed through the line—but they never returned. These are the fresh troops from the reserves—determined because of the knowledge that on their action hangs the fate of Kuropatkin and his army. So that day's success remained with the Russians, in spite of all our efforts. Well, they deserved it. At the suggestion of an officer of the Staff Corps we volunteered to reach the works the same night. Men came to their officers and begged to let them go and fill up the trenches with their corpses, so that those following them might walk over their bodies into the defences. At the men's earnest request a deputation of officers and men was sent to the Divisional Commander, who gave them the requested permission, not without some hesitation. . . . At midnight the men threw off their great winter coats, and white distinguishing bands were put on the sleeves in readiness to move. With drawn swords the officers led, with fixed bayonets the men follow in our usual formation. First grenade men in a line at certain intervals, then the main body in column of sixes, with a grenade man at every few paces in the ranks. With a tremendous yell we stormed into the earthworks. What followed I cannot bear to recite. How many of us returned? A few, a very few. And the works? Intact still? As we rested came the enemy's counter-attack,—the officer in command of this section knows his business well. . . . After half a day's desultory firing and leisurely fighting our battalion received an order to take Tahoshitu [Tashichaou], which the enemy held in force. In this my company form the first line. I talk of battalions and companies; but a battalion, particularly ours at this stage, furnished about as many men as a company. We moved through a hail of rifle and machine-gun bullets, which now began to resemble some perfectly natural phenomenon, as of sunshine or of rain, and it was mere child's play compared with the experiences of the awful night of the 6th."

And we almost imagine that similar accounts of the fearful stresses of the battle in this particular engagement might have been written from every other portion of the field. This much is certain, that until midday on the 7th Kuropatkin still fought with the hope of success. For four days he had held Nogi,—he was still holding Oku, but of Nodzu he knew nothing,—and Linievitch still reported the Russian left secure. But it will be noticed that we have made no mention of Nodzu. Again was this intrepid leader to furnish the turning influence in the struggle.

Early on March 5 the gunners with Nodzu reported the Russian intrenchments just south of Mukden to be practicable—that is, practicable for Japanese assault. They had been submitted for the last ten days to possibly the heaviest artillery bombardment that had ever been concentrated on a line of field-works. The very intensity of the fire had done much to lessen the power of the resistance of the troops holding these works; and over and above this, every available man had been withdrawn by Kuropatkin to throw into the operations against the flank attacks. Nodzu, with that military instinct to which we have already referred, knew exactly the right moment when to throw in his unexpected weight. We find him on March 6 still with his left at Sha-ho-pu.

On the following day, almost without a check, his men are up and over the shattered breast-works which they had been watching for the last six months; and before Kuropatkin quite realises what is happening, and at the very moment that Nogi is beseeching Oku to come to his assistance, Nodzu, with troops that are practically fresh, has thrown himself over the Hun-ho and is practically into Mukden.

Simultaneously with this news of an advance,

which was almost as disastrous and decisive as the general advance ordered by Wellington on the historic field of Waterloo, there reached Kuropatkin information that his railway communication was severed just south of Tieling. One cannot envy the General his feelings at this moment. It is true that the railway was only cut by a patrol detached from Nogi's left, but when the news arrived at the Russian headquarters Kuropatkin had just been called from superintending a counter-attack against Tashichaou to organise a resistance against this new terror advancing directly from the south. Then it was that he penned the message which, sent by an alternative line, leaked out in St Petersburg, "I am surrounded." Was there ever a more miserable statement of a situation placed on record than the despairing echo contained in that message?

On the night of March 7 Kuropatkin gave the fateful order that the whole army should fall back on Tieling. It must have been a great wrench to this earnest soldier thus to acknowledge to his own troops, to the enemy, and to posterity, that he was outmanœuvred, out-numbered, and beaten; that he could only hope to save himself by flight, and by the excellent roads which he had had constructed between Tieling, Mukden, and Fu-shun.

But Kuropatkin accepted the situation with all the fortitude of a brave man; he did not desert the cause as if it were absolutely lost. He did not, like some other great captains in history, place himself in the forefront of the flight, but turned with all the dogged nature and desperate courage of which the Slav is capable to do his best to repeat the story of Liauyang.

Collecting together the troops that had held his centre, he threw them in to the support of the brave legions that had held Nogi at bay for the last five days. It was under the cover of this rear-guard that he hoped to emulate his Liauyang retirement and withdraw his army, with some measure of success, behind the intrenchments he had established at Tieling.

It will be remembered that in a previous chapter we commented on the fact that, while the Japanese intrenched their second and third positions within an easy distance of their first line, Kuropatkin had chosen to allow his army a stretch of forty miles before they could hope to reach the field-works, which were destined to be their second line of resistance. It was these forty miles of open which killed Kuropatkin's army, which rendered the devotion of his rear-guard useless, and which practically turned the withdrawal of his baggage and his rear-guards into a rout.

Again did Nodzu prove the deciding factor. The majority of the accounts which have reached this country contain the suggestion that it was Nogi who cut off Kuropatkin's rear-guard and was responsible for the great capture of prisoners and military equipment. A careful study of all the reports furnished, however, goes to prove that this impression is quite wrong. As he had intended, Kuropatkin was able to hold Nogi to the very end. In fact, pivoted upon his own right wing in retirement, Kuropatkin swung round in front of Nogi. If it had not been for the wonderful rapidity and energy of Nodzu's advance, the withdrawal from Mukden would, as Kuropatkin had hoped, have gone down to history as a successful retreat, worthy of a parallel with that of Liauyang.

It was not in Nogi's army, which, the reader must remember, a few hours previously had been urgently soliciting aid and reinforcements, to press a pursuit, or to cut off as desperate troops as those which Kuropatkin personally conducted into their position as his rear-guard. But Nodzu, pressing on, not even waiting to assist Kuroki into Fu-shun, pushed north until he struck the railway at Pu-ho, midway between Mukden and Tieling. All through the 8th and 9th this intrepid soldiery,—which had turned the scale at Tehlitz, had assaulted and pierced the Russian centre at Liauyang and on the Sha-ho, and, here again, had defeated the enemy, and unexpectedly placed itself athwart the line of retreat of Kuropatkin's rear-guard,— staggered on in face of a Manchurian snow blizzard,—on, until midday on

March 10, when the battle of Mukden was finally lost and won.

There are many misconceptions with regard to this great battle. It was a decisive blow against Russian prestige and military power in the Far East. It was a heavy defeat and a crowning disaster to a disastrous campaign. But it was not the crushing, withering, exterminating blow that it has so generally been represented to have been in this country. After examining the evidence of foreign officers who were present on this occasion, we come to the conclusion that the battle of Mukden was almost as disastrous in its military paralysis to the victors as to the vanquished. In fact, if we are to look for the prime factor which conduced to the surprising peace which was subsequently arranged at Portsmouth, we will not be far wrong if we trace the cause of Japan's magnanimity to the paralysing effect of the battle of Mukden on her military resources.

At the time wonderful speculations were rife as to the fate of Linievitch with the Siberian Army Corps. Kawamura was supposed to have dropped from the clouds and to have immediately engulfed a third of Kuropatkin's army in disaster. In reality, of course, we find that Linievitch, learning that Kuropatkin's centre had given way, was himself forced to retire; but knowing the fate that would await him if he debouched directly into Mukden's plain, he withdrew his army more composedly by way of the Wankao passes.

It now behoves us to count the cost of this stupendous struggle. Again we are flung upon the rocks of uncertainty, and are faced with the original difficulty of making the reports and estimates of eye-witnesses coincide with the official returns. According to the Japanese estimates, they captured on the field of Mukden just over 40,000 Russian prisoners. They reckon that the Russians left some 30,000 dead on the field, and that altogether the Russian casualties, in killed and wounded and missing, amounted to 170,000 men. We are asked to believe — that is, we are told in the official Japanese accounts — that this result was attained by a loss to the Japanese themselves of only 50,000 men in all manner of casualties. Already in previous articles we have given it as our opinion that, in spite of the assurances from correspondents in Japan, in spite of the fact that the Japanese have held funeral rites for a specified number of departed souls, we cannot believe that an organisation so crafty and careful in its dissemination of military news would have gratuitously handed to its enemy a correct statement of its losses.

We will refer the reader, who may be sceptical of the truth of our assertions, to the quotation which we have used from the Japanese officer who was with Nogi on Kuropatkin's right flank. It will be noted that he states that the battalions in his division were reduced to the strength of companies. There is one point that we notice in a consecutive study of Japan's methods of conducting operations which is here worthy of comment. It is the remarkable manner in which their staff manages to equally distribute the stress of battle through every unit in the army. Therefore we may take it as granted that the officer whom we have already quoted did not belong to a division which during the battle of Mukden was engaged to a degree out of proportion to other units in the entire army. This reflection, coupled with the expression of opinion by expert European officers who were present at the battle, leads us to believe that the success at Mukden cost the Japanese in casualties at least as much as it cost their enemy.

On March 10 the Japanese officially entered Mukden. On the same date Kawamura, instead of falling from the skies and overwhelming Linievitch, entered Fu-shun. With the occupation of Mukden, the ancient capital of the Manchu dynasty, it may be said that the military campaign ended, since the conclusion of peace has rendered it impossible either for the Russians to re-establish their military prestige or for the Japanese to add to their laurels on land.

This being the case, it will not be necessary to follow in much detail the events which followed the battle of Mukden. On March 16 the Japanese, after one unsuccessful attempt, occupied Tieling, the Russians having evacuated before them. On the following day Kuropatkin was relieved of his command, and his place taken by General Linievitch, and on March 21 the Japanese occupied Chang-tu-fu. This latter occupation, to all military intents and purposes, marks the limit of the Japanese military occupation in Manchuria.

From the moment that they lost Mukden, the whole of the Russian hopes for the time being centred in their fleet, which, under Rojdestvensky, had arrived on March 17 at Nossé Bay. The history of this fleet and its disastrous voyage to the Far East, culminating with its total annihilation in the Straits of Tsushima, has already been dealt with in these pages.

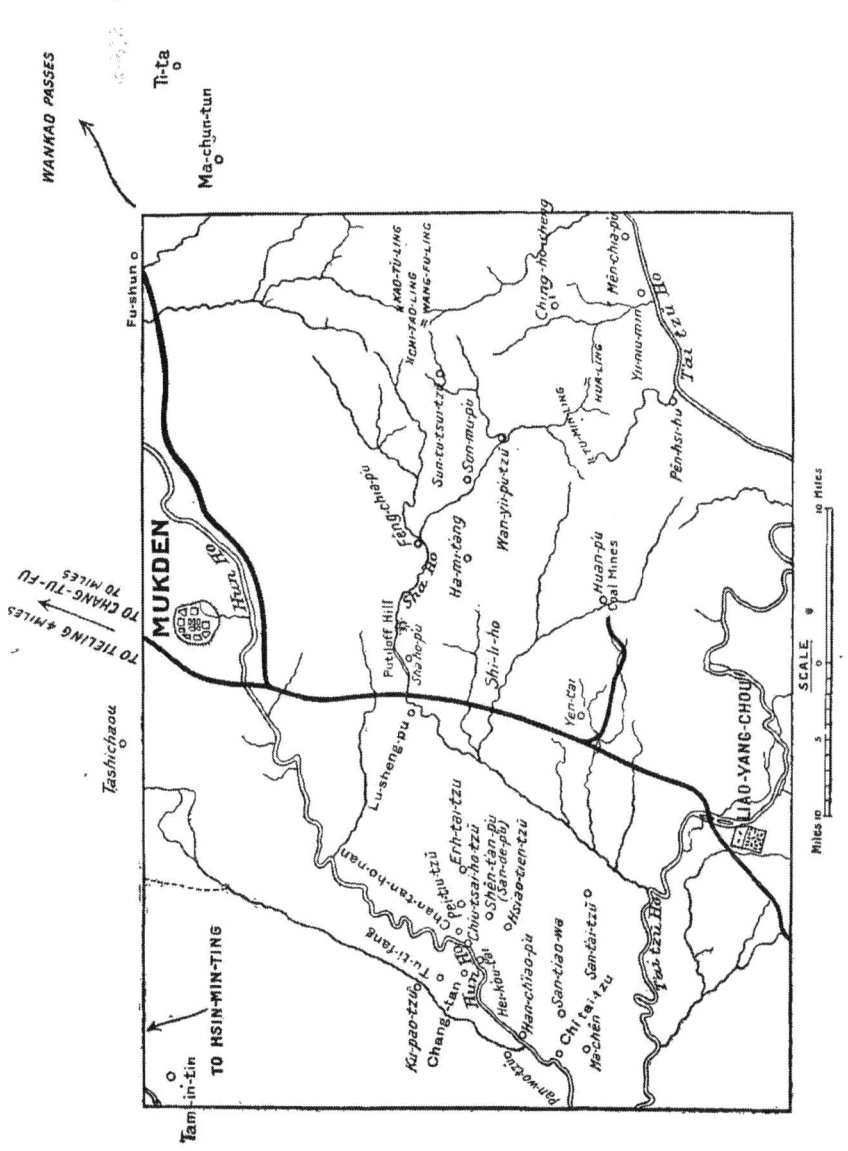

THE SOUTHERN APPROACHES TO MUKDEN.

SCALE 1 : 10000 000.
Kilometres.

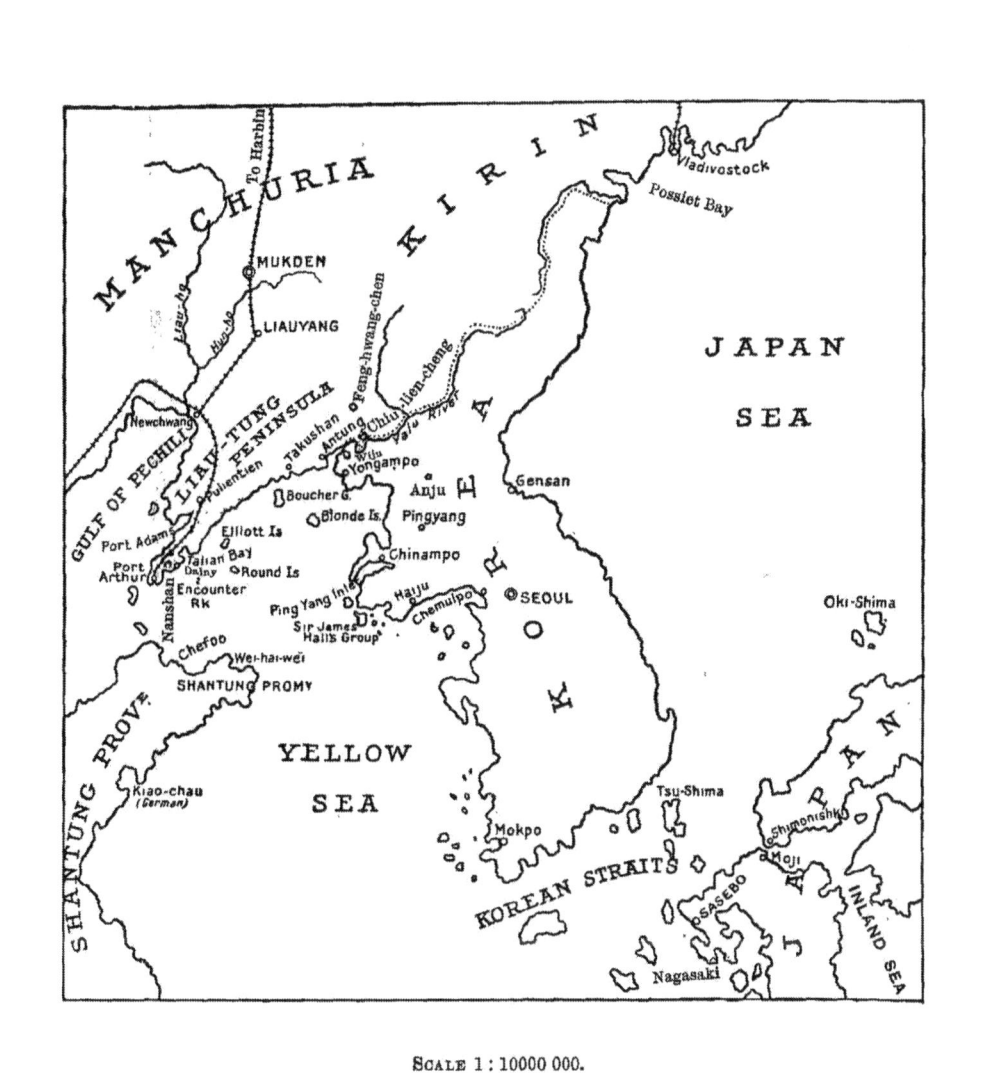

The following publications have been largely consulted in the compilation of this work:—

'The Times' war reports.
The Russo-Japanese War, by T. Cowen (Arnold).
With Kuroki in Manchuria, by F. Palmer (Methuen).
The Campaign with Kuropatkin, by Douglas Story (Werner Laurie).
A Secret Agent in Port Arthur, by W. Greener (Constable).
A Modern Campaign, by D. Fraser (Methuen).
The Yellow War, by the Author of 'On the Heels of De Wet' (Blackwood).
The Principles of Land Defence, by Capt. H. Thuillier, R.E. (Longmans).
Port Arthur: Three Months with the Besiegers, by F. Villiers (Longmans).
The Russo-Japanese War (Kinkodo Publishing Co., Tokio).
The Russian Navy in the Russo-Japanese War, by Capt. Klado, I.R.N. (Hurst & Blackett).
The Naval Annual, Edited by T. A. Brassey (Griffin).
An Eyewitness in Manchuria, by Lord Brooke (Eveleigh Nash).
Manchuria: Its People, Resources, and Recent History, by Alexander Hosie (Methuen).

PRINTED BY WILLIAM BLACKWOOD AND SONS.

QUESTIONS AND ANSWERS IN THE THEORY AND PRACTICE OF MILITARY TOPOGRAPHY. By Major J. H. BOWHILL. Crown 8vo, 4s. 6d. net. Portfolio containing 34 Working Plans and Diagrams, 3s. 6d. net.

THE EFFECT OF MARITIME COMMAND ON LAND CAMPAIGNS SINCE WATERLOO. By Colonel C. E. CALLWELL. With Plans. Post 8vo, 6s. net.

TACTICS OF TO-DAY. By the Same. Sixth Impression. Crown 8vo, 2s. 6d. net.

MILITARY OPERATIONS AND MARITIME PREPONDERANCE: Their Relations and Interdependence. By the Same. Demy 8vo, 15s. net.

HISTORY OF THE INDIAN MUTINY. By G. W. FORREST, C.I E., Ex-Director of Records, Government of India. 2 vols. demy 8vo, 38s. net.

SEPOY GENERALS: Wellington to Roberts. By the Same. With Portraits. Crown 8vo, 6s.

THE SIKHS. By General Sir JOHN J. H. GORDON, K.C.B. With Illustrations. Demy 8vo, 7s. 6d. net.

THE OPERATIONS OF WAR EXPLAINED AND ILLUSTRATED. By General Sir EDWARD BRUCE HAMLEY, K.C.B., K.C.M.G. Second Edition of Fifth Edition. With Maps and Plans. 4to, 30s. Also in 2 parts: Part I., 10s. 6d.; Part II., 21s.

ON THE HEELS OF DE WET. By The Intelligence Officer. Sixth Impression. Crown 8vo, 6s. People's Edition, royal 8vo, paper cover, 6d.

MODERN STRATEGY. By Lieut.-Col. WALTER H. JAMES, *P.S.C.*, late R.E. With 6 Maps. Second Edition, thoroughly revised and brought up to date. Royal 8vo, 16s. net.

THE DEVELOPMENT OF TACTICS FROM 1740 TO THE PRESENT DAY. By the Same. Demy 8vo. [*In the press.*

HISTORY OF THE INVASION OF THE CRIMEA. By A. W. KINGLAKE. Complete in 9 vols., crown 8vo. Cheap reissue at 3s. 6d. each.
    Abridged Edition for Military Students. Revised by Lieut.-Col. Sir GEORGE SYDENHAM CLARKE, K.C.M.G., R.E. Demy 8vo, 15s. net.
    Atlas to accompany above. Folio, 9s. net.

HISTORY OF THE INVASION OF THE CRIMEA. By the Same. Demy 8vo. Vol. VI. Winter Troubles. With a Map, 16s. Vols. VII. and VIII. From the Morrow of Inkerman to the Death of Lord Raglan. With an Index to the Whole Work. With Maps and Plans. 28s.

WORDS BY AN EYEWITNESS: The Struggle in Natal. By "LINESMAN." Eleventh Impression, with Three Additional Chapters. Crown 8vo, 6s.
    People's Edition, royal 8vo, paper covers, 6d.

THE MECHANISM OF WAR. By the Same. Crown 8vo, 3s. 6d.

A PRIMER OF TACTICS, FORTIFICATION, TOPOGRAPHY, AND MILITARY LAW. By Lieut.-Colonel C. P. LYNDEN-BELL. With Diagrams. Crown 8vo, 3s. net.

THE SURRENDER OF NAPOLEON. Being the Narrative of the Surrender of Buonaparte, and of his residence on Board H.M.S. Bellerophon; with a detail of the principal events that occurred in that Ship between the 24th of May and the 8th of August 1815. By REAR-ADMIRAL SIR FREDERICK LEWIS MAITLAND, K.C.B. A New Edition. Edited, with a Life of the Author, by WILLIAM KIRK DICKSON. In 1 vol. post 8vo, with Portraits and other Illustrations. Demy 8vo, 15s. net.

HISTORY OF INDIA. From the Earliest Period to the Present Time. By JOHN CLARK MARSHMAN, C.S.I. Third and Cheaper Edition. Post 8vo, with Map, 6s.

MILITARY TOPOGRAPHY. Illustrated by Practical Examples of a Practical Subject. By MAJOR-GENERAL W. E. MONTAGUE, C.B., P.S.C., late Garrison Instructor Intelligence Department, Author of 'Campaigning in South Africa.' With Forty-one Diagrams. Crown 8vo, 5s.

THE YELLOW WAR. By O. Crown 8vo, 6s. Pop. Edition, 6d.

THE 9th (QUEEN'S ROYAL) LANCERS, from 1715 to 1903. By FRANK H. REYNARD. Royal 8vo, £2, 2s. net.

A BOOK OF THE SNIPE. By SCOLOPAX. Illustrated. Crown 8vo, 5s. net.

THINGS SEEN: Impressions of Men, Cities, and Books. By the late G. W. STEEVENS. Edited by G. S. STREET. With a Memoir by W. E. HENLEY, and a Photogravure reproduction of Collier's Portrait. Memorial Edition. Crown 8vo, 6s.

FROM CAPETOWN TO LADYSMITH, AND EGYPT IN 1898. By the SAME. Memorial Edition. Crown 8vo, 6s.

IN INDIA. By the SAME. With Map. Memorial Edition. Crown 8vo, 6s.

WITH KITCHENER TO KHARTUM. By the SAME. With 8 Maps and Plans. Memorial Edition. Crown 8vo, 6s.

GLIMPSES OF THREE NATIONS. By the SAME. Memorial Edition. Crown 8vo, 6s.

MONOLOGUES OF THE DEAD. By the SAME. Memorial Edition. Crown 8vo, 3s. 6d.

FROM CAPETOWN TO LADYSMITH: An Unfinished Record of the South African War. By the SAME. Edited by VERNON BLACKBURN. With Maps. Crown 8vo, 3s. 6d.

THE PUNJAB IN PEACE AND WAR. By S. S. THORBURN. Demy 8vo, 12s. 6d. net.

THE ARABIAN HORSE: His Country and People. By Major-General W. TWEEDIE, C.S.I., Bengal Staff Corps; for many years H.B.M.'s Consul-General, Baghdad, and Political Resident for the Government of India in Turkish Arabia. In one vol. royal 4to, with Seven Coloured Plates and other Illustrations, and a Map of the Country. Price £3, 3s. net.

WILLIAM BLACKWOOD & SONS, EDINBURGH AND LONDON.

Catalogue

of

Messrs Blackwood & Sons'

Publications

PERIODS OF EUROPEAN LITERATURE: A Complete and CONTINUOUS HISTORY OF THE SUBJECT. Edited by PROFESSOR SAINTSBURY. In 12 crown 8vo vols., each 5s. net.

 I. THE DARK AGES. By Professor W. P. KER.
 II. THE FLOURISHING OF ROMANCE AND THE RISE OF ALLEGORY. (12TH AND 13TH CENTURIES.) By GEORGE SAINTSBURY, M.A., Hon. LL.D., Aberdeen, Professor of Rhetoric and English Literature in Edinburgh University.
 III. THE FOURTEENTH CENTURY. By F. J. SNELL.
 IV. THE TRANSITION PERIOD. By G. GREGORY SMITH.
 V. THE EARLIER RENAISSANCE. By THE EDITOR.
 VI. THE LATER RENAISSANCE. By DAVID HANNAY.
 VIII. THE AUGUSTAN AGES. By OLIVER ELTON.
 IX. THE MID-EIGHTEENTH CENTURY. By J. H. MILLAR.
 XI. THE ROMANTIC TRIUMPH. By T. S. OMOND.

The other Volumes are:—

VII. THE FIRST HALF OF THE SEVENTEENTH CENTURY. Prof. H. J. C. Grierson.
X. THE ROMANTIC REVOLT. Prof. C. E. Vaughan.
XII. THE LATER NINETEENTH CENTURY. The Editor.

PHILOSOPHICAL CLASSICS FOR ENGLISH READERS. Edited by WILLIAM KNIGHT, LL.D., Professor of Moral Philosophy in the University of St Andrews. *Re-issue in Shilling Volumes net.*

DESCARTES, ... Prof. Mahaffy.	VICO, ... Prof. Flint.
BUTLER . . . . Rev. W. L. Collins.	HOBBES, . . . Prof. Croom Robertson.
BERKELEY, . . Prof. Campbell Fraser.	HUME, ... Prof. Knight.
FICHTE, ... Prof. Adamson.	SPINOZA, ... Principal Caird.
KANT, ... Prof. Wallace.	BACON: Part I., ... Prof. Nichol.
HAMILTON, ... Prof. Veitch.	BACON: Part II., . . . Prof. Nichol.
HEGEL, ... The Master of Balliol.	LOCKE, . . . Prof. Campbell Fraser.
LEIBNIZ, . . . John Theodore Merz.	

FOREIGN CLASSICS FOR ENGLISH READERS. Edited by Mrs OLIPHANT. CHEAP RE-ISSUE. In limp cloth, fcap. 8vo, price 1s. each net.

DANTE, by the Editor. — VOLTAIRE, by General Sir E. B. Hamley, K.C.B. — PASCAL, by Principal Tulloch. — PETRARCH, by Henry Reeve, C.B. — GOETHE, by A. Hayward, Q.C. — MOLIÈRE, by the Editor and F. Tarver, M.A. — MONTAIGNE, by Rev. W. L. Collins. — RABELAIS, by Sir Walter Besant. — CALDERON, by E. J. Hasell. — SAINT SIMON, by C. W. Collins. — CERVANTES, by the Editor. — CORNEILLE AND RACINE, by Henry M. Trollope. — MADAME DE SÉVIGNÉ, by Miss Thackeray. — LA FONTAINE, AND OTHER FRENCH FABULISTS, by Rev. W. Lucas Collins, M.A. — SCHILLER, by James Sime, M.A. — TASSO, by E. J. Hasell. — ROUSSEAU, by Henry Grey Graham. — ALFRED DE MUSSET, by C. F. Oliphant.

ANCIENT CLASSICS FOR ENGLISH READERS. Edited by the REV. W. LUCAS COLLINS, M.A. CHEAP RE-ISSUE. In limp cloth, fcap. 8vo, price 1s. each net.

Contents of the Series. — HOMER: ILIAD, by the Editor. — HOMER: ODYSSEY, by the Editor. — HERODOTUS, by G. C. Swayne. — CÆSAR, by Anthony Trollope. — VIRGIL, by the Editor. — HORACE, by Sir Theodore Martin. — ÆSCHYLUS, by Bishop Copleston. — XENOPHON, by Sir Alex. Grant. — CICERO, by the Editor. — SOPHOCLES, by C. W. Collins. — PLINY, by Rev. A. Church and W. J. Brodribb. — EURIPIDES, by W. B. Donne. — JUVENAL, by E. Walford. — ARISTOPHANES, by the Editor. — HESIOD AND THEOGNIS, by J. Davies. — PLAUTUS AND TERENCE, by the Editor. — TACITUS, by W. B. Donne. — LUCIAN, by the Editor. — PLATO, by C. W. Collins. — GREEK ANTHOLOGY, by Lord Neaves. — LIVY, by the Editor. — OVID, by Rev. A. Church. — CATULLUS, TIBULLUS, AND PROPERTIUS, by J. Davies. — DEMOSTHENES, by W. J. Brodribb. — ARISTOTLE, by Sir Alex. Grant. — THUCYDIDES, by the Editor. — LUCRETIUS, by W. H. Mallock. — PINDAR, by Rev. F. D. Morice.

CATALOGUE

OF

MESSRS BLACKWOOD & SONS'

PUBLICATIONS.

ACTA SANCTORUM HIBERNIÆ; Ex Codice Salmanticensi. Nunc primum integre edita opera CAROLI DE SMEDT et JOSEPHI DE BACKER, e Soc. Jesu, Hagiographorum Bollandianorum; Auctore et Sumptus Largiente JOANNE PATRICIO MARCHIONE BOTHAE. In One handsome 4to Volume, bound in half roxburghe, £2, 2s.; in paper cover, 31s. 6d.

ADAMSON. The Development of Modern Philosophy. With other Lectures and Essays. By ROBERT ADAMSON, LL.D., late Professor of Logic in the University of Glasgow. Edited by Professor W. R. SORLEY, University of Cambridge. In 2 vols. demy 8vo, 18s. net.

AFLALO. A Sketch of the Natural History (Vertebrates) of the British Islands. By F. G. AFLALO, F.R.G.S., F.Z.S., Author of 'A Sketch of the Natural History of Australia, &c. With numerous Illustrations by Lodge and Bennett. Crown 8vo, 6s. net.

AIKMAN. Manures and the Principles of Manuring. By C. M. AIKMAN, D.Sc., F.R.S.E., &c., formerly Professor of Chemistry, Glasgow Veterinary College, and Examiner in Chemistry, University of Glasgow, &c. Second Impression. Crown 8vo, 6s. 6d.

Farmyard Manure: Its Nature, Composition, and Treatment. Crown 8vo, 1s. 6d.

ALISON.

History of Europe. By Sir ARCHIBALD ALISON, Bart., D.C.L.

1. From the Commencement of the French Revolution to the Battle of Waterloo.
   LIBRARY EDITION, 14 vols., with Portraits. Demy 8vo, £10, 10s.
   ANOTHER EDITION, in 20 vols. crown 8vo, £6.
   PEOPLE'S EDITION, 13 vols. crown 8vo, £2, 11s.

2. Continuation to the Accession of Louis Napoleon.
   LIBRARY EDITION, 8 vols. 8vo, £6, 7s. 6d.
   PEOPLE'S EDITION, 8 vols. crown 8vo. 34s.

Epitome of Alison's History of Europe. Thirtieth Thousand, 7s. 6d.

Atlas to Alison's History of Europe. By A. Keith Johnston.
   LIBRARY EDITION, demy 4to, £3, 3s.
   PEOPLE'S EDITION, 31s. 6d.

ANCIENT CLASSICS FOR ENGLISH READERS. Edited by Rev. W. LUCAS COLLINS, M.A. Price 1s. each net. *For List of Vols. see p. 2.*

ANDERSON. Matriculation Roll of St Andrews University. Edited by J. MAITLAND ANDERSON In 1 vol. demy 8vo, 18s. net

ANNALIST. Musings without Method: A Record of 1900 and 1901. By ANNALIST. Large crown 8vo, 7s. 6d.

ATKINSON. Local Government in Scotland. By MABEL ATKINSON, M.A. In 1 vol. demy 8vo, 12s. 6d. net.

AYTOUN.
Lays of the Scottish Cavaliers, and other Poems. By W. EDMONDSTOUNE AYTOUN, D.C.L., Professor of Rhetoric and Belles-Lettres in the University of Edinburgh. New Edition. Fcap. 8vo, 3s. 6d.
CHEAP EDITION. 1s. Cloth, 1s. 3d.

An Illustrated Edition of the Lays of the Scottish Cavaliers From designs by Sir NOEL PATON. Cheaper Edition. Small 4to, 10s. 6d.

BAKER. A Palace of Dreams and other Verse. By ADA BARTRICK BAKER. Crown 8vo, 5s.

BANKS. The Ethics of Work and Wealth. By D. C. BANKS. Crown 8vo, 5s. net.

BARBOUR. Thoughts from the Writings of R. W. BARBOUR. Pott 8vo, limp leather, 2s. 6d. net.

BARCLAY. A New Theory of Organic Evolution. By JAMES W. BARCLAY. In 1 vol. crown 8vo, 3s. 6d. net.

BARRINGTON.
The King's Fool. By MICHAEL BARRINGTON. Crown 8vo, 6s.
The Reminiscences of Sir Barrington Beaumont, Bart. A Novel. Crown 8vo, 6s.

BARTLETT. The Siege and Capitulation of Port Arthur. By E. ASHMEAD BARTLETT. Demy 8vo, 21s. net.

BELL. My Strange Pets, and other Memories of Country Life. By RICHARD BELL of Castle O'er. Demy 8vo, 6s. net.

BELLESHEIM. History of the Catholic Church of Scotland. From the introduction of Christianity to the Present Day. By ALPHONS BELLESHEIM, D.D., Canon of Aix-la-Chapelle. Translated, with Notes and Additions, by D. OSWALD HUNTER BLAIR, O.S.B., Monk of Fort Augustus. Cheap Edition. Complete in 4 vols. demy 8vo, with Maps. Price 21s. net.

BLACKBURN.
A Burgher Quixote. By DOUGLAS BLACKBURN, Author of 'Prinsloo of Prinsloosdorp.' Second Impression. With Frontispiece. Crown 8vo, 6s.

Richard Hartley: Prospector. Crown 8vo, 6s.

BLACKWOOD.
Annals of a Publishing House. William Blackwood and his Sons; Their Magazine and Friends. By Mrs OLIPHANT. With Four Portraits. Third Edition. Demy 8vo. Vols. I. and II. £2, 2s.
Annals of a Publishing House. Vol. III. John Blackwood. By his Daughter Mrs BLACKWOOD PORTER. With 2 Portraits and View of Strathtyrum. Demy 8vo, 21s.
Blackwood's Magazine, from Commencement in 1817 to October 1904. Nos. 1 to 1079, forming 178 Volumes.
Tales from Blackwood. First Series. Price One Shilling each, in Paper Cover. Sold separately at all Railway Bookstalls.
They may also be had bound in 12 vols., cloth, 18s. Half calf, richly gilt, 30s. Or the 12 vols. in 6, roxburghe, 21s. Half red morocco, 28s.

BLACKWOOD.
  Tales from Blackwood. Second Series. Complete in Twenty-four Shilling Parts. Handsomely bound in 12 vols., cloth, 30s. In leather back, roxburghe style, 37s. 6d. Half calf, gilt, 52s. 6d. Half morocco, 55s.
  Tales from Blackwood. Third Series. Complete in Twelve Shilling Parts. Handsomely bound in 6 vols., cloth, 15s.; and in 12 vols. cloth, 18s. The 6 vols. in roxburghe 21s. Half calf, 25s. Half morocco, 28s.
  Travel, Adventure, and Sport. From 'Blackwood's Magazine.' Uniform with 'Tales from Blackwood.' In Twelve Parts, each price 1s. Handsomely bound in 6 vols., cloth, 15s. And in half calf, 25s.
  New Educational Series. *See separate Educational Catalogue.*
  New Uniform Series of Novels (Copyright).
    Crown 8vo, cloth. Price 3s. 6d. each. Now ready:—

WENDERHOLME. By P. G. Hamerton.
THE STORY OF MARGRÉDEL. By D. Storrar Meldrum.
MISS MARJORIBANKS. By Mrs Oliphant.
THE PERPETUAL CURATE, and THE RECTOR By the Same.
SALEM CHAPEL, and THE DOCTOR'S FAMILY. By the Same.
A SENSITIVE PLANT. By E. D. Gerard.
LADY LEE'S WIDOWHOOD. By General Sir E. B. Hamley.
KATIE STEWART, and other Stories. By Mrs Oliphant.
VALENTINE AND HIS BROTHER. By the Same.
SONS AND DAUGHTERS. By the Same.

MARMORNE. By P. G. Hamerton.
REATA. By E. D. Gerard.
BEGGAR MY NEIGHBOUR. By the Same.
THE WATERS OF HERCULES. By the Same.
FAIR TO SEE. By L. W. M. Lockhart.
MINE IS THINE. By the Same.
DOUBLES AND QUITS. By the Same.
ALTIORA PETO. By Laurence Oliphant.
PICCADILLY. By the Same. With Illustrations.
LADY BABY. By D. Gerard.
THE BLACKSMITH OF VOE. By Paul Cushing.
MY TRIVIAL LIFE AND MISFORTUNE. By A Plain Woman.
POOR NELLIE. By the Same.

  Standard Novels. Uniform in size and binding. Each complete in one Volume.

    FLORIN SERIES, Illustrated Boards. Bound in Cloth, 2s. 6d.

TOM CRINGLE'S LOG. By Michael Scott.
THE CRUISE OF THE MIDGE. By the Same.
CYRIL THORNTON. By Captain Hamilton.
ANNALS OF THE PARISH. By John Galt.
THE PROVOST, &c. By the Same.
SIR ANDREW WYLIE. By the Same.
THE ENTAIL. By the Same.
MISS MOLLY. By Beatrice May Butt.
REGINALD DALTON. By J. G. Lockhart.

PEN OWEN. By Dean Hook.
ADAM BLAIR. By J. G. Lockhart.
LADY LEE'S WIDOWHOOD. By General Sir E. B. Hamley.
SALEM CHAPEL. By Mrs Oliphant.
THE PERPETUAL CURATE. By the Same.
MISS MARJORIBANKS. By the Same.
JOHN: A Love Story. By the Same.

    SHILLING SERIES, Illustrated Cover. Bound in Cloth, 1s. 6d.

THE RECTOR, and THE DOCTOR'S FAMILY. By Mrs Oliphant.
THE LIFE OF MANSIE WAUCH. By D. M. Moir.
PENINSULAR SCENES AND SKETCHES. By F. Hardman.

SIR FRIZZLE PUMPKIN, NIGHTS AT MESS, &c.
THE SUBALTERN.
LIFE IN THE FAR WEST. By G. F. Ruxton.
VALERIUS: A Roman Story. By J. G. Lockhart.

BON GAULTIER'S BOOK OF BALLADS. A new Edition, with Autobiographical Introduction by Sir THEODORE MARTIN, K.C.B. With Illustrations by Doyle, Leech, and Crowquill. Small quarto, 5s. net.

BOWHILL. Questions and Answers in the Theory and Practice of Military Topography. By Major J. H. BOWHILL. Crown 8vo, 4s. 6d. net. Portfolio containing 34 working plans and diagrams, 3s. 6d. net.

BROOKS. Daughters of Desperation. By HILDEGARD BROOKS. Small crown 8vo, 3s. 6d. net.

BRUCE. Life of John Collingwood Bruce. By Right Hon. Sir GAINSFORD BRUCE. Demy 8vo, 10s. 6d. net.

BRUCE. Our Heritage: Individual, Social, and Religious. By W. S. BRUCE, D.D., Croall Lecturer for 1903. Crown 8vo, 2s. 6d. net.

BUCHAN. The First Things. Studies in the Embryology of Religion and Natural Theology. By Rev. JOHN BUCHAN, John Knox Church, Glasgow. Crown 8vo, 5s.

BUCHAN.

The African Colony: Studies in the Reconstruction. By JOHN BUCHAN. 1 vol. demy 8vo, 15s. net.

The Watcher by the Threshold, and other Tales. Second Impression. Crown 8vo, 6s.

BURBIDGE.

Domestic Floriculture, Window Gardening, and Floral Decorations. Being Practical Directions for the Propagation, Culture, and Arrangement of Plants and Flowers as Domestic Ornaments. By F. W. BURBIDGE. Second Edition. Crown 8vo, with numerous Illustrations, 7s. 6d.

BURTON.

The History of Scotland: From Agricola's Invasion to the Extinction of the last Jacobite Insurrection. By JOHN HILL BURTON, D.C.L., Historiographer-Royal for Scotland. Cheaper Edition. In 8 vols. Crown 8vo, 2s. 6d. net each. Being issued in Monthly volumes.

The Book-Hunter. A New Edition, with specially designed Title-page and Cover by JOSEPH BROWN. Printed on antique laid paper. Post 8vo, 3s. 6d.

The Scot Abroad. Uniform with 'The Book-Hunter.' Post 8vo, 3s. 6d.

BUTE.

The Roman Breviary: Reformed by Order of the Holy Œcumenical Council of Trent; Published by Order of Pope St Pius V.; and Revised by Clement VIII. and Urban VIII.; together with the Offices since granted. Translated out of Latin into English by JOHN, MARQUESS OF BUTE, K.T. New Edition, Revised and Enlarged. In 4 vols. crown 8vo, and in 1 vol. crown 4to. [*In the press.*

The Altus of St Columba. With a Prose Paraphrase and Notes By JOHN, MARQUESS OF BUTE, K.T. In paper cover, 2s. 6d.

Sermones, Fratris Adæ, Ordinis Præmonstratensis, &c. Twenty-eight Discourses of Adam Scotus of Whithorn, hitherto unpublished; to which is added a Collection of Notes by the same, illustrative of the rule of St Augustine. Edited, at the desire of the late MARQUESS OF BUTE, K.T., LL.D., &c., by WALTER DE GRAY BIRCH, LL.D., F.S.A., of the British Museum, &c. Royal 8vo, 25s. net.

Catalogue of a Collection of Original MSS. formerly belonging to the Holy Office of the Inquisition in the Canary Islands. Prepared under the direction of the late MARQUESS OF BUTE, K.T., LL.D., by WALTER DE GRAY BIRCH, LL.D., F.S.A. 2 vols. royal 8vo, £3, 3s. net.

BUTE, MACPHAIL, AND LONSDALE. The Arms of the Royal and Parliamentary Burghs of Scotland. By JOHN, MARQUESS OF BUTE, K.T., J. R. N. MACPHAIL, and H. W. LONSDALE. With 131 Engravings on wood, and 11 other Illustrations. Crown 4to. £2, 2s. net.

BUTE, STEVENSON, AND LONSDALE. The Arms of the Baronial and Police Burghs of Scotland. By JOHN, MARQUESS OF BUTE, K.T., J. H. STEVENSON, and H. W. LONSDALE. With numerous Illustrations. Crown 4to, £2, 2s. net.

BUTT. Miss Molly. By BEATRICE MAY BUTT. Cheap Edition, 2s.

CAIRD. Sermons. By JOHN CAIRD, D.D., Principal of the University of Glasgow. Seventeenth Thousand. Fcap. 8vo, 5s.

CALDWELL. Schopenhauer's System in its Philosophical Significance (the Shaw Fellowship Lectures, 1893). By WILLIAM CALDWELL, M.A., D.Sc., Professor of Moral and Social Philosophy, Northwestern University, U.S.A.; formerly Assistant to the Professor of Logic and Metaphysics, Edin., and Examiner in Philosophy in the University of St Andrews. Demy 8vo, 10s. 6d. net.

CALLWELL.

The Effect of Maritime Command on Land Campaigns since Waterloo. By Lt.-Col. C. E. CALLWELL, R.G.A. With Plans. Post 8vo, 6s. net.

Tactics of To-day. Sixth Impression. Crown 8vo, 2s. 6d. net.

Military Operations and Maritime Preponderance: Their Relations and Interdependence. Demy 8vo, 15s. net.

CAMPBELL. Balmerino and its Abbey. A Parish History, With Notices of the Adjacent District. By JAMES CAMPBELL, D.D., F.S.A. Scot., Minister of Balmerino; Author of 'A History of the Celtic Church in Scotland.' A New Edition. With an Appendix of Illustrative Documents, a Map of the Parish, and upwards of 40 Illustrations. Demy 8vo, 30s. net.

CAREY.

Monsieur Martin: A Romance of the Great Northern War. By WYMOND CAREY. Crown 8vo, 6s.

For the White Rose. Crown 8vo, 6s.

CARLYLE. A History of Mediæval Political Theory in the West. By R. W. CARLYLE, C.I.E., Balliol College, Oxford; and A. J. CARLYLE, M.A., Chaplain and Lecturer (late Fellow) of University College, Oxford. In 3 vols. demy 8vo. Vol. I.—A History of Political Theory from the Roman Lawyers of the Second Century to the Political Writers of the Ninth. By A. J. CARLYLE. 15s. net.

"CHASSEUR." A Study of the Russo-Japanese War. By "CHASSEUR." Demy 8vo. [*In the press.*

CHESNEY. The Dilemma. By General Sir GEORGE CHESNEY, K.C.B. A New Edition. Crown 8vo, 2s.

CHRONICLES OF WESTERLY. A Provincial Sketch. By the Author of 'Culmshire Folk,' 'John Orlebar,' &c. New Edition. Crown 8vo, 6s.

CHURCH SERVICE SOCIETY.

A Book of Common Order: being Forms of Worship issued by the Church Service Society. Seventh Edition, carefully revised. In 1 vol. crown 8vo, cloth, 3s. 6d.; French morocco, 5s. Also in 2 vols. crown 8vo, cloth, 4s.; French morocco, 6s. 6d.

Daily Offices for Morning and Evening Prayer throughout the Week. Crown 8vo, 3s. 6d.

Order of Divine Service for Children. Issued by the Church Service Society. With Scottish Hymnal. Cloth, 3d.

CLIFFORD.

Sally: A Study; and other Tales of the Outskirts. By HUGH CLIFFORD, C.M.G. Crown 8vo, 6s.

Bush-Whacking, and other Sketches. Second Impression. Crown 8vo, 6s.

CLODD. Thomas Henry Huxley. "Modern English Writers." By EDWARD CLODD. Crown 8vo, 2s. 6d.

CLOUSTON.

The Lunatic at Large. By J. STORER CLOUSTON. Fourth Impression. Crown 8vo, 6s. PEOPLE'S EDITION, royal 8vo, 6d.

The Adventures of M. D'Haricot. Second Impression. Crown 8vo, 6s. PEOPLE'S EDITION, royal 8vo, 6d.

Our Lady's Inn. Crown 8vo, 6s.

Garmiscath. Crown 8vo, 6s.

COLLINS.

A Scholar of his College. By W. E. W. COLLINS. Crown 8vo, 6s.

The Don and the Undergraduate. A Tale of St Hilary's College, Oxford. Second Impression. Crown 8vo, 6s.

Episodes of Rural Life. Crown 8vo 6s.

CONRAD.

Lord Jim. A Tale. By JOSEPH CONRAD, Author of 'The Nigger of the Narcissus,' 'An Outcast of the Islands,' 'Tales of Unrest,' &c. Second Impression. Crown 8vo, 6s.

Youth: A Narrative; and Two other Stories. Second Impression. Crown 8vo, 6s.

COOPER. Liturgy of 1637, commonly called Laud's Liturgy. Edited by the Rev. Professor COOPER, D.D., Glasgow. Crown 8vo, 7s. 6d. net.

CORNFORD. R. L. Stevenson. "Modern English Writers." By L. COPE CORNFORD. Second Edition. Crown 8vo, 2s. 6d.

COTTON. The Company of Death. By ALBERT LOUIS COTTON. Crown 8vo, 6s.

COUNTY HISTORIES OF SCOTLAND. In demy 8vo volumes of about 350 pp. each. With Maps. Price 7s. 6d. net.

Fife and Kinross. By ÆNEAS J. G. MACKAY, LL.D., Sheriff of these Counties.

Dumfries and Galloway. By Sir HERBERT MAXWELL, Bart., M.P. Second Edition.

Moray and Nairn. By CHARLES RAMPINI, LL.D., Sheriff of Dumfries and Galloway.

Inverness. By J. CAMERON LEES, D.D.

Roxburgh, Selkirk, and Peebles. By Sir GEORGE DOUGLAS, Bart.

Aberdeen and Banff. By WILLIAM WATT, Editor of Aberdeen 'Daily Free Press.'

COUNTY HISTORIES OF SCOTLAND..
Perth and Clackmannan. By JOHN CHISHOLM, M.A., Advocate.
[In the press.
Edinburgh and Linlithgow. By WILLIAM KIRK DICKSON,
Advocate. [In the press.

COWELL. Day-Book from 'The Fairie Queene.' By A. COWELL.

CRAIK. A Century of Scottish History. From the Days before the '45 to those within living Memory. By Sir HENRY CRAIK, K.C.B., M.A. (Oxon.), Hon. LL.D. (Glasgow). 2 vols. demy 8vo, 30s. net.

CRAWFORD. Saracinesca. By F. MARION CRAWFORD, Author of 'Mr Isaacs,' &c., &c. Crown 8vo, 3s. 6d. Also at 6d.

CRAWFORD. The Mysteries of Christianity. By the late THOMAS J. CRAWFORD, D.D., Professor of Divinity in the University of Edinburgh. Crown 8vo, 7s. 6d.

CREED. The Fight. By SYBIL CREED. **Crown 8vo, 6s.**

CROSS.
Impressions of Dante and of the New World. By J. W. CROSS. Post 8vo, 6s.
The Rake's Progress in Finance. Crown 8vo, 2s. net.

CUMMING.
Memories. By C. F. GORDON CUMMING. Demy 8vo. Illustrated, 20s net.
At Home in Fiji. Post 8vo. Illustrated. Cheap Edition, 6s.
A Lady's Cruise in a French Man-of-War. Post 8vo. Illustrated. Cheap Edition. 6s.
Fire-Fountains. 2 vols. post 8vo. Illustrated, 25s.
Granite Crags. Post 8vo. Illustrated. Cheap Edition. 6s.
Wanderings in China. Small post 8vo. Cheap Edition. 6s.

DAVIDSON. Herbart's Psychology and Educational Theory. By JOHN DAVIDSON. Demy 8vo, 5s. net.

DESCARTES. The Method, Meditations, and Principles of Philosophy of Descartes. Translated from the Original French and Latin. With a New Introductory Essay, Historical and Critical, on the Cartesian Philosophy. By Professor VEITCH, LL.D., Glasgow University. Eleventh Edition. 6s. 6d.

DICKSON. Life of Major-General Sir R. Murdoch Smith, K.C.M.G. By WILLIAM KIRK DICKSON. Demy 8vo, 15s. net.

DODDS AND MACPHERSON. The Licensing Acts (Scotland) Consolidation and Amendment Act, 1903. Annotated by Mr J. M. DODDS, of the Scottish Office; Joint-Editor of the 'Parish Council Guide for Scotland,' and Mr EWAN MACPHERSON, Advocate, Legal Secretary to the Lord Advocate. In 1 vol. crown 8vo, 5s. net.

DOUGLAS.
The Ethics of John Stuart Mill. By CHARLES DOUGLAS, M.A., D.Sc., M.P., late Lecturer in Moral Philosophy, and Assistant to the Professor of Moral Philosophy in the University of Edinburgh. Post 8vo, 6s. net.
John Stuart Mill: A Study of his Philosophy. Crown 8vo 4s. 6d. net.

ECCOTT.
>   Fortune's Castaway. By W. J. ECCOTT. Crown 8vo, 6s.
>   His Indolence of Arras. Crown 8vo, 6s.

ELIOT.
>   **George Eliot's Life, Related in Her Letters and Journals.**
>   Arranged and Edited by her husband, J. W. CROSS. With Portrait and other Illustrations. Third Edition. 3 vols. post 8vo, 42s.
>
>   **George Eliot's Life. With Portrait and other Illustrations.**
>   New Edition, in one volume. Crown 8vo, 7s. 6d.
>
>   **Life and Works of George Eliot (Warwick Edition).** 14 volumes, cloth, limp, gilt top, 2s. net per volume; leather, limp, gilt top, 2s. 6d. net per volume; leather, gilt top, with book-marker, 3s. net per volume.

ADAM BEDE. 826 pp.	MIDDLEMARCH. 2 vols. 664 and 630 pp.
THE MILL ON THE FLOSS. 828 pp.	DANIEL DERONDA. 2 vols. 616 and 636 pp.
FELIX HOLT, THE RADICAL. 718 pp.	THE SPANISH GYPSY; JUBAL
ROMOLA. 900 pp.	ESSAYS; THEOPHRASTUS SUCH.
SCENES OF CLERICAL LIFE. 624 pp.	LIFE. 2 vols., 626 and 580 pp.
SILAS MARNER; BROTHER JACOB; THE LIFTED VEIL. 560 pp.	

>   **Works of George Eliot (Standard Edition).** 21 volumes, crown 8vo. In buckram cloth, gilt top, 2s. 6d. per vol.; or in roxburghe binding, 3s. 6d. per vol.
>   ADAM BEDE. 2 vols.—THE MILL ON THE FLOSS. 2 vols.—FELIX HOLT, THE RADICAL. 2 vols.—ROMOLA. 2 vols.—SCENES OF CLERICAL LIFE. 2 vols.—MIDDLEMARCH. 3 vols.—DANIEL DERONDA. 3 vols.—SILAS MARNER. 1 vol.—JUBAL. 1 vol.—THE SPANISH GYPSY. 1 vol.—ESSAYS. 1 vol.—THEOPHRASTUS SUCH. 1 vol.
>
>   **Life and Works of George Eliot (Cabinet Edition).** 24 volumes, crown 8vo, price £6. Also to be had handsomely bound in half and full calf. The Volumes are sold separately, bound in cloth, price 5s. each.
>
>   **Novels by George Eliot. Popular Copyright Edition.** In new uniform binding, price 3s. 6d. each.

ADAM BEDE.	SILAS MARNER; THE LIFTED VEIL; BROTHER JACOB.
THE MILL ON THE FLOSS.	
SCENES OF CLERICAL LIFE.	MIDDLEMARCH.
ROMOLA.	DANIEL DERONDA.
FELIX HOLT, THE RADICAL.	

>   Essays. New Edition. Crown 8vo, 5s.
>   Impressions of Theophrastus Such. New Edition. Crown 8vo, 5s.
>   The Spanish Gypsy. New Edition. Crown 8vo, 5s.
>   The Legend of Jubal, and other Poems, Old and New. New Edition. Crown 8vo, 5s.
>   Silas Marner. New Edition, with Illustrations by Reginald Birch. Crown 8vo, 6s. Cheap Edition, 2s. 6d. People's Edition, royal 8vo, paper cover, price 6d.
>   Scenes of Clerical Life. Pocket Edition, 3 vols. pott 8vo, 1s. net each; bound in leather, 1s. 6d. net each. Cheap Edition, 3s. Illustrated Edition, with 20 Illustrations by H. R. Millar, crown 8vo, 2s.; paper covers, 1s. People's Edition, royal 8vo, in paper cover, price 6d.
>   Felix Holt. People's Edition. Royal 8vo, in paper cover, 6d.
>   Adam Bede. Pocket Edition. In 1 vol. pott 8vo, 1s. net; bound in leather, in 3 vols., 4s. 6d. net. People's Edition, royal 8vo, in paper cover, price 6d. New Edition, crown 8vo, paper cover, 1s.; crown 8vo, with Illustrations, cloth, 2s.

ELIOT.
   The Mill on the Floss. Pocket Edition, 2 vols. pott 8vo,
      cloth, 3s. net; limp leather, 4s. 6d. net. People's Edition, royal 8vo, in paper cover, price 6d. New Edition, paper covers, 1s.; cloth, 2s.
   Romola. People's Edition. Royal 8vo, in paper cover, price 6d.
   Silas Marner; Brother Jacob; Lifted Veil. Pocket Edition.
      Pott 8vo, cloth, 1s. 6d. net; limp leather, 2s. 3d. net.
   Wise, Witty, and Tender Sayings, in Prose and Verse. Selected from the Works of GEORGE ELIOT. New Edition. Fcap. 8vo, 3s. 6d.

ELLIS.
   Barbara Winslow, Rebel. By BETH ELLIS. Crown 8vo, 6s.
   Madame, Will You Walk? Crown 8vo, 6s.

ELTON. The Augustan Ages. "Periods of European Literature." By OLIVER ELTON, B.A., Lecturer in English Literature, Owen's College Manchester. Crown 8vo, 5s. net.

FAHIE. A History of Wireless Telegraphy. Including some Bare-wire Proposals for Subaqueous Telegraphs. By J. J. FAHIE, Member of the Institution of Electrical Engineers, London, and of the Société Internationale des Electriciens, Paris; Author of 'A History of Electric Telegraphy to the Year 1837,' &c. With Illustrations. Third Edition, Revised. Crown 8vo, 6s.

FAITHS OF THE WORLD, The. A Concise History of the Great Religious Systems of the World. By various Authors. Crown 8vo, 5s.

FERGUSSON. Scots Poems. By ROBERT FERGUSSON. With Photogravure Portrait. Pott 8vo, gilt top, bound in cloth, 1s. net; leather, 1s. 6d. net.

FERRIER. Philosophical Remains. Crown 8vo, 14s.

FISHER. One London Season. By CAROLINE FISHER. Crown 8vo, 6s.

FLINT.
   Philosophy as Scientia Scientiarum. A History of Classifications of the Sciences. By ROBERT FLINT, Corresponding Member of the Institute of France, Hon. Member of the Royal Society of Palermo, Professor in the University of Edinburgh, &c. 12s. 6d. net.
   Studies on Theological, Biblical, and other Subjects. 7s. 6d. net.
   Historical Philosophy in France and French Belgium and Switzerland. 8vo, 21s.
   Agnosticism. Demy 8vo, 18s. net.
   Theism. Being the Baird Lecture for 1876. Tenth Edition Revised. Crown 8vo, 7s. 6d.
   Anti-Theistic Theories. Being the Baird Lecture for 1877. Fifth Edition. Crown 8vo, 10s. 6d.
   Sermons and Addresses. Demy 8vo, 7s. 6d

FORBES. Helena: a Novel. By Mrs H. O. FORBES. Crown 8vo, 6s.

FORD. A History of Cambridge University Cricket Club. By W. J. FORD, Author of 'A History of Middlesex County Cricket,' &c. With Illustrations. Demy 8vo, 15s. net.

FOREIGN CLASSICS FOR ENGLISH READERS. Edited by Mrs OLIPHANT. Price 1s. each net. *For List of Volumes, see page 2.*

FORREST.

History of the Indian Mutiny. By G. W. FORREST, C.I.E., Ex-Director of Records, Government of India. 2 vols. demy 8vo, 38s. net.

Sepoy Generals: Wellington to Roberts. With Portraits. Crown 8vo, 6s.

FORSTER. Where Angels Fear to Tread. By E. M. FORSTER. Crown 8vo, 6s.

FOULIS. Erchie: My Droll Friend. By HUGH FOULIS. Paper covers, 1s. net; cloth, 1s. 6d. net.

FRANKLIN. My Brilliant Career. By MILES FRANKLIN. Fourth Impression. Crown 8vo, 6s.

FRASER.

Philosophy of Theism. Being the Gifford Lectures delivered before the University of Edinburgh in 1894-96. By ALEXANDER CAMPBELL FRASER, D.C.L. Oxford; Emeritus Professor of Logic and Metaphysics in the University of Edinburgh. Second Edition, Revised. Post 8vo, 6s. 6d. net.

Biographia Philosophica. In 1 vol. demy 8vo, 6s. net.

FRENCH COOKERY FOR ENGLISH HOMES. Third Impression. Crown 8vo, limp cloth, 2s. 6d. Also in limp leather, 3s.

GALLOWAY. Studies in the Philosophy of Religion. By GEORGE GALLOWAY, B.D. Demy 8vo, 7s. 6d. net.

GENERAL ASSEMBLY OF THE CHURCH OF SCOTLAND.

Scottish Hymnal, With Appendix Incorporated. Published for use in Churches by Authority of the General Assembly. 1. Large type, cloth, red edges, 2s. 6d.; French morocco, 4s. 2. Bourgeois type, limp cloth, 1s.; French morocco, 2s. 3. Nonpareil type, cloth, red edges, 6d.; French morocco, 1s. 4d. 4. Paper covers, 3d. 5. Sunday-School Edition, paper covers, 1d., cloth, 2d. No. 1, bound with the Psalms and Paraphrases, French morocco, 8s. No. 2, bound with the Psalms and Paraphrases, cloth, 2s.; French morocco, 3s.

Prayers for Social and Family Worship. Prepared by a Special Committee of the General Assembly of the Church of Scotland. Entirely New Edition, Revised and Enlarged. Fcap. 8vo, red edges, 2s.

Prayers for Family Worship. A Selection of Four Weeks' Prayers. New Edition. Authorised by the General Assembly of the Church of Scotland. Fcap. 8vo, red edges, 1s. 6d.

One Hundred Prayers. Prepared by the Committee on Aids to Devotion. 16mo, cloth limp, 6d.

Morning and Evening Prayers for Affixing to Bibles. Prepared by the Committee on Aids to Devotion. 1d. for 6, or 1s. per 100.

Prayers for Soldiers and Sailors. Prepared by the Committee on Aids to Devotion. Thirtieth Thousand. 16mo, cloth limp. 2d. net.

Prayers for Sailors and Fisher-Folk. Prepared and Published by Instruction of the General Assembly of the Church of Scotland. Fcap. 8vo, 1s. net.

GERARD.

Reata: What's in a Name. By E. D. GERARD. Cheap Edition. Crown 8vo, 3s. 6d.

Beggar my Neighbour. Cheap Edition. Crown 8vo, 3s. 6d.

GERARD.
> The Waters of Hercules. Cheap Edition. Crown 8vo, 3s. 6d.
> A Sensitive Plant. Crown 8vo, 3s. 6d.

GERARD.
> A Foreigner. An Anglo-German Study. By E. GERARD (Madame de Laszowska). Crown 8vo, 6s.
> Bis: Some Tales Retold. Crown 8vo, 6s.

GERARD.
> One Year. By DOROTHEA GERARD (Madame Longard de Longgarde). Crown 8vo, 6s.
> The Impediment. Crown 8vo, 6s.
> A Forgotten Sin. Crown 8vo, 6s.
> A Spotless Reputation. Third Edition. Crown 8vo, 6s.
> The Wrong Man. Second Edition. Crown 8vo, 6s.
> Lady Baby. Cheap Edition. Crown 8vo, 3s. 6d.
> Recha. Crown 8vo, 6s.

GIBBON.
> Souls in Bondage. By PERCEVAL GIBBON. Crown 8vo, 6s.
> The Vrouw Grobelaar's Leading Cases. Crown 8vo, 6s.

GILLESPIE. The Humour of Scottish Life. By Very Rev. JOHN GILLESPIE, LL.D. Crown 8vo, 3s. 6d. net.

GLEIG. Personal Reminiscences of the First Duke of Wellington, with Sketches of some of his Guests and Contemporaries. By Rev. G. R. GLEIG, author of 'The Subaltern.' Demy 8vo, 15s. net.

GOODALL. Association Football. By JOHN GOODALL. Edited by S. ARCHIBALD DE BEAR. With Diagrams. Fcap. 8vo, 1s.

GORDON. The Sikhs. By General Sir JOHN J. H. GORDON, K.C.B. With Illustrations. Demy 8vo, 7s. 6d. net.

GOUDIE. The Celtic and Scandinavian Antiquities of Shetland. By GILBERT GOUDIE, F.S.A. Scot. Demy 8vo, 7s. 6d. net.

GRAHAM.
> Manual of the Elections (Scot.) (Corrupt and Illegal Practices) Act, 1890. With Analysis, Relative Act of Sederunt, Appendix containing the Corrupt Practices Acts of 1883 and 1885, and Copious Index. By J. EDWARD GRAHAM, Advocate. 8vo, 4s. 6d.
> A Manual of the Acts relating to Education in Scotland. (Founded on that of the late Mr Craig Sellar.) Demy 8vo, 18s.

GRAND.
> A Domestic Experiment. By SARAH GRAND, Author of 'The Heavenly Twins,' 'Ideala: A Study from Life.' Crown 8vo, 6s.
> Singularly Deluded. Crown 8vo, 6s.

GREEN. Elizabeth Grey. By E. M. GREEN. Crown 8vo, 6s.

GRIER.

In Furthest Ind. The Narrative of Mr. EDWARD CARLYON of Ellswether, in the County of Northampton, and late of the Honourable East India Company's Service, Gentleman. Wrote by his own hand in the year of grace 1697. Edited, with a few Explanatory Notes. By SYDNEY C. GRIER. Post 8vo, 6s. Cheap Edition, 2s.

His Excellency's English Governess. Third Impression. Cr. 8vo, 6s. Cheap Edition, 2s.

An Uncrowned King: A Romance of High Politics. Second Impression. Crown 8vo, 6s. Cheap Edition, 2s.

Peace with Honour. Third Impression. Crown 8vo, 6s. Cheap Edition, 2s.

A Crowned Queen: The Romance of a Minister of State. Second Impression. Crown 8vo, 6s. Cheap Edition, 2s.

Like Another Helen. Second Impression. Cr. 8vo, 6s. Cheap Edition, 2s.

The Kings of the East: A Romance of the near Future. Second Impression. Crown 8vo, 6s. Cheap Edition, 2s.

The Warden of the Marches. Third Impression. Crown 8vo, 6s. Cheap Edition, 2s. Popular Edition, 6d.

The Prince of the Captivity. Second Impression. Crown 8vo, 6s.

The Advanced-Guard. Third Impression. Crown 8vo, 6s.

The Great Proconsul: The Memoirs of Mrs Hester Ward, formerly in the family of the Hon. Warren Hastings, Esquire, late Governor-General of India. Crown 8vo, 6s.

The Letters of Warren Hastings to his Wife. Demy 8vo, 15s. net.

GROOT. Jan Van Dyck. By J. MORGAN-DE-GROOT. Crown 8vo, 6s.

GUNN. Stock Exchange Securities. By N. B. Gunn. Demy 8vo, 2s. net

HALDANE. How we Escaped from Pretoria. By Lieut.-Colonel AYLMER HALDANE, D.S.O., 2nd Battalion Gordon Highlanders. New Edition, revised and enlarged. With numerous Illustrations, Plans, and Map. Crown 8vo, 1s.

HALIBURTON. Horace in Homespun. By HUGH HALIBURTON. A New Edition, containing additional Poems. With 26 Illustrations by A. S. Boyd. Post 8vo, 6s. net.

HAMLEY.

The Operations of War Explained and Illustrated. By General Sir EDWARD BRUCE HAMLEY, K.C.B., K.C.M.G. Second Edition of Fifth Edition. With Maps and Plans. 4to, 30s. Also in 2 parts: Part I., 10s. 6d.; Part II., 21s.

Thomas Carlyle: An Essay. Second Edition. Crown 8vo, 2s. 6d.

On Outposts. Second Edition. 8vo, 2s.

HAMLEY.
>   Lady Lee's Widowhood. New Edition. Crown 8vo, 2s.
>   Our Poor Relations. A Philozoic Essay. With Illustrations, chiefly by Ernest Griset. Crown 8vo, cloth gilt, 3s. 6d.

HANNAY. The Later Renaissance. "Periods of European Literature." By DAVID HANNAY. Crown 8vo, 5s. net.

HARRADEN.
>   Ships that Pass in the Night. By BEATRICE HARRADEN. Illustrated Edition. Crown 8vo, 3s. 6d.
>   The Fowler. Illustrated Edition. Crown 8vo, 3s. 6d. People's Edition, paper covers, 6d.
>   In Varying Moods: Short Stories. Illustrated Edition. Crown 8vo, 3s. 6d.
>   Hilda Strafford, and The Remittance Man. Two Californian Stories. Illustrated Edition. Crown 8vo, 3s. 6d.
>   Untold Tales of the Past. With 40 Illustrations by H. R. Millar. Square crown 8vo, gilt top, 5s. net.
>   Katharine Frensham. Crown 8vo, 6s. People's Edition, paper covers, 6d.

HARRIS.
>   The Disappearance of Dick. By WALTER B. HARRIS. With 17 Illustrations. Crown 8vo, 5s.
>   The Career of Harold Ensleigh. Crown 8vo, 6s.

HARTLEY. Wild Sport with Gun, Rifle, and Salmon-Rod. By GILFRID W. HARTLEY. With numerous Illustrations in photogravure and half-tone from drawings by G. E. LODGE and others. Demy 8vo, 6s. net.

HAY-NEWTON. Readings on the Evolution of Religion. By Mrs F. HAY-NEWTON. Crown 8vo, 5s.

HEMANS.
>   The Poetical Works of Mrs Hemans. Copyright Edition. Royal 8vo, with Engravings, cloth, gilt edges, 5s.
>   Select Poems of Mrs Hemans. Fcap., cloth, gilt edges, 3s.

HENDERSON. The Young Estate Manager's Guide. By RICHARD HENDERSON, Member (by Examination) of the Royal Agricultural Society of England, the Highland and Agricultural Society of Scotland, and the Surveyors' Institution. With an Introduction by R. Patrick Wright, F.R.S.E., Professor of Agriculture, Glasgow and West of Scotland Technical College. With Plans and Diagrams. Crown 8vo, 5s.

HENDERSON. The Minstrelsy of the Scottish Border. By Sir WALTER SCOTT. A New Edition. Edited by T. F. Henderson, Author of 'A History of Scottish Vernacular Literature.' With a New Portrait of Sir Walter Scott. In 4 vols., demy 8vo, £2, 2s. net.

HERFORD. Browning (Modern English Writers). By Professor HERFORD. Crown 8vo, 2s. 6d.

HERKLESS AND HANNAY. The College of St Leonard's. By JOHN HERKLESS and ROBERT KERR HANNAY. Post 8vo, 7s. 6d. net.

HEWISON. The Isle of Bute in the Olden Time. With Illustrations, Maps, and Plans. By JAMES KING HEWISON, D.D., R.S.A. (Scot.), Minister of Rothesay. Vol. I., Celtic Saints and Heroes. Crown 4to, 15s. net. Vol. II., The Royal Stewards and the Brandanes. Crown 4to, 15s. net.

HOME PRAYERS. By Ministers of the Church of Scotland and Members of the Church Service Society. Second Edition. Fcap. 8vo, 3s.

HUNT. A Handy Vocabulary: English-Afrikander, Afrikander-English. For the Use of English-speaking People in South Africa. By G. M. G. HUNT. Small 8vo, 1s.

HUTCHINSON. Hints on the Game of Golf. By HORACE G. HUTCHINSON. Twelfth Edition, Revised. Fcap. 8vo, cloth, 1s.

HUTTON.
Frederic Uvedale. By EDWARD HUTTON. Crown 8vo, 6s.
Italy and the Italians. With Illustrations. Second Edition. Large crown 8vo, 6s.

IDDESLEIGH. Life, Letters, and Diaries of Sir Stafford Northcote, First Earl of Iddesleigh. By ANDREW LANG. With Three Portraits and a View of Pynes. Third Edition. 2 vols. post 8vo, 31s. 6d.
POPULAR EDITION. With Portrait and View of Pynes. Post 8vo, 3s. 6d.

INNES.
Free Church Union Case. Judgment of the House of Lords. With Introduction by A. TAYLOR INNES. Demy 8vo, 1s. net.
The Law of Creeds in Scotland. A Treatise on the Relations of Churches in Scotland, Established and not Established, to the Civil Law. Demy 8vo, 10s. net.

INTELLIGENCE OFFICER.
On the Heels of De Wet. By THE INTELLIGENCE OFFICER. Sixth Impression. Crown 8vo, 6s. People's Edition, royal 8vo, paper cover, 6d.
The Boy Galloper. With Illustrations. In 1 vol. cr. 8vo, 6s.
The Yellow War. Crown 8vo, 6s. Popular Edition, paper covers, 6d.

IRONS. The Psychology of Ethics. By DAVID IRONS, M.A., Ph.D., Professor of Philosophy in Bryn Mawr College, Penn. Crown 8vo, 5s. net.

JAMES. William Wetmore Story and his Friends. From Letters, Diaries, and Recollections. By HENRY JAMES. With 2 Portraits. In two vols. post 8vo, 24s. net.

JAMES.
Modern Strategy. By Lieut.-Col. WALTER H. JAMES, P.S.C., late R.E. With 6 Maps. Second Edition, thoroughly revised and brought up to date. Royal 8vo, 16s. net.
The Development of Tactics from 1740 to the Present Day. Demy 8vo. [*In the press.*]

JOHNSTON.
The Chemistry of Common Life. By Professor J. F. W. JOHNSTON. New Edition, Revised. By ARTHUR HERBERT CHURCH, M.A. Oxon. Author of 'Food: its Sources, Constituents, and Uses,' &c. With Maps and 102 Engravings. Crown 8vo, 7s. 6d.
Elements of Agricultural Chemistry. An entirely New Edition from the Edition by Sir CHARLES A. CAMERON, M.D., F.R.C.S.I. &c. Revised and brought down to date by C. M. AIKMAN, M.A., B.Sc., F.R.S.E., Professor of Chemistry, Glasgow Veterinary College. 17th Edition. Crown 8vo, 6s. 6d.
Catechism of Agricultural Chemistry. An entirely New Edition from the Edition by Sir CHARLES A. CAMERON. Revised and Enlarged by C. M. AIKMAN, M.A., &c. 95th Thousand. With numerous Illustrations. Crown 8vo, 1s.

JOHNSTON. Agricultural Holdings (Scotland) Acts, 1883 to 1900; and the Ground Game Act, 1880. With Notes, and Summary of Procedure, &c. By CHRISTOPHER N. JOHNSTON, M.A., Advocate. Fifth Edition. Demy 8vo, 6s. net.

JOKAI. Timar's Two Worlds. By MAURUS JOKAI. Authorised Translation by Mrs HEGAN KENNARD. Cheap Edition. Crown 8vo, 6s.

KENNEDY. Hurrah for the Life of a Sailor! Fifty Years in the Royal Navy. By Admiral Sir WILLIAM KENNEDY, K.C.B. With Illustrations from Sketches by the Author. Fifth Impression. Demy 8vo, 12s. 6d.
CHEAPER EDITION, small demy 8vo, 6s.

KER. The Dark Ages. "Periods of European Literature." By Professor W. P. KER. In 1 vol. crown 8vo, 5s. net.

KERR.
Memories: Grave and Gay. By JOHN KERR, LL.D. With Portrait and other Illustrations. Cheaper Edition, Enlarged. Crown 8vo, 2s. 6d. net.
Other Memories: Old and New. Crown 8vo. 3s. 6d. net.

KINGLAKE.
History of the Invasion of the Crimea. By A. W. KINGLAKE. Complete in 9 vols., crown 8vo. Cheap reissue at 3s. 6d. each.
—— Abridged Edition for Military Students. Revised by Lieut.-Col. Sir GEORGE SYDENHAM CLARKE, K.C.M.G., R.E. Demy 8vo, 15s. net.
—— —— Atlas to accompany above. Folio, 9s. net.
History of the Invasion of the Crimea. Demy 8vo. Vol. VI. Winter Troubles. With a Map, 16s. Vols. VII. and VIII. From the Morrow of Inkerman to the Death of Lord Raglan. With an Index to the Whole Work. With Maps and Plans. 28s
Eothen. A New Edition, uniform with the Cabinet Edition of the 'History of the Invasion of the Crimea.' 6s.
CHEAPER EDITION. With Portrait and Biographical Sketch of the Author. Crown 8vo, 2s. 6d. net.

KINNEAR. The New House of Commons. By ALFRED KINNEAR. Second Edition, Extended. Crown 8vo, 3s. 6d. net.

KNEIPP. My Water-Cure. As Tested through more than Thirty Years, and Described for the Healing of Diseases and the Preservation of Health. By SEBASTIAN KNEIPP. With a Portrait and other Illustrations. Authorised English Translation from the Thirtieth German Edition, by A. de F. With an Appendix, containing the Latest Developments of Pfarrer Kneipp's System, and a Preface by E. Gerard. Crown 8vo, 3s. 6d.

LAMB. Saints and Savages: The Story of Five Years in the New Hebrides. By ROBERT LAMB, M.A. (N.Z.), M.B., B.D. (Edin.). With Illustrations by Julian R. Ashton, Sydney, N.S.W. Post 8vo, 6s.

LANG.
A History of Scotland from the Roman Occupation. By ANDREW LANG. Vol. I. With a Photogravure Frontispiece and Four Maps. Second Edition. Demy 8vo, 15s. net.
Vol. II. With a Photogravure Frontispiece. 15s. net.
Vol. III. With a Photogravure Frontispiece. 15s. net.
Tennyson. "Modern English Writers." 2nd Ed. Cr. 8vo, 2s. 6d.
POPULAR EDITION, paper covers, 6d. net.
Life, Letters, and Diaries of Sir Stafford Northcote, First Earl of Iddesleigh. With Three Portraits and a View of Pynes. Third Edition. 2 vols. post 8vo, 31s. 6d.
POPULAR EDITION. With Portrait and View of Pynes. Post 8vo, 3s. 6d.
The Highlands of Scotland in 1750. From Manuscript 104 in the King's Library, British Museum. With an Introduction by ANDREW LANG. Crown 8vo, 5s. net.

B

LANG.
  The Expansion of the Christian Life. The Duff Lecture for 1897. By the Rev. J. MARSHALL LANG, D.D., Principal of the University of Aberdeen. Crown 8vo, 5s.
  The Church and its Social Mission. Being the Baird Lecture for 1901. Crown 8vo, 6s. net.

LAWSON.
  The Country I Come From. By HENRY LAWSON. Crown 8vo, 6s.
  Joe Wilson and his Mates. Crown 8vo, 6s.

LAWSON. British Economics in 1904. By W. R. LAWSON. Crown 8vo, 6s. net.

LEHMANN. Crumbs of Pity, and other Verses; to which are added Six Lives of Great Men. By R. C. LEHMANN, author of 'Anni Fugaces,' &c. Crown 8vo, 5s. net.

LEIGHTON. The Life History of British Serpents, and their Local Distribution in the British Isles. By GERALD R. LEIGHTON, M.D. With 50 Illustrations. Crown 8vo, 5s. net.

LEISHMAN. The Westminster Directory. Edited, with an Introduction and Notes, by the Very Rev. T. LEISHMAN, D.D. Crown 8vo, 4s. net.

LESSING. Children of Men. By BRUNO LESSING. Crown 8vo, 5s. net.

LEYDEN. Journal of a Tour in the Highlands and Western Islands of Scotland in 1800. By JOHN LEYDEN. Edited, with a Bibliography, by JAMES SINTON. Crown 8vo, 6s. net.

LINDSAY.
  Recent Advances in Theistic Philosophy of Religion. By Rev. JAMES LINDSAY, M.A., B.D., B.Sc., F.R.S.E., F.G.S., Minister of the Parish of St Andrew's, Kilmarnock. Demy 8vo, 12s. 6d. net.
  The Progressiveness of Modern Christian Thought. Crown 8vo, 6s.
  Essays, Literary and Philosophical. Crown 8vo, 3s. 6d.
  The Significance of the Old Testament for Modern Theology. Crown 8vo, 1s. net.
  The Teaching Function of the Modern Pulpit. Crown 8vo, 1s. net

"LINESMAN."
  Words by an Eyewitness: The Struggle in Natal. By "LINESMAN." Eleventh Impression, with Three Additional Chapters. Crown 8vo, 6s.
  The Mechanism of War. Crown 8vo, 3s. 6d.

LOBBAN. An Anthology of English Verse from Chaucer to the Present Day. By J. H. LOBBAN, M.A. Crown 8vo, gilt top, 5s.

LOCKHART.
  Doubles and Quits. By LAURENCE W. M. LOCKHART. Crown 8vo, 3s. 6d. A New Edition, Crown 8vo, 2s.
  Fair to See. New Edition. Crown 8vo, 3s. 6d.
  Mine is Thine. New Edition. Crown 8vo, 3s. 6d.

LYNDEN-BELL. A Primer of Tactics, Fortification, Topography, and Military Law. By Lieut.-Colonel C. P. LYNDEN-BELL. With Diagrams. Crown 8vo, 3s. net.

MABIE.
Essays on Nature and Culture. By HAMILTON WRIGHT MABIE. With Portrait. Fcap. 8vo, 3s. 6d.
Books and Culture. Fcap. 8vo, 3s. 6d.

MACDONALD. A Manual of the Criminal Law (Scotland) Procedure Act, 1887. By NORMAN DORAN MACDONALD. Revised by the LORD JUSTICE-CLERK. 8vo, 10s. 6d.

MACDOUGALL AND DODDS. A Manual of the Local Government (Scotland) Act, 1894. With Introduction, Explanatory Notes, and Copious Index. By J. PATTEN MACDOUGALL, Legal Secretary to the Lord Advocate, and J. M. DODDS. New and Revised Edition. [*In preparation.*

MACKENZIE. Studies in Roman Law. With Comparative Views of the Laws of France, England, and Scotland. By LORD MACKENZIE, one of the Judges of the Court of Session in Scotland. Seventh Edition, Edited by JOHN KIRKPATRICK, M.A., LL.B., Advocate, Professor of History in the University of Edinburgh. 8vo, 21s.

MACKINLAY, J. M. Influence of the Pre-Reformation Church on Scottish Place-Names. By J. M. MACKINLAY, F.S.A. Scot. Demy 8vo, 12s. 6d. net.

MACLAGAN, R. C. The Perth Incident of 1396. By R. C. MACLAGAN, M.D. Demy 8vo, 5s. net.

MACLEOD. The Doctrine and Validity of the Ministry and Sacraments of the National Church of Scotland. By the Very Rev. DONALD MACLEOD, D.D. Being the Baird Lecture for 1903. Crown 8vo, 6s. net.

MACPHERSON. Books to Read and How to Read Them. By HECTOR MACPHERSON. Second Impression. Crown 8vo, 3s. 6d. net.

MAIN. Three Hundred English Sonnets. Chosen and Edited by DAVID M. MAIN. New Edition. Fcap. 8vo, 3s. 6d.

MAIR.
A Digest of Laws and Decisions, Ecclesiastical and Civil, relating to the Constitution, Practice, and Affairs of the Church of Scotland. With Notes and Forms of Procedure. By the Rev. WILLIAM MAIR, D.D., lately Minister of the Parish of Earlston. New Edition, Revised. In 1 vol. crown 8vo, 12s. 6d. net.

Speaking; or, From Voice Production to the Platform and Pulpit. Third Edition, Revised. Crown 8vo, 3s.

MAITLAND. The Surrender of Napoleon. Being the Narrative of the Surrender of Buonaparte, and of his residence on board H.M.S. Bellerophon; with a detail of the principal events that occurred in that Ship between the 24th of May and the 8th of August 1815. By Rear-Admiral Sir FREDERICK LEWIS MAITLAND, K.C.B. A New Edition. Edited, with a Life of the Author, by WILLIAM KIRK DICKSON. In 1 vol. post 8vo, with Portraits and other Illustrations. Demy 8vo 15s. net.

MARSHMAN. History of India. From the Earliest Period to the present time. By JOHN CLARK MARSHMAN, C.S.I. Third and Cheaper Edition. Post 8vo, with Map, 6s.

MARTIN.

Poems of Giacomo Leopardi. Translated by Sir THEODORE MARTIN, K.C.B. Crown 8vo, 5s. net.

The Æneid of Virgil. Books I.-VI. Translated by Sir THEODORE MARTIN, K.C.B. Post 8vo, 7s. 6d.

Goethe's Faust. Part I. Translated into English Verse. Second Edition, crown 8vo, 6s. Ninth Edition, fcap. 8vo, 3s. 6d.

Goethe's Faust. Part II. Translated into English Verse. Second Edition, Revised. Fcap. 8vo, 6s.

The Works of Horace. Translated into English Verse, with Life and Notes. 2 vols. New Edition. Crown 8vo, 21s.

Poems and Ballads of Heinrich Heine. Done into English Verse. Third Edition. Small crown 8vo, 5s.

The Song of the Bell, and other Translations from Schiller, Goethe, Uhland, and Others. Crown 8vo, 7s. 6d.

Madonna Pia: A Tragedy; and Three Other Dramas. Crown 8vo, 7s. 6d.

Catullus. With Life and Notes. Second Edition, Revised and Corrected. Post 8vo, 7s. 6d.

The 'Vita Nuova' of Dante. Translated with an Introduction and Notes. Fourth Edition. Small crown 8vo, 5s.

Aladdin: A Dramatic Poem. By ADAM OEHLENSCHLAEGER. Fcap. 8vo, 5s.

Correggio: A Tragedy. By OEHLENSCHLAEGER. With Notes. Fcap. 8vo, 3s.

Helena Faucit (Lady Martin). By Sir THEODORE MARTIN, K.C.B., K.C.V.O. With Five Photogravure Plates. Second Edition. Demy 8vo, 10s. 6d. net.

MARTIN. On some of Shakespeare's Female Characters. By HELENA FAUCIT, Lady MARTIN. Dedicated by permission to Her Most Gracious Majesty the Queen. With a Portrait by Lehmann. Seventh Edition, with a new Preface. Demy 8vo, 7s. 6d.

MATHESON.

Can the Old Faith Live with the New? or, The Problem of Evolution and Revelation. By the Rev. GEORGE MATHESON, D.D. Third Edition. Crown 8vo, 7s. 6d.

The Psalmist and the Scientist; or, Modern Value of the Religious Sentiment. Third Edition. Crown 8vo, 5s.

Spiritual Development of St Paul. Fourth Edition. Cr. 8vo, 5s.

The Distinctive Messages of the Old Religions. Second Edition. Crown 8vo, 5s.

Sacred Songs. Third Edition. Crown 8vo, 2s. 6d.

MAXWELL.

The Honourable Sir Charles Murray, K.C.B. A Memoir. By the Right Hon. Sir HERBERT MAXWELL, Bart., M.P., F.S.A., &c. With Five Portraits. Demy 8vo, 18s.

Life and Times of the Rt. Hon. William Henry Smith, M.P. With Portraits and numerous Illustrations by Herbert Railton, G. L. Seymour, and Others. 2 vols. demy 8vo, 25s.

POPULAR EDITION. With a Portrait and other Illustrations. Crown 8vo, 3s. 6d.

MAXWELL.
  Dumfries and Galloway. Being one of the Volumes of the County Histories of Scotland. With Four Maps. Second Edition. Demy 8vo, 7s. 6d. net.
  Scottish Land-Names: Their Origin and Meaning. Being the Rhind Lectures in Archæology for 1893. Post 8vo, 6s.
  A Duke of Britain. A Romance of the Fourth Century. Fourth Edition. Crown 8vo 6s.
  The Chevalier of the Splendid Crest. Third Edition. Crown 8vo, 6s.

MELDRUM.
  The Conquest of Charlotte. By DAVID S. MELDRUM. Third Impression. Crown 8vo, 6s.
  Holland and the Hollanders. With numerous Illustrations and a Map. Second Edition. Square 8vo, 6s.
  The Story of Margrédel: Being a Fireside History of a Fifeshire Family. Cheap Edition Crown 8vo, 3s. 6d.
  Grey Mantle and Gold Fringe. Crown 8vo, 6s.

MELLONE.
  Studies in Philosophical Criticism and Construction. By SYDNEY HERBERT MELLONE, M.A. Lond., D.Sc. Edin. Post 8vo, 10s. 6d. net.
  Leaders of Religious Thought in the Nineteenth Century. Crown 8vo, 6s. net.
  An Introductory Text-Book of Logic. Crown 8vo, 5s.

MERZ. A History of European Thought in the Nineteenth Century. By JOHN THEODORE MERZ. Vol. I., post 8vo, 10s. 6d. net. Vol. II., 15s. net.

MEYNELL. John Ruskin. "Modern English Writers." By Mrs MEYNELL. Third Impression. Crown 8vo, 2s. 6d.

MICHIE. The Englishman in China during the Victorian Era. As Illustrated in the Life of Sir Rutherford Alcock, K.C.B., D.C.L. By ALEXANDER MICHIE. With Illustrations, Portraits, and Maps. 2 vols. demy 8vo, 38s. net.

MICKLETHWAIT. The Licensing Act, 1904. By St J. G. MICKLETHWAIT, M.A., B.C.L., Barrister-at-Law. Crown 8vo, 2s. 6d. net.

MILL.
  The Colonel Sahib. A Novel. By GARRETT MILL. Second Impression. Crown 8vo, 6s.
  Ottavia. Second Impression. Crown 8vo, 6s.
  Mr Montgomery: Fool. Crown 8vo, 6s.
  In the Hands of the Czar. Crown 8vo, 6s.

MILLAR. The Mid-Eighteenth Century. "Periods of European Literature." By J. H. MILLAR. Crown 8vo, 5s. net.

MILN. A Woman and Her Talent. By LOUISE JORDAN MILN. Crown 8vo, 6s.

MITCHELL. The Scottish Reformation. Being the Baird Lecture for 1899. By the late ALEXANDER F. MITCHELL, D.D., LL.D. Edited by D. HAY FLEMING, LL.D. With a Biographical Sketch of the Author, by James Christie, D.D. Crown 8vo, 6s.

MODERN ENGLISH WRITERS. In handy crown 8vo volumes, tastefully bound, price 2s. 6d. each.

  Matthew Arnold. By Professor SAINTSBURY. Second Impression.

  R. L. Stevenson. By L. COPE CORNFORD. Second Impression.

  John Ruskin. By Mrs MEYNELL. Third Impression.

  Tennyson. By ANDREW LANG. Second Edition.

  Huxley. By EDWARD CLODD.

  Thackeray. By CHARLES WHIBLEY.

  Browning. By Prof. C. H. HERFORD.

In Preparation.

GEORGE ELIOT. By A. T. Quiller-Couch. | FROUDE. By John Oliver Hobbes.

MOIR. Life of Mansie Wauch, Tailor in Dalkeith. By D. M. MOIR. With CRUIKSHANK's Illustrations. Cheaper Edition. Crown 8vo, 2s. 6d. Another Edition, without Illustrations, fcap. 8vo, 1s. 6d.

MOMERIE.

  Dr Alfred Momerie. His Life and Work. By Mrs MOMERIE. Demy 8vo, 12s. 6d. net.

  The Origin of Evil, and other Sermons. By Rev. ALFRED WILLIAMS MOMERIE, M.A., D.Sc., LL.D. Eighth Edition, Enlarged. Crown 8vo, 5s.

  Personality. The Beginning and End of Metaphysics, and a Necessary Assumption in all Positive Philosophy. Fifth Ed., Revised. Cr. 8vo, 3s.

  Agnosticism. Fourth Edition, Revised. Crown 8vo, 5s.

  Preaching and Hearing; and other Sermons. Fourth Edition, Enlarged. Crown 8vo, 5s.

  Belief in God. Fourth Edition. Crown 8vo, 3s.

  The Future of Religion, and other Essays. Second Edition. Crown 8vo, 3s. 6d.

  The English Church and the Romish Schism. Second Edition. Crown 8vo, 2s. 6d.

MONTAGUE. Military Topography. Illustrated by Practical Examples of a Practical Subject. By Major-General W. E. MONTAGUE, C.B., P.S.C., late Garrison Instructor Intelligence Department, Author of 'Campaigning in South Africa.' With Forty-one Diagrams. Crown 8vo, 5s.

MOWBRAY. Seventy Years at Westminster. With other Letters and Notes of the late Right Hon. Sir JOHN MOWBRAY, Bart., M.P. Edited by his Daughter. With Portraits and other Illustrations. Large crown 8vo, 7s. 6d.

MUNRO. Uniform Edition Novels.

  John Splendid. The Tale of a Poor Gentleman and the Little Wars of Lorn. Sixth Impression. Crown 8vo, 3s. 6d.

  Children of Tempest: A Tale of the Outer Isles. By NEIL MUNRO. Crown 8vo, 3s. 6d.

  Shoes of Fortune. Crown 8vo, 3s. 6d.

  The Lost Pibroch, and other Sheiling Stories. Fourth Impression. Crown 8vo, 3s. 6d.

  Doom Castle: A Romance. Second Impression. Crown 8vo, 3s. 6d.

  Gilian the Dreamer. Crown 8vo, 3s. 6d.

MUNRO.
Rambles and Studies in Bosnia-Herzegovina and Dalmatia. By ROBERT MUNRO, M.A., M.D., LL.D., F.R.S.E. Second Edition, Revised and Enlarged. With numerous illustrations. Demy 8vo, 12s. 6d. net.

Prehistoric Problems. With numerous Illustrations. Demy 8vo, 10s. net.

MUNRO. On Valuation of Property. By WILLIAM MUNRO, M.A., Her Majesty's Assessor of Railways and Canals for Scotland. Second Edition, Revised and Enlarged. 8vo, 3s. 6d.

MURRAY.
Selections from the Writings of Sir Charles Murray. 2 vols. demy 8vo, 30s. net.

Travels in North America. Demy 8vo, 15s. net.

Hassan; or, The Child of the Pyramid. Demy 8vo, 15s. net.

The Prairie-Bird. Demy 8vo, 15s. net.

MY TRIVIAL LIFE AND MISFORTUNE: A Gossip with no Plot in Particular. By A PLAIN WOMAN. Cheap Edition. Crown 8vo, 3s. 6d.

By the SAME AUTHOR.

POOR NELLIE. Cheap Edition. Crown 8vo, 3s. 6d.

MYRES. A Manual of Classical Geography. By JOHN L. MYRES. Crown 8vo. [*In the press.*

NEWCOMBE. Village, Town, and Jungle Life in India By A. C. NEWCOMBE. Demy 8vo, 12s. 6d. net.

NICHOLSON.
A Manual of Zoology, for the Use of Students. With a General Introduction on the Principles of Zoology. By HENRY ALLEYNE NICHOLSON, M.D., D.Sc., F.L.S., F.G.S., Regius Professor of Natural History in the University of Aberdeen. Seventh Edition, Rewritten and Enlarged. Post 8vo, pp. 956, with 555 Engravings on Wood, 18s.

Text-Book of Zoology, for Junior Students. Fifth Edition. Rewritten and Enlarged. Crown 8vo, with 358 Engravings on Wood, 10s. 6d

A Manual of Palæontology, for the Use of Students. With a General Introduction on the Principles of Palæontology. By Professor H. ALLEYNE NICHOLSON and RICHARD LYDEKKER, B.A. Third Edition, entirely Rewritten and greatly Enlarged. 2 vols. 8vo, £3, 3s.

NICHOLSON.
Toth. A Romance. By JOSEPH SHIELD NICHOLSON, M.A., D.Sc., Professor of Commercial and Political Economy and Mercantile Law in the University of Edinburgh. Third Edition. Crown 8vo, 4s. 6d.

A Dreamer of Dreams. A Modern Romance. Second Edition. Crown 8vo, 6s.

NICOL. Recent Archæology and the Bible. Being the Croall Lectures for 1898. By the Rev. THOMAS NICOL, D.D., Professor of Divinity and Biblical Criticism in the University of Aberdeen; Author of 'Recent Explorations in Bible Lands.' Demy 8vo, 9s. net.

NISBET. The Forester: A Practical Treatise on British Forestry and Arboriculture for Landowners, Land Agents, and Foresters. By JOHN NISBET, D.Œc. In 2 volumes, royal 8vo, with 285 Illustrations, 42s. net.

NOBLE.
The Edge of Circumstance. By EDWARD NOBLE. Crown 8vo, 6s.

Waves of Fate. Crown 8vo, 6s.

NOYES.
    Poems by ALFRED NOYES. 7s. 6d. net.
    The Forest of Wild Thyme : A Tale for Children under Ninety.
        Crown 8vo, 5s. net.

O. The Yellow War. By O. Crown 8vo, 6s.

OLIPHANT.
    Masollam : A Problem of the Period. A Novel. By LAURENCE
        OLIPHANT . 3 vols. post 8vo, 25s. 6d.
    Altiora Peto. Cheap Edition. Crown 8vo, boards, 2s. 6d.;
        cloth, 3s. 6d. Illustrated Edition. Crown 8vo, cloth, 6s.
    Piccadilly. With Illustrations by Richard Doyle. New Edi-
        tion, 3s. 6d. Cheap Edition, boards, 2s. 6d.
    Episodes in a Life of Adventure ; or, Moss from a Rolling
        Stone. Cheaper Edition. Post 8vo, 3s. 6d.
    The Land of Gilead. With Excursions in the Lebanon.
        With Illustrations and Maps. Demy 8vo, 21s.
    Memoir of the Life of Laurence Oliphant, and of Alice
        Oliphant, his Wife. By Mrs M. O. W. OLIPHANT. Seventh Edition. 2 vols.
        post 8vo, with Portraits. 21s.
        POPULAR EDITION. With a New Preface. Post 8vo, with Portraits. 7s. 6d.

OLIPHANT.
    The Autobiography and Letters of Mrs M. O. W. Oliphant.
        Arranged and Edited by Mrs HARRY COGHILL. With Two Portraits. Cheap
        Edition. Crown 8vo, 6s.
    Annals of a Publishing House. William Blackwood and his
        Sons; Their Magazine and Friends. By Mrs OLIPHANT. With Four Portraits.
        Third Edition. Demy 8vo. Vols. I. and II. £2, 2s.
    A Widow's Tale, and other Stories. With an Introductory
        Note by J. M. BARRIE. Second Edition. Crown 8vo, 6s.
    Who was Lost and is Found. Second Edition. Crown
        8vo, 6s.
    Miss Marjoribanks. New Edition. Crown 8vo, 3s. 6d.
    The Perpetual Curate, and The Rector. New Edition. Crown
        8vo, 3s. 6d.
    Salem Chapel, and The Doctor's Family. New Edition.
        Crown 8vo, 3s. 6d
    Chronicles of Carlingford. 3 vols. crown 8vo, in uniform
        binding, gilt top, 3s. 6d. each.
    Katie Stewart, and other Stories. New Edition. Crown 8vo,
        cloth, 3s. 6d.
    Katie Stewart. Illustrated boards, 2s. 6d.
    Valentine and his Brother. New Edition. Crown 8vo, 3s. 6d.
    Sons and Daughters. Crown 8vo, 3s. 6d.
    Stories of the Seen and the Unseen. Old Lady Mary—The
        Open Door—The Portrait—The Library Window. Fcap. 8vo, 3s. 6d.

OMOND. The Romantic Triumph. "Periods of European
    Literature." By T. S. OMOND. Crown 8vo, 5s. net.

O'NEILL. Songs of the Glens of Antrim. By MOIRA O'NEILL.
Ninth Impression. Crown 8vo, 3s. 6d.

PAGE.
Intermediate Text-Book of Geology. By Professor LAPWORTH.
Founded on Dr Page's 'Introductory Text-Book of Geology.' Crown 8vo, 5s.
Advanced Text-Book of Geology. New Edition. Revised and enlarged by Professor LAPWORTH. Crown 8vo. [In the press.
Introductory Text-Book of Physical Geography. Crown 8vo, 2s. 6d.
Advanced Text-Book of Physical Geography. Crown 8vo, 5s.
Physical Geography Examinator. Crown 8vo, sewed, 9d.

PARKER. Miss Lomax: Millionaire. By BESSIE PARKER.
Crown 8vo, 6s.

PAUL. History of the Royal Company of Archers, the Queen's Body-Guard for Scotland. By Sir JAMES BALFOUR PAUL, Advocate of the Scottish Bar. Crown 4to, with Portraits and other Illustrations. £2, 2s.

PEARSE. The Hearseys: Five Generations of an Anglo-Indian Family. By Colonel HUGH PEARSE. Demy 8vo, 15s. net.

PEILE. Lawn Tennis as a Game of Skill. By Lieut.-Col. S. C. F. PEILE, B.S.C. Revised Edition, with new Scoring Rules. Fcap. 8vo, cloth, 1s.

PERIODS OF EUROPEAN LITERATURE. Edited by Professor SAINTSBURY. *For List of Volumes, see page 2.*

PHILOSOPHICAL CLASSICS FOR ENGLISH READERS.
Edited by WILLIAM KNIGHT, LL.D., Professor of Moral Philosophy, University of St Andrews. Cheap Re-issue in Shilling Volumes net.
[*For List of Volumes, see page 2.*

PITCAIRN. The History of the Fife Pitcairns, with Transcripts from Old Charters. By CONSTANCE PITCAIRN. Demy 8vo, £2, 2s. net.

POLLOK. The Course of Time: A Poem. By ROBERT POLLOK, A.M. New Edition. With Portrait. Fcap. 8vo, gilt top, 2s. 6d.

PRESTWICH. Essays: Descriptive and Biographical. By GRACE, Lady PRESTWICH, Author of 'The Harbour Bar' and 'Enga.' With a Memoir by her sister, LOUISA E. MILNE. With Illustrations. Demy 8vo, 10s. 6d.

PRESTWICH. Life and Letters of Sir Joseph Prestwich, M.A. D.C.L., F.R.S. Formerly Professor of Geology in the University of Oxford. Written and Edited by his WIFE. With Portraits and other Illustrations. Demy 8vo, 21s.

PRINGLE-PATTISON.
Scottish Philosophy. A Comparison of the Scottish and German Answers to Hume. Balfour Philosophical Lectures, University of Edinburgh. By A. SETH PRINGLE-PATTISON, LL.D., Professor of Logic and Metaphysics in Edinburgh University. Third Edition. Crown 8vo, 5s.
Hegelianism and Personality. Balfour Philosophical Lectures. Second Series. Second Edition. Crown 8vo, 5s.
Man's Place in the Cosmos, and other Essays. Second Edition, Enlarged. Post 8vo, 6s. net.
Two Lectures on Theism. Delivered on the occasion of the Sesquicentennial Celebration of Princeton University. Crown 8vo, 2s. 6d.

PUBLIC GENERAL STATUTES AFFECTING SCOTLAND
from 1707 to 1847, with Chronological Table and Index. 8 vols. large 8vo, £3, 3s.
Also Published Annually with General Index.

RANJITSINHJI. The Jubilee Book of Cricket. By PRINCE RANJITSINHJI.
POPULAR EDITION. With 107 full-page Illustrations. Sixth Edition. Large crown 8vo, 6s.
SIXPENNY EDITION. With a selection of the Illustrations.

REID. Christian Prayer. By WILLIAM A. REID. With Introduction by the Very Rev. Professor CHARTERIS, D.D., LL.D. Crown 8vo, 5s. net.

REYNARD. The 9th (Queen's Royal) Lancers, from 1715 to 1903. By FRANK H. REYNARD. Royal 8vo, £2, 2s. net.

ROBERTSON.
The Poetry and the Religion of the Psalms. The Croall Lectures, 1893-94. By JAMES ROBERTSON, D.D., Professor of Oriental Languages in the University of Glasgow. Demy 8vo, 12s.
The Early Religion of Israel. As set forth by Biblical Writers and Modern Critical Historians. Being the Baird Lecture for 1888-89. Fourth Edition. Crown 8vo, 10s. 6d.

ROBERTSON.
A History of German Literature. By JOHN G. ROBERTSON, Professor of German, University of London. Demy 8vo, 10s. 6d. net.
Schiller after a Century. Crown 8vo, 2s. 6d. net.

ROBINSON. Life of Sir John Beverley Robinson, Bart. By Major-General C. W. ROBINSON. Demy 8vo, 16s. net.

ROBINSON. Wild Traits in Tame Animals. Being some Familiar Studies in Evolution. By LOUIS ROBINSON, M.D. With Illustrations by STEPHEN T. DADD. Cheaper Edition. Demy 8vo, 6s.

RONALDSHAY.
On the Outskirts of Empire in Asia. By the EARL OF RONALDSHAY, F.R.G.S. With numerous Illustrations and Maps. Royal 8vo, 21s. net
Sport and Politics under an Eastern Sky. With numerous Illustrations and Maps. Royal 8vo, 21s. net.

RUTLAND.
Notes of an Irish Tour in 1846. By the DUKE OF RUTLAND, G.C.B. (LORD JOHN MANNERS). New Edition. Crown 8vo, 2s. 6d.
Correspondence between the Right Honble. William Pitt and Charles Duke of Rutland, Lord-Lieutenant of Ireland, 1781-1787. With Introductory Note by JOHN DUKE OF RUTLAND. 8vo, 7s. 6d.
The Collected Writings of Janetta, Duchess of Rutland. With Portrait and Illustrations. 2 vols. post 8vo, 15s. net.
Impressions of Bad-Homburg. Comprising a Short Account of the Women's Associations of Germany under the Red Cross. By the DUCHESS OF RUTLAND (LADY JOHN MANNERS). Crown 8vo, 1s. 6d.
Some Personal Recollections of the Later Years of the Earl of Beaconsfield, K.G. Sixth Edition. 6d.
Employment of Women in the Public Service. 6d.

RUTLAND.
Some of the Advantages of Easily Accessible Reading and Recreation Rooms and Free Libraries. With Remarks on Starting and Maintaining them. Second Edition. Crown 8vo, 1s.
A Sequel to Rich Men's Dwellings, and other Occasional Papers. Crown 8vo, 2s. 6d.
Encouraging Experiences of Reading and Recreation Rooms, Aims of Guilds, Nottingham Social Guide, Existing Institutions, &c., &c. Crown 8vo, 1s.

SAINTSBURY.
A History of Criticism and Literary Taste in Europe. From the Earliest Texts to the Present Day. By GEORGE SAINTSBURY, M.A. (Oxon.), Hon. LL.D. (Aberd.), Professor of Rhetoric and English Literature in the University of Edinburgh. In 3 vols. demy 8vo. Vol. I.—Classical and Mediæval Criticism. 16s. net.
Vol. II.—From the Renaissance to the Decline of Eighteenth Century Orthodoxy. 20s. net.
Vol. III.—Nineteenth Century. 20s. net.
Matthew Arnold. "Modern English Writers." Second Edition. Crown 8vo, 2s. 6d
The Flourishing of Romance and the Rise of Allegory (12th and 13th Centuries). "Periods of European Literature." Crown 8vo, 5s. net.
The Earlier Renaissance. "Periods of European Literature." Crown 8vo, 5s. net.

"SCOLOPAX." A Book of the Snipe. By SCOLOPAX. Illustrated. Crown 8vo, 5s. net.

SCOTT. Tom Cringle's Log. By MICHAEL SCOTT. New Edition. With 19 Full-page Illustrations. Crown 8vo, 3s. 6d.

SCUDAMORE. Belgium and the Belgians. By CYRIL SCUDAMORE. With Illustrations. Square crown 8vo, 6s.

SERMONS TO BRITONS ABROAD: Preached in a Foreign Station of a Scottish Church. Crown 8vo, 3s. 6d. net.

SERREL. With Hound and Terrier in the Field. By ALYS F. SERREL. Edited by FRANCES SLAUGHTER. With numerous Illustrations. Demy 8vo, 15s. net.

SETH. A Study of Ethical Principles. By JAMES SETH, M.A., Professor of Moral Philosophy in the University of Edinburgh. Sixth Edition, Revised. Post 8vo, 7s. 6d.

SHARPLEY. Aristophanes—Pax. Edited, with Introduction and Notes, by H. SHARPLEY. Demy 8vo, 12s. 6d. net.

SHAW. Securities over Moveables. Four Lectures delivered at the Request of the Society of Accountants in Edinburgh, the Institute of Accountants and Actuaries in Glasgow, and the Institute of Bankers in Scotland, in 1902-3. Demy 8vo, 3s. 6d. net.

"SIGMA." Personalia: Political, Social and Various. By "SIGMA." In 1 vol. crown 8vo, 5s. net.

SIMPSON. Side-Lights on Siberia. Some account of the Great Siberian Iron Road: The Prisons and Exile System. By J. Y. SIMPSON, M.A., D.Sc. With numerous Illustrations and a Map. Demy 8vo, 16s.

SINCLAIR. The Thistle and Fleur de Lys: A Vocabulary of Franco-Scottish Words. By ISABEL G. SINCLAIR. Crown 8vo, 3s. net.

SKELTON. The Handbook of Public Health. A New Edition, Revised by JAMES PATTEN MACDOUGALL, Advocate, Secretary to the Local Government Board for Scotland, Joint-Author of 'The Parish Council Guide for Scotland,' and ABIJAH MURRAY, Chief Clerk of the Local Government Board for Scotland. In Two Parts. Crown 8vo. Part I.—The Public Health (Scotland) Act, 1897, with Notes. 3s. 6d. net.

SLATER. Footpaths thro' the Veld. By F. C. SLATER. Crown 8vo, 5s. net.

SMITH.
The Transition Period. "Periods of European Literature." By G. GREGORY SMITH. Crown 8vo, 5s. net.
Specimens of Middle Scots. Post 8vo, 7s. 6d. net.

SMITH. Retrievers, and how to Break them. By Lieutenant-Colonel Sir HENRY SMITH, K.C.B. With an Introduction by Mr S. E. SHIRLEY, President of the Kennel Club. Dedicated by special permission to H.R.H. the Duke of Cornwall and York. New Edition, enlarged. With additional Illustrations. Crown 8vo. 2s.

SNELL. The Fourteenth Century. "Periods of European Literature." By F. J. SNELL. Crown 8vo, 5s. net.

SOLBÉ. Hints on Hockey. By F. DE LISLE SOLBÉ. English International Team: 1897, 1898, 1899, 1900. With Diagrams. Fcap. 8vo, 1s.

"SON OF THE MARSHES, A."
From Spring to Fall; or, When Life Stirs. By "A SON OF THE MARSHES." Cheap Uniform Edition. Crown 8vo, 3s. 6d.
Within an Hour of London Town: Among Wild Birds and their Haunts. Edited by J. A. OWEN. Cheap Uniform Edition. Cr. 8vo, 3s. 6d.
With the Woodlanders and by the Tide. Cheap Uniform Edition. Crown 8vo, 3s. 6d.
On Surrey Hills. Cheap Uniform Edition. Crown 8vo, 3s. 6d.
Annals of a Fishing Village. Cheap Uniform Edition. Crown 8vo, 3s. 6d.

SORLEY.
The Ethics of Naturalism. By W. R. SORLEY, M.A., Fellow of Trinity College, Cambridge, Professor of Moral Philosophy, University of Cambridge. Second Edition. Crown 8vo, 6s.
Recent Tendencies in Ethics. Crown 8vo, 2s. 6d. net.

SPROTT.
The Worship and Offices of the Church of Scotland. By GEORGE W. SPROTT, D.D., Minister of North Berwick. Crown 8vo, 6s.
The Book of Common Order of the Church of Scotland, commonly known as John Knox's Liturgy. With Historical Introduction and Illustrative Notes. Crown 8vo, 4s. 6d. net.
Scottish Liturgies of the Reign of James VI. Edited, with an Introduction and Notes. Crown 8vo, 4s. net.
Euchologion: A Book of Common Order. Crown 8vo, 4s. 6d. net.

STEEVENS.
Things Seen: Impressions of Men, Cities, and Books. By the late G. W. STEEVENS. Edited by G. S. STREET. With a Memoir by W. E. HENLEY, and a Photogravure reproduction of Collier's Portrait. Memorial Edition. Crown 8vo, 6s.
From Capetown to Ladysmith, and Egypt in 1898. Memorial Edition. Crown 8vo, 6s.

STEEVENS.
  In India. With Map. Memorial Edition. Crown 8vo, 6s.
  With Kitchener to Khartum. With 8 Maps and Plans.
    Memorial Edition. Crown 8vo, 6s.
  The Land of the Dollar. Memorial Edition. Crown 8vo, 6s.
  Glimpses of Three Nations. Memorial Edition. Cr. 8vo, 6s.
  Monologues of the Dead. Memorial Edition. Crown 8vo, 3s. 6d.
  With the Conquering Turk. With 4 Maps. Ch. Ed. Cr. 8vo, 6s.
  From Capetown to Ladysmith: An Unfinished Record of the
    South African War. Edited by VERNON BLACKBURN. With Maps. Crown 8vo, 3s. 6d.

STEPHENS.
  The Book of the Farm; detailing the Labours of the Farmer,
    Farm-Steward, Ploughman, Shepherd, Hedger, Farm-Labourer, Field-Worker, and Cattle-man. Illustrated with numerous Portraits of Animals and Engravings of Implements, and Plans of Farm Buildings. Fourth Edition. Revised, and in great part Re-written, by JAMES MACDONALD, F.R.S.E., Secretary Highland and Agricultural Society of Scotland. Complete in Six Divisional Volumes, bound in cloth, each 10s. 6d., or handsomely bound, in 3 volumes with leather back and gilt top, £3, 3s.
  The Book of Farm Implements and Machines. By J. SLIGHT
    and R. SCOTT BURN, Engineers. Edited by HENRY STEPHENS. Large 8vo, £2, 2s.

STEWART. Haud Immemor. Reminiscences of Legal and
  Social Life in Edinburgh and London, 1850-1900. By CHARLES STEWART. With 10 Photogravure Plates. Royal 8vo, 7s. 6d

STEWART AND CUFF. Practical Nursing. By ISLA STEWART,
  Matron of St Bartholomew's Hospital, London; and HERBERT E. CUFF, M.D., F.R.C.S., Medical Superintendent North-Eastern Fever Hospital, Tottenham, London. With Diagrams. In 2 vols. crown 8vo. Vol. I. Second Edition. 3s. 6d. net. Vol. II., 3s. 6d. net.
    Also in 1 Volume, 5s. net.

STIRLING. Our Regiments in South Africa, 1899-1902. Their
  Record, based on the Despatches. By JOHN STIRLING. In 1 vol. demy 8vo, 12s. 6d. net.

STODDART. John Stuart Blackie: A Biography. By ANNA
  M. STODDART. POPULAR EDITION, with Portrait. Crown 8vo, 3s. 6d.

STORMONTH.
  Dictionary of the English Language, Pronouncing, Etymo-
    logical, and Explanatory. By the Rev. JAMES STORMONTH. Revised by the Rev. P. H. PHELP. Library Edition. New and Cheaper Edition, with Supplement. Imperial 8vo, handsomely bound in half morocco, 18s. net.

STORMONTH.
  Etymological and Pronouncing Dictionary of the English
    Language. Including a very Copious Selection of Scientific Terms. For use in Schools and Colleges, and as a Book of General Reference. The Pronunciation carefully revised by the Rev. P. H. PHELP, M.A. Cantab. Sixteenth Edition. Revised. Crown 8vo, pp. 1000. 5s. net.
  Handy Dictionary. New Edition, thoroughly Revised. By
    WILLIAM BAYNE. 16mo, 1s.

STORY. The Apostolic Ministry in the Scottish Church (The
  Baird Lecture for 1897). By R. H. STORY, D.D., Principal of the University of Glasgow, and Chaplain to the Queen. Crown 8vo, 7s. 6d.

STORY. William Wetmore Story and his Friends. From Letters, Diaries, and Recollections. By HENRY JAMES. With 2 Portraits. In 2 vols. post 8vo, 24s. net.

STRONG. Sonnets and Songs. By Archibald T. STRONG, M.A. Crown 8vo, 5s. net.

SYNGE. The Story of the World. By M. B. SYNGE. With Coloured Frontispieces and numerous Illustrations by E. M. SYNGE, A.R.E., and Maps. 2 vols, 3s. 6d. each net.

TAYLOR. The Story of my Life. By the late Colonel MEADOWS TAYLOR, Author of 'The Confessions of a Thug,' &c., &c. Edited by his Daughter. Cheap Edition. Crown 8vo, 3s. 6d.

THEOBALD. A Text-Book of Agricultural Zoology. By FRED. V. THEOBALD. With numerous Illustrations. Crown 8vo, 8s. 6d.

THOMSON. Handy Book of the Flower-Garden. By DAVID THOMSON. Crown 8vo, 5s.

THOMSON. A Practical Treatise on the Cultivation of the Grape Vine. By WILLIAM THOMSON, Tweed Vineyards. Tenth Edition. 8vo, 5s.

THOMSON. History of the Fife Light Horse. By Colonel ANSTRUTHER THOMSON. With numerous Portraits. Small 4to, 21s. net.

THORBURN. The Punjab in Peace and War. By S. S. THORBURN. Demy 8vo, 12s. 6d. net.

THURSTON.
 The Circle. By KATHERINE CECIL THURSTON. Fifth Impression. Crown 8vo, 6s. People's Edition, paper covers, 6d.
 John Chilcote, M.P. Fourteenth Impression, crown 8vo, 6s. People's Edition, paper covers, 6d.

TIELE. Elements of the Science of Religion. Part I.—Morphological. Part II.—Ontological. Being the Gifford Lectures delivered before the University of Edinburgh in 1896-98. By C. P. TIELE, Theol. D., Litt. D. (Bonon.), Hon. M.R.A.S., &c., Professor of the Science of Religion, in the University of Leiden. In 2 vols. post 8vo, 7s. 6d. net. each.

TRANSACTIONS OF THE HIGHLAND AND AGRICULTURAL SOCIETY OF SCOTLAND. Published annually, price 5s.

TRAVERS.
 The Way of Escape. A Novel. By GRAHAM TRAVERS (Margaret Todd, M.D.) Second Impression. Crown 8vo, 6s.
 Mona Maclean, Medical Student. A Novel. Fourteenth Edition. Crown 8vo, 6s. Cheaper Edition, 2s. 6d.
 Windyhaugh. Fourth Edition. Crown 8vo, 6s.
 Fellow Travellers. Fourth Edition. Crown 8vo, 6s.

TROTTER.
- A Leader of Light Horse. Life of Hodson of Hodson's Horse. By Captain L. J. TROTTER, Author of 'Life of John Nicholson, Soldier and Statesman.' With a Portrait and 2 Maps. Demy 8vo, 16s.
- The Bayard of India. Life of Lieut.-General Sir James Outram, Bart., G.C.B., G.C.S.I. With Portrait. Demy 8vo, 16s. net.

TULLOCH. Recollections of Forty Years' Service. By Major-General Sir ALEXANDER BRUCE TULLOCH, K.C.B., C.M.G. Demy 8vo, 15s. net.

TULLOCH.
- Modern Theories in Philosophy and Religion. By JOHN TULLOCH, D.D., Principal of St Mary's College in the University of St Andrews, and one of her Majesty's Chaplains in Ordinary in Scotland. 8vo. 15s.
- Memoir of Principal Tulloch, D.D, LL.D. By Mrs OLIPHANT, Author of 'Life of Edward Irving.' Third and Cheaper Edition. 8vo, with Portrait, 7s. 6d.

TWEEDIE. The Arabian Horse: His Country and People. By Major-General W. TWEEDIE, C.S.I., Bengal Staff Corps; for many years H.B.M.'s Consul-General, Baghdad, and Political Resident for the Government of India in Turkish Arabia. In one vol. royal 4to, with Seven Coloured Plates and other Illustrations, and a Map of the Country. Price £3, 3s. net.

VETCH. Life, Letters, and Diaries of Lieut.-General Sir Gerald Graham, V.C., G.C.B., R.E. By Colonel R. H. VETCH, C.B., late Royal Engineers. With Portraits, Plans, and his Principal Despatches. Demy 8vo, 21s.

WADDELL.
- Christianity as an Ideal. By Rev. P. HATELY WADDELL, B.D. Crown 8vo, 3s. 6d.
- Essays on Faith. Crown 8vo, 3s. 6d.

WARREN'S (SAMUEL) WORKS:—
- Diary of a Late Physician. Cloth, 2s. 6d.; boards, 2s.
- Ten Thousand A-Year. Cloth, 3s. 6d.; boards, 2s. 6d.
- Now and Then. The Lily and the Bee. Intellectual and Moral Development of the Present Age. 4s. 6d.
- Essays: Critical, Imaginative, and Juridical. 5s.

WATT. By Still Waters. By MACLEAN WATT. 1s. 6d. net. Leather, 2s. net.

WENLEY. Aspects of Pessimism. By R. M. WENLEY, M.A., D.Sc., D.Phil., Professor of Philosophy in the University of Michigan, U.S.A. Crown 8vo, 6s.

WHIBLEY. Thackeray. "Modern English Writers." By CHARLES WHIBLEY. Crown 8vo, 2s. 6d.

WHITE.
 The Young Gerande. By EDMUND WHITE. In 1 vol. crown 8vo, 6s.
 Bray of Buckholt. Crown 8vo, 6s.

WHITE. Mountains of Necessity. By HESTER WHITE. Crown 8vo, 6s.

WILLIAMSON. Ideals of Ministry. By A. WALLACE WILLIAMSON, D.D., St Cuthbert's, Edinburgh. Crown 8vo, 3s. 6d.

WILSON. The Prophets and Prophecy to the Close of the Eighth Century B.C. By the Rev. ALEXANDER WILSON, M.A., Minister of Ythan Wells, Aberdeenshire. With Introductory Preface by the Rev. ALLAN MENZIES, D.D., Professor of Biblical Criticism in the University of St Andrews. Fcap. 8vo, 1s. net.

WILSON.
 Works of Professor Wilson. Edited by his Son-in-Law, Professor FERRIER. 12 vols. crown 8vo, £2, 8s.
 Christopher in his Sporting-Jacket. 2 vols., 8s.
 Isle of Palms, City of the Plague, and other Poems. 4s.
 Lights and Shadows of Scottish Life, and other Tales. 4s.
 Essays, Critical and Imaginative. 4 vols., 16s.
 The Noctes Ambrosianæ. 4 vols., 16s.
 Homer and his Translators, and the Greek Drama. Crown 8vo, 4s.

WORSLEY.
 Homer's Odyssey. Translated into English Verse in the Spenserian Stanza. By PHILIP STANHOPE WORSLEY, M.A. New and Cheaper Edition. Post 8vo, 7s. 6d. net.
 Homer's Iliad. Translated by P. S. Worsley and Prof. Conington. 2 vols. crown 8vo, 21s.

WOTHERSPOON.
 Kyrie Eleison ("Lord, have Mercy"). A Manual of Private Prayers. With Notes and Additional Matter. By H. J. WOTHERSPOON, M.A., of St Oswald's, Edinburgh. Cloth, red edges, 1s. net; limp leather, 1s. 6d. net.
 Before and After. Being Part I. of 'Kyrie Eleison.' Cloth, limp, 6d. net.
 The Second Prayer Book of King Edward the Sixth (1552) and the Liturgy of Compromise. Edited by Rev. G. W. SPROTT, D.D. Crown 8vo, 4s. net.

YATE. Khurasan and Sistan. By Lieut.-Col. C. E. YATE, C.S.I., C.M.G., F.R.G.S., Indian Staff Corps, Agent to the Governor-General and Chief Commissioner for Baluchistan, late Agent to the Governor-General of India, and Her Britannic Majesty's Consul-General for Khurasan and Sistan. With Map and 25 Illustrations, and Portraits. Demy 8vo, 21s.

ZACK.
 On Trial. By ZACK. Second Edition. Crown 8vo, 6s.
 Life is Life, and other Tales and Episodes. Second Edition. Crown 8vo, 6s.

10/05.